Great and Glorious Days

*Schellenberg, Blenheim, Ramillies,
Oudenarde and Malplaquet*

GREAT AND GLORIOUS DAYS

SCHELLENBERG, BLENHEIM, RAMILLIES, OUDENARDE AND MALPLAQUET

by

James Falkner 26 SEP 2002

Foreword by His Grace The Duke of Marlborough

British Library Cataloguing in Publication Data:
A catalogue record for this book is available
from the British Library

Copyright © James Falkner 2002
Foreword copyright © The Duke of Marlborough 2002
Maps copyright © Spellmount Ltd 2002

ISBN 1-86227-148-8

First published in the UK in 2002 by
Spellmount Limited
The Old Rectory
Staplehurst
Kent TN12 0AZ

Tel: 01580 893730
Fax: 01580 893731
E-mail: enquiries@spellmount.com
Website: www.spellmount.com

1 3 5 7 9 8 6 4 2

Typeset in Palatino by MATS, Southend-on-Sea, Essex
Printed in Great Britain by
TJ International Ltd, Padstow, Cornwall

Contents

List of Maps		vii
Foreword		ix
Introduction		xi
I	The Coming Man	1
II	The Trouble with Spain: The War of the Spanish Succession	9
III	To the Aid of Austria: The Long March to the Danube	19
IV	The Hill of the Bell: The Storm of the Schellenberg	29
V	Marshal Tallard is in My Coach: The Battle of Blenheim	49
VI	The Toils of War: Marlborough's Campaigns from the Danube to Ramillies	87
VII	The Glorious Success: The Battle of Ramillies	95
VIII	Endless Dusty Roads: The Lack of Success in 1707	127
IX	The Devil Must Have Carried Them: The Battle of Oudenarde	131
X	Terrible Dark Winter: The Great Frost and the Missed Peace	163
XI	A Very Murdering Battle: The Battle of Malplaquet	167

XII	Like Hounds Upon a Hare: The Closing Campaigns and the Fall of Marlborough	201
XIII	Time's Shadowy Fingers: Marlborough's Battles in Review	207
XIV	The Sound of a Distant Drum: Marlborough's Army	213
Appendix I:	Marlborough's British Regiments	219
Appendix II:	Who was Who on Marlborough's Battlefields	221
Bibliography		227
Index		231

List of Maps

Map 1   The Netherlands: Campaigns of 1704–9   11

Map 2   Marlborough's March to the Danube and
             Operations in Bavaria, 1704   21

Map 3   The Schellenberg 2 July 1704   31

Map 4   Blenheim 13 August 1704   55

Map 5   Ramillies 23 May 1706   99

Map 6   Oudenarde 11 July 1708   139

Map 7   The Manoeuvres before Malplaquet   169

Map 8   Malplaquet 11 September 1709   175

Unless otherwise stated, the illustrations are from the author's collection
© James Falkner

Foreword

by

His Grace The Duke of Marlborough

Blenheim Palace.

The lst Duke of Marlborough, very often regarded as the greatest military commander this nation has produced, made no effort himself to leave any account for posterity of his outstanding military achievement. As his famous descendant, Sir Winston Churchill, pointed out, Marlborough was content to leave Blenheim Palace, the great House built for him by a grateful nation after the Battle of Blenheim, to speak for him.

I am particularly pleased, therefore, to introduce this new book which vividly helps to make the case for Marlborough's military genius.

Leaving aside as it does the political intrigue, the personal issues and the failing health which clouded Marlborough's later years, the strength and interest of this account lie for me in its purposeful concentration specifically on his military career, in particular on his major battles: Blenheim, Ramillies, Oudenarde and Malplaquet, together with the Schellenberg, upon which the Duke's reputation rests.

The clear description of the events of each battle as it unfolds makes compellingly clear even to the reader with no previous awareness of Marlborough's achievement just how great was his mastery of strategy and tactics. Intriguingly too, we see how vital were his personal charm, persuasiveness and calm in influencing cautious and often reluctant allies to support him in dynamic action. His personal bravery is also clear: we are rather taken aback, perhaps to realise that even as army commander he more than once narrowly escaped death.

I welcome this very readable book which strikes to the heart of where the lst Duke of Marlborough's reputation justifiably lies.

Marlborough

Introduction

He commanded the armies of Europe against France.[1]

Widely regarded as the foremost soldier of his generation, John Churchill, the 1st Duke of Marlborough campaigned successfully against the most capable and renowned generals that King Louis XIV of France could send into the field. During the period between 1704 and 1709 the Duke fought and won five major battles, two in southern Germany and three in present day Belgium. These years of the War of the Spanish Succession were Marlborough's years; his was the military genius of the age.

When Marlborough took the field as Queen Anne's Captain-General in 1702, he was a comparatively untried and untested commander. England was a small and hardly to be trusted participant in a Grand Alliance to limit the power of France. Her troops had a reputation for great bravery, but with an unfortunate habit of being led by mediocre generals. Six years later, by the time the Battle of Oudenarde had been fought and won in July 1708, Great Britain was the main partner in that same Grand Alliance and Queen Anne's treasury had become the paymaster of the Allied armies. Moreover, Marlborough was the leader, both militarily and diplomatically, of a mighty confederate effort to curb the power and ambition of Louis XIV. Energetic, imaginative, cultured and urbane, the Duke was equally at home in the courtly capitals of the Protestant states of Europe, and on the teeming battlefields of Belgium and Germany.

In action Marlborough was bold and determined, yet also calculating and patient. Despite the fairly unsophisticated weapons and means of communication and transportation of the day, he scanned very wide horizons indeed, and his tactical methods were stunningly effective. The Duke understood the need to fight decisive battles in a very modern sense, and in a way that was shared by few of his contemporaries. With a careful eye to detail, and a keen compassion for the marching soldiers he commanded, he proved capable of out-witting, out-marching, and out-fighting his opponents with stunning certainty.

Throughout this exciting period Marlborough had to contend not only with skilful opponents at the head of valiant armies, but with his own obstinate and obstructive allies. In this respect his diplomatic skills in dealing with the states that made up the Grand Alliance matched those virtues he displayed on the battlefield. In time, although he could not win the war for them, the Duke enjoyed their trust and respect. Unfortunately, Marlborough had also to endure suspicion and intrigue at home in London, where powerful and jealous enemies conspired against him. His own countrymen forgot his services and capabilities soon enough, although the Duke's soldiers never stopped loving him. Fatally, the valuable friendship he enjoyed with Queen Anne, upon which his position largely depended, became fragile and eventually failed.

The Duke of Marlborough was by no means perfect. He was given to intrigue, and always had an eye to his own personal advancement. In this he was typical of his age – the Duke was a self made man who had known poverty in his youth, and it was said that he would save sixpence and walk home in the rain rather than take a sedan-chair. However, his personal interests rarely, if ever, interfered with the faithful discharge of his duty, and he declined tempting offers that might have jeopardized the common cause against France.

The soldiers that Marlborough led onto the battlefield came from a dozen states and more. Most of the Protestant rulers of western Europe joined in the huge military effort against Louis XIV. As the war went on, and the Duke added victory to victory, professional soldiers from across the continent hurried to join his armies to have their share in the glory. The skills they brought materially added to what Marlborough could attempt and achieve. The muster roll of his army, from great commanders like Prince Eugene of Savoy, and the Dutch Veld-Marshal Henry of Nassau, Count Overkirk, to the humblest soldier who wielded a musket in the ranks such as the Hampshire farmer Tom Kitcher and the Irish-woman soldier Christian Davies, represent much of what was the military life of the age. Fortunately some left informative memoirs, and study of these lively journals soon dispels any notion that warfare under Marlborough was slow, dull or quaint. These men and women were serious soldiers, and they fought to win.

The Duke of Marlborough's quiet and subtly effective diplomatic victories in this period helped immeasurably to hold together the Grand Alliance through all the complexities and strains of continental war. More dramatically, Marlborough procured by battle a decisive victory for the Alliance that others could have picked up, had they chosen to do so. His martial triumphs on the battlefield are mighty examples of the art of generalship in war and they are the subject of this book.

NOTES

1.   Churchill, W S, *Marlborough: His Life and Times*, 1947, Vol. I, p.15.

CHAPTER I

The Coming Man

You are a rascal. I forgive you, for you do it to get a living.

Just after 1.00 am on Sunday 5 June 1650, John Churchill, who one day would become the 1st Duke of Marlborough, was born in the groaning chair at Ash House, near Axminster in Devon, England.[1] He was the eldest son of Sir Winston Churchill, an impoverished Royalist officer who was broken in fortune by the English Civil War, and his parliamentarian wife, Elizabeth (a descendant of the great Elizabethan seaman, Sir Francis Drake). The young boy-child was christened on 12 June 1650, in the private chapel in Ash House.

Because of the difficult family circumstances, the young Churchills (John had five brothers and five sisters, although not all survived) were obliged to make their own way in the world. Winston Churchill's connections at court after the Restoration of King Charles II (who remembered his friends) enabled him to put his eldest son in fortune's way. In 1665, after some education in Dublin and at St Paul's School in London, the young John was placed as a page in the household of James, Duke of York, the brother of the King. His elder sister, Arabella Churchill, also had a place in the Duke's household, playing an intimate part in his private life as his mistress.[2]

On 14 September 1667 John Churchill was granted a commission, a 'pair of colours', as an Ensign in the King's Own Company of Colonel Russell's Regiment of Foot Guards (subsequently the Grenadier Guards), and he began his career as a soldier. He took the place of John Howard Esquire, who had to resign his commission because of his Roman Catholic faith. Churchill promptly went on campaign to Tangier in 1668, serving on attachment with the Gouvernor's Regiment. Precise dates are uncertain but Churchill had returned to England by 1671 and resumed his life at Court, attaining something of a devastating reputation amongst the dazzling beauties there.

Perhaps on account of his amorous intrigues Churchill was engaged in two duels in 1671, with a Mr Fenwick in January and with Captain Henry Herbert in August. On the latter occasion he was slightly wounded. Rather more profitably employed the following year, he served under the

1

Duke of York during the naval battles fought against the Dutch, as part of Charles II's alliance with France. During the bitterly fought battle at Solebay off the Suffolk coast on 7 June 1672, the young man gained a reputation for gallantry with the 1st Company of Foot Guards on the reeking shot-torn decks of the Duke of York's flagship, *The Prince*. He was rewarded with a captaincy in the Lord High Admiral's Regiment, over the heads of officers with more service and experience. Already jealous eyes were cast at the rapid progress of this handsome and apparently fortunate young man, who enjoyed such easy favour at Court.[3]

Churchill then went to war in France. He was a member of the small English army, under the command of James, Duke of Monmouth (the illegitimate son of Charles II), that the King provided to Louis XIV for active service in his current land campaign against the Dutch. Serving as Captain of grenadiers in Monmouth's own regiment, John Churchill's bravery and skill attracted the notice of the formidable French commander, the Vicomte de Turenne. He earned the soubriquet of 'Le Bel Anglais' amongst the French soldiers, apparently coined from a quip of Turenne's.

The handsome English officer was introduced to Louis XIV at this time. The King in later years remembered him well, although his initial impression of the young man was that he was rather too taken up with the highly spiced pleasures to be found at Court to make anything much of himself. Churchill also made the acquaintance of many of the French officers he would fight and beat when he was England's Captain-General thirty years later. During the repulse of one Dutch sortie, at Maastricht on 24 June 1673, Monmouth and Churchill distinguished themselves by their gallantry, under the very eyes of the French King. Captain d'Artagnan of the Mousquetières, the hero of Alexandre Dumas' novels, was killed in this affair, and amongst the young French volunteers who took part in the desperate action was Claude-Louis-Hector Villars. Ironically, Marlborough would one misty September day thirty-six years later confront and controversially defeat Villars who, as a Marshal of France, commanded the French army at Malplaquet on the border between France and the Spanish Netherlands.

By 1674 Churchill was once again enjoying the nefarious pleasures of the Court in London. With his startling good looks and great charm, he remained much in demand amongst the ladies of the place, and he conducted a warm and entertaining affair with his voluptuous cousin, Barbara Villiers, the King's particular mistress – an affair of which the cynical old monarch was no doubt aware. Churchill was reputedly obliged one evening to jump from the lady's bedroom window in his shirt to avoid meeting his King in embarrassing circumstances. Apparently in recognition of his discretion on this occasion, and possibly for other services provided, Villiers gave Churchill £4,500. The young man, used to relative poverty in a high spending world, would have been grateful for the cash gifts that the passionate Villiers bestowed on him at any time, and he promptly bought an annuity with the money. He was cautious with money – a virtue for which his enemies were inclined to sneer at him later in his career. The Merry Monarch understood his handsome courtier rather well and was amused by the escapade. He patted his cheek with the wry comment 'You are a rascal. I forgive you, for you do it to get a living.'[4]

In April 1674 Churchill entered the actual service of Louis XIV when Charles II asked the French King to grant the young man a colonelcy in the Royal English Regiment, an infantry corps in the French army. In this role Churchill was present at the Battle of Sinsheim on 16 June 1674, under Turenne. He fought also at Entzheim the following October, when the courage of the English regiments secured a bloody victory for the French commander over an Imperial German army. In the winter campaign that followed, Churchill was with Turenne when the Viscount seized the province of Alsace for France. In this series of campaigns, Churchill learned much of his trade as a soldier under the great Marshal, and he learned it well. He was Lieutenant-Colonel and an acknowledged commander in his 25th year, although he was about to enter a long period of uncertainty, intrigue and suspicion during which his rise to prominence and fortune was often in doubt. He would attain the ripe old age (for the period) of 52 years before he was fully the commanding general of an army on a campaign.

Churchill apparently had an offer of permanent service in Louis XIV's army, but rejected the notion as an Englishman could not hope to rise far in the French service. By the summer of 1675 he was in London again, with the role of Gentleman of the Bedchamber in the suite of his patron, the Duke of York. He was also Lieutenant-Colonel of the Duke of York's Regiment of Foot. At this time he met and fell in love with the sparkling Sarah Jennings, then a 15-year-old Maid of Honour to James's young second wife, Mary of Modena. She was also a close friend of the Princess Anne, youngest daughter of James and his first wife, Ann Hyde. Sarah was at first reluctant to accept the dashing young soldier, perhaps suspecting that his intentions were less than honourable. Despite this doubt the romance prospered and John Churchill and Sarah Jennings married in the winter of 1677–8 secretly, as both sets of parents wanted a more advantageous marriage for their children. This was undoubtedly a love match; neither of the young persons had wealth to speak of or particular connections, and many of their friends thought the whole thing rather strange. Still, the marriage was a particularly devoted one.

In later life Sarah wrote on one of her husband's old letters, 'I believe I was married when this was writ [22 February 1678] but it was not known to any one but the Duchess [Mary of Modena].'[5] John and Sarah drew strength and comfort from each other in unmeasured degrees throughout their marriage. Sarah was a dynamic and vibrant woman, often impossibly difficult to deal with, yet Churchill adored her. To Sarah, John Churchill was all that she could wish for in a man, although his unlimited patience often frustrated her, and their wonderful passion for each other remained undimmed to the end of their life together.

Alliances were shifting, and in 1678 Churchill was sent with Sidney Godolphin to Holland, to confer with the Stadholder, William of Orange, on plans to counter French expansion. This is an indication of the growing reliance that was placed on his diplomatic abilities, and was the first contact between Churchill and the Dutchman. Churchill was made Baron Churchill of Aymouth, in the Scottish Peerage, in December 1682. The following year the King's Own Regiment of (Royal) Dragoons were raised and Churchill became their first Colonel. Eyebrows were raised at a supposedly 'foot' officer getting the lucrative appointment of a mounted regiment (even though the dragoons were regarded as a humbler breed than the 'Horse' who were thought of as proper cavalry). A rather unkind doggerel rhyme at this time runs: 'Let's cut our meat with spoons, the sense is as good, as that Churchill should, be put to command the Dragoons.'[6] Churchill continued in the service of the Duke of York, throughout the growing difficulties that his steadfast adherence to the Roman Catholic faith caused. To an increasing degree, James came to depend upon him.

When Charles II died in January 1685, Churchill was sent to take the news to the French King in Versailles, and he walked in the Coronation procession of King James II as Gentleman of the Bedchamber. On 24 May 1685 the new King rewarded his loyal service when he was made Baron Churchill of Sandridge. Soon afterwards the Duke of Monmouth landed in Lyme Bay in Dorsetshire and quickly raised the west of England in revolt.

On Sunday 25 July 1685 Churchill had command, with the elderly French Catholic Louis Duras, Earl of Feversham, of the royal army at the defeat of Monmouth's rebel troops at Sedgemoor Dyke in Somersetshire. While Judge Jeffreys and others went on to make a shambles of parts of the West Country in ruthless suppression of rebellion, Churchill went back to London, having now arrived as a man of influence. Feversham got the Order of the Garter, but Churchill received a commission as Major-General, and the lucrative command of the First Troop of Horse Guards, the most prestigious colonelcy in the regular army at that time. He was also awarded a Somersetshire estate (worth £250 per annum). The previous owner, John Huber Esquire, swung on the gallows for his part in the late rebellion.

Popular unrest followed, as James pursued an unwise course of imposing Catholic officers on the army, Catholic appointees to the judiciary and Catholic peers on the Privy Council in London. William of

Orange (who was married to James II's eldest daughter, Mary) was waiting in the wings, and the King's actions were a dangerous and unpopular course to take. In response to the growing public unrest, a permanent military camp was established at Hounslow in Middlesex to the west of London. Churchill was present there with the King, and accompanied him on a progress that was undertaken to assess the mood of the country. It was noticed that Churchill pulled faces at a royal review of the troops. The King pretended not to see, but it was not a good sign.[7]

William of Orange landed in Torbay on 15 November 1688 and James ordered Feversham to muster the royal army at Salisbury in Wiltshire to oppose him. On 7 November James made Churchill a Lieutenant-General, but he left the King all the same on 4 December. Churchill certainly agonised over the decision, and was in very good company, only doing what many officers in the royal army did. Still, he owed everything to his benefactor; however unwise and stubborn James II was, he might have looked for something better, for his position was thereby fatally undermined. James remarked to Feversham, on learning of Churchill's departure from the Royal encampment: 'You knew him better than I my Lord, when you advised me to have him arrested with those who might have accompanied him in his flight, but I did not expect this terrible blow.'[8]

James II returned to London, to find that the Princess Anne, his younger and favourite daughter, had fled to Nottingham in company with Sarah Churchill. Soon afterwards he sent his Queen and infant son to France, and on 21 December 1688, having rather unwisely ordered Feversham to effectively disband his army, he followed. This was apparently to avoid civil war, but there was plenty of potential for anarchy instead. However, Churchill began to issue orders to the English troops, many of whom still regarded James to be their lawful King, for all his faults. Trouble, particularly with William's over-bearing Dutch troops, was thus largely avoided.

On 1 January 1689 (not New Year's Day at that time) Churchill was one of sixty-six peers assembled to welcome William of Orange at Westminster Abbey in London. William and Mary were proclaimed King and Queen of England on Wednesday 22 February 1689. Gazetted Lieutenant-General (again) by William, Churchill was given the task of re-organising the English Army (the Scots and Irish had separate establishments). Amongst the other rewards that came his way, were membership of the Privy Council, and the title of Earl of Marlborough. He remained a Gentleman of the Bedchamber, only the King was changed – the English Catholic was supplanted by a Dutch Calvinist.

On 15 May 1689 England, in alliance with Holland, declared war on France. The new Earl found himself fighting for the first time against French troops. On 27 August Marlborough distinguished himself with his gallant conduct at the Battle of Walcourt in the Spanish Netherlands. His cautious use of the steady English infantry, his employment of their well controlled musketry volleys, and the careful keeping back of cavalry reserves out of the thick of the fight until just the right moment, would all became hallmarks of his tactical style in future years.

Meanwhile, James II was campaigning in Ireland to regain the throne so rashly given up the previous year. Marlborough was not present at the Battles of the Boyne or Aughrim, where James's campaign foundered, but he was sent by Queen Mary, acting as Regent in London, to the command of 6,000 troops at the capture of Cork in September 1689, and again at Kinsale in October.

In 1691 Marlborough was sent by William III to co-ordinate with the Dutch a renewed campaign against France. Suddenly, on 20 January 1692, he fell from Royal favour and was dismissed in disgrace:

> I believe your grace will be surprised to hear that my Lord Marlborough is out of all his employment, and the manner was very disagreeable to him; for in his waiting week, which is this, after having put on the King's shirt in the morning, before twelve o'clock, my Lord Nottingham was sent to him, to tell him that the King had no further need of his service.[9]

Sarah was the close friend of the Princess Anne, and there had been a violent row the previous evening between her and Queen Mary. Perhaps this was the cause of the dismissal, but Marlborough was in regular correspondence with James II in exile (perhaps hedging his bets in case of another Stuart restoration), and he certainly trod thin ice with William as a consequence. Matters were not helped by ever present jealousy and rivalry between the King's Dutch favourites and the English courtiers.

Marlborough was committed to the Tower of London on 15 May 1692. The charge was high treason. Although this was serious stuff, the evidence against him was flimsy, and William seems to have been taking simple precautions, as there were persistent rumours of a Jacobite expedition to restore James II to the throne. He may also have been taking the opportunity to rein in this ambitious and gifted man. By October Marlborough was set free and the charges against him forgotten but, out of office, he kicked his heels quietly in semi-retirement for the next four years.

At this time there occurred the strange incident of the Camaret Bay letter. Supposedly provided by Marlborough to the Jacobite agent, Sackville, on 14 May 1694, the missive disclosed plans for an attack upon the French port of Brest. The attack itself, on 16 June, was an expensive failure and the commander of the expedition, Lieutenant-General Tollemarche, was amongst those killed. Hard evidence seems very scarce as to real misconduct by Marlborough, given that he was out of office at the time and was not immediately a party to military plans of this kind. In addition, Louis XIV had plenty of other sources for this sort of information. Doubts about his complete innocence persisted all the same, given Marlborough's continued correspondence with the exiled court at St Germain. Some thought it quite possible that he sent news of the plans after the information was of any use, but soon enough to curry favour with James II. If that were so it was questionable conduct certainly, but hardly the cause of the disaster that overtook the Allied expedition.

Marlborough's friends were active in trying to persuade William to take him back into his service. The King was not convinced; he wrote to the Earl of Shrewsbury on 16 July 1694:

> In regard to what you wrote to me in your last, concerning Lord Marlborough, I can say no more than that I do not think it for the good of my service, to entrust the command of my troops to him.[10]

The death of Queen Mary of smallpox in January 1695 rather changed matters, for she died childless. William could no longer ignore the Princess Anne, as she was now heir to the English throne. (No child by a second marriage of William's would be eligible to take the crown on his death.) Marlborough and his wife were Anne's closest friends and their fortunes revived accordingly. With the constant assistance of people like Shrewsbury and the Earl of Albemarle (the King's young Dutch favourite and a good friend of Marlborough) the Earl regained his offices, and on 29 April 1698 he was appointed the governor of the young Duke of Gloucester, Anne's only surviving son and, after herself, the heir to the throne. In short, Marlborough had the upbringing of the future King in his hands.

William's letter of appointment for the governorship contained flowery compliments to Marlborough ('My Lord, teach him to be like yourself'), but their relationship seemed cool, even though the King felt obliged to make use of his obvious talents.[11] Marlborough wrote to Shrewsbury on 22 May 1700:

> The King's coldness to me still continues; so that I should have been glad to have had your friendly advice; for to have friends and acquaintances unreasonably jealous, and the King at the same time angry, is what I know not how to bear.[12]

Nonetheless, when William went to Holland in July, he appointed Marlborough to be one of the Lord Justices responsible for the government of England while he was abroad. When the Duke of Gloucester died of smallpox the following month, the King wrote a kind and reassuring letter to Marlborough – a simple sign of his reinstatement to Royal favour. William realised that, in the uncertain times that loomed ahead, he had need of this untrusted but capable man.

As war with France over the succession in Spain grew more and more likely, Marlborough was appointed General of Infantry on 12 June 1701, and Ambassador-Extraordinary and Plenipotentiary to the United Provinces of Holland. The following month Marlborough accompanied the King on a visit to the Hague, and he was closely involved in the negotiations which led to the Treaty of Grand Alliance. In 1702, as the terrible danger of war with France came nearer, Princess Anne ascended the throne of England on the accidental death of her Dutch brother-in-law. With this change it seemed possible that all William's carefully laid plans to combine the strength of England and Holland to oppose Louis XIV might be lost. This did not happen – those plans had been negotiated with the States-General of Holland by John Churchill at the direction of the deceased King, and preparations for war proceeded during the period of Anne's accession with scarcely a skipped beat.

NOTES

1. Edwards, H, *A Life of Marlborough*, 1926, p.4.
2. One of the meaner criticisms of the Duke was that he climbed to fame and fortune under the patronage of a man who seduced his rather plain sister. Well, to be the mistress of a nobleman has, for much of human history, been the necessary choice of many gently born young ladies who, in their own fashion, had to make their way in life. The son of the union of the Duke of York and Arabella Churchill was James Fitzjames, the Duke of Berwick. He was a superb soldier, a Marshal of France, and became one of Marlborough's most accomplished opponents.
3. Edwards, p. 12.
4. Wolseley, G, *The Life of Marlborough*, Vol. I, 1894, p.158; Rowse, A, *The Early Churchills*, 1956, p.158.
5. Edwards, p.22.
6. Wolseley, p.353.
7. Chandler, D, *Marlborough as Military Commander*, 1973, p 24.
8. ibid., p.25.
9. Edwards, p. 59.
10. ibid., p. 86.
11. ibid., p. 90.
12. ibid., p.96.

CHAPTER II

The Trouble with Spain
The War of the Spanish Succession

The Pyrenees have ceased to exist

On 1 November 1700 the invalid King Carlos II of Spain died. He was nicknamed 'The Sufferer' and lived far longer than anyone really expected. In his sad bewilderment he gave to Europe a grim legacy. Carlos was childless and it was intended that the throne of Spain, when he left it, should be bestowed on a young Bavarian prince, Joseph Ferdinand. This was not at all contentious – most of the rulers of Europe were agreed on the wisdom of this course. Unfortunately, the young prince died in February 1699 before he could ascend the throne. Louis XIV of France and William III of England so feared that war would result that they agreed the Second Partition Treaty in June 1699, augmenting the Treaty of Ryswick of 1697 (which had brought to an end the last European war). This allowed the Austrian Archduke Charles to have the Spanish throne in return for certain important concessions to French interests elsewhere, particularly in northern Italy. This seemed a sensible and practical solution to a complex problem, although the Austrian Emperor thought that too much was being handed to France.

As it was, Carlos perversely left the throne to Philip, Duke of Anjou and the young second grandson of Louis XIV. The danger inherent in this offer was obvious, quite apart from the fact that the Archduke Charles was a rival claimant. Spain had extensive possessions in Italy, the Low Countries and the Americas, and she controlled much of the lucrative slave trade from West Africa. For Louis XIV's grandson to sit on the throne in Madrid would mark an extraordinary extension of French influence and power. France was already the single most populous and powerful country in Europe, and Louis XIV had a long history of ambition for territorial and political expansion – the most recent being the bitterly fought wars in the Netherlands, which had staggered to a tired end in the imperfect treaties of 1697 and 1699.

The news of the death of Carlos, and the dramatic offer of his throne to Philip of Anjou, reached Fontainebleau on 8 November 1700. Despite his ambitions for France, Louis XIV was very astute, and he could well see the trouble that acceptance of the proffered throne would bring. The recently concluded Second Partition Treaty contained agreements, not only that Archduke Charles should have the Spanish throne, but that certain Barrier Towns in the Spanish Netherlands (present-day Belgium) would be garrisoned by the Dutch. This was their security against French invasion from the south. For a French-born King to sit on the throne of Spain must put the security of these important towns in some doubt and would neatly abrogate the Treaty, not only on the succession itself, but on the Barrier too. Acceptance of the offer would risk offending the Austrians, the Dutch and William III. In simple fact Louis XIV would alarm every Protestant Prince in Europe whose fears of mighty Catholic France would rise once more – renewed war might result.

Despite all these sombre considerations, Louis XIV reluctantly gave his consent to Anjou's acceptance of the offered throne. Apparently the Dauphin, the King's eldest son, urged that his own young son should be permitted to claim this glittering inheritance. Louis gave way, and on 16 November 1700 Castel del Rey, the Spanish envoy at Versailles, was invited to kneel and kiss the hand of the young French Prince, now his new King, Philip V of Spain. The Duc de St Simon, who witnessed the scene, wrote:

> Contrary to all precedent, the King caused the double doors of his cabinet [private chambers] to be thrown open, and ordered all the crowd assembled without to enter; then, glancing majestically over the numerous company: 'Gentlemen' said he, indicating the Duc d'Anjou, 'This is the King of Spain.'[1]

The assembled notables then went to prayers in the King's private chapel. There was only one kneeling cushion, always used by Louis XIV. He offered it to his grandson, now a monarch in his own right, but the young man blushingly declined the cushion that his grandfather offered, and so both men knelt on the carpet.

Preparations moved quickly for the triumphal procession of King Philip and his entourage to Madrid. All might yet have been well, given careful diplomacy, but for a number of significant miscalculations by the normally sure-footed French ruler.

Reports that Louis XIV emotionally embraced his grandson on his departure from Versailles and declared 'The Pyrenees have ceased to exist', were widely believed. (It seems more likely that Castel del Rey incautiously blurted this out on being presented to his new King.) This might have been dismissed as loose private talk, without serious meaning, but the French King soon began to meddle in the affairs of Spain. Anxious to protect his grandson's new possessions in the Spanish Netherlands, in

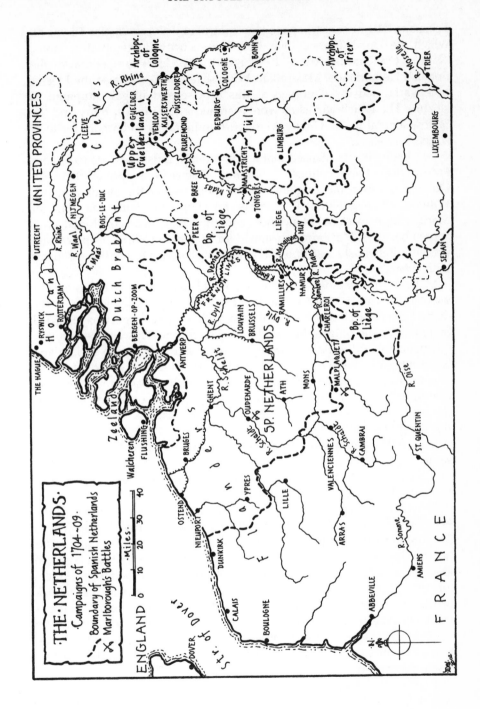

THE·NETHERLANDS·
Campaigns of 1704~09.
---- Boundary of Spanish Netherland
✗ Marlborough's Battles

·Miles·
0   10   20   30   40

February 1701 he sent troops to take control of the very Barrier Towns on which the Dutch pinned their hopes of security (Luxembourg, Mons, Namur, Oudenarde, Ath and Nieuport). The Governor-General of the Spanish Netherlands, Maximilian Wittelsbach, who was also the Elector of Bavaria, actively connived at this unwise and illegal campaign of seizure. The Dutch garrisons were marched away into captivity and the States-General in the Hague were left humiliatingly to bargain for their soldiers' release.

Gradually, it was realised that a firm attempt must be made to oppose France over these actions. A Grand Alliance was formed between Holland, Austria and England (at this point rather the junior partner). William III negotiated the terms for England, with the Earl of Marlborough in close attendance, and the Treaty was concluded on 7 September 1701. Marlborough signed for England in William's place, and was simultaneously instrumental in keeping Sweden out of the argument with France.

Matters grew rapidly worse when, on 13 September 1701, Louis XIV went to the Court at St Germain and emotionally acknowledged to the dying King James II that his son, the Chevalier de St George, was regarded by France as the rightful heir to the English throne. This was yet another infringement of the Barrier Treaty, and caused indignation in England when it became known. Louis XIV had managed to give grave offence to Austria, Holland and England in turn. The French ambassador in London, Camille d'Houton, Marquis de Tallard, was promptly expelled which was unfortunate, as his quiet and skilled diplomacy had been of real value at this dangerous time.

Louis XIV learned of the Treaty of Grand Alliance five days after it was signed, although its detailed provisions only became known to him some time later, when the Swedish Ambassador gave him the news.[2] Meantime, William III did not live to see another war. He died on 8 March 1702 from the effects of a fall from his horse near Hampton Court in Middlesex. The Princess Anne came to the English throne, and she proved to be just as resolute in furthering the common cause against France. Two days after her brother-in-law's death, Anne sent Marlborough to the Hague to ensure that the States-General were still steadfast for the Alliance. Matters moved rapidly forward and the Garter King of Arms and his heralds proclaimed a State of War with France and Spain at the gates of St James's Palace in London at 1.00 pm on 4 May 1702. A similar declaration was made at the Hague and in Vienna that same day. On hearing the news, Louis XIV remarked rather drily: 'I must be growing old if ladies are now declaring war on me.'[3]

Importantly, Queen Anne confirmed the Earl of Marlborough (as he still was at this time) as Captain-General and Commander in Chief of her army to be deployed in the Low Countries. The Dutch were persuaded to approve his authority over their own troops on campaign. He was accepted despite the claims of several veteran generals of their own who also aspired to the command, for the States-General had grown used to his reassuring manners during the negotiations for the Alliance.

Declaring war on Louis XIV was one thing, pursuing an effective strategy was quite another. It was intended by the Allied powers that campaigns against France would proceed simultaneously in northern Italy, Spain, along the River Rhine and in the Savoyard Alps. However, Holland was under most immediate threat. The natural fear of the Dutch was of an early invasion of their southern provinces now that the Barrier Towns were lost to their control. Once already in the previous forty years they had breached their precious sea-dykes and drowned their land, rather than submit to French troops. Louis XIV undoubtedly hoped to take advantage of the temporary confusion in Allied councils now William III was dead, and he planned a rapid campaign to knock the States-General out of the war. A bruising invasion of southern Holland by the able veteran Marshal Boufflers and 60,000 veteran French troops might soon have the Dutch looking for a separate peace. To counter this offensive threat the main Allied effort would unavoidably have to be in the north

Once the campaign was underway, Boufflers made short work of out-manoeuvring the Dutch field commander, Godart van Rede Ginkel, the Earl of Athlone. He was an able soldier, having served William III as his commander in Ireland on campaign against James II, but he was no match for the skilful French Marshal. Before very long the Anglo-Dutch army was penned against Nijmegen on the lower Rhine, but Boufflers found that his campaign began to drag. Soon afterwards Marlborough arrived in the field as the chosen commander of the Anglo-Dutch forces. Athlone also aspired to that command, and he looked on Marlborough's arrival with a keen and jealous eye. However, before long he was won over by the Duke's easy charm and subtle skills, and he wrote later that year:

> The success of this campaign is solely due to this incomparable Commander in Chief, since I confess that I, serving as second in command, opposed in all circumstances his opinions and proposals.[4]

Early in June 1702 Marlborough assumed the command of the now reinforced Allied army near Nijmegen. He had about 60,000 troops, nearly one quarter of whom were English, Scots, Welsh and Irish. The remainder were Dutch (the largest contingent, including many Scots and Swiss soldiers), Germans and Danes. Boufflers' army lay in the enclave of Cleves, apparently in an ideal position to dictate events. This was an illusion, for the French commander, perhaps through over-confidence, was badly over extended, and he had no substantial magazines or forward depots near at hand. Any threat to his lengthy lines of communication and supply back to the Spanish Netherlands and Brussels would seriously unbalance his deployment.

Marlborough struck on 26 July 1702, advancing rapidly south-westwards towards Liège. Momentarily dazzled by the unexpected speed of the Allied move, Boufflers feared for the safety of his communications. He drew his army back across the heaths of Peer towards the River Meuse (Maas). This rather hurried march took the French troops perilously across the front of Marlborough's army, drawn up in battle array nearby. In the event, Boufflers only escaped a severe mauling because the Dutch field deputies forbade the use of their troops in any 'hazardous' enter-prise. These field deputies took it upon themselves to stand at Marlborough's elbow and offer criticism and advice and, on occasions, to veto his plans for action. Marlborough swallowed his disappointment as best he could in the interests of Allied harmony, but he could not resist the chance to take the field deputies 'Who made it their business to prevent engagements and forbid the commander in chief to fight battles.'[5] and their generals to a vantage point from where they could watch the out-manoeuvred French scurry past: '. . . in the greatest confusion and disorder imaginable.'[6] The cautious Dutch fairly acknowledged the opportunity they had allowed to slip away, but in practice they would amply prove that this was a lesson that they needed a great deal of time to learn fully.

With this skilful movement Marlborough forced the French army away from the Lower Rhine, and the important cities of Liège and Cologne. Large areas of Guelderland were recovered for the Allies at little cost other than that of worn shoe leather, and the Earl obtained valuable strategic depth in which to manoeuvre and defend the southern borders of Holland. Marlborough's soldiers took heart from what was a very obvious success for their commander, while a significant psychological advantage was gained over Boufflers, who was rather shaken by this abrupt turn of events.

Although the pace of operations rather stalled in the months that followed, Marlborough was created a Duke by the Queen for his successful efforts in the Low Countries (somewhat to his wife's alarm, at the likely expense of maintaining such a dignity). Meanwhile, the Dutch persisted in their caution, objecting to aggressive campaigning, and looking instead for steady and careful manoeuvres. This was an early turning point for the Allies in the war, for the new Duke was effectively prevented from forcing his opponents to accept pitched battle in either 1702 or 1703. The Dutch attitude was understandable, for a botched battle would destroy the only army they had to defend their republic. Marlborough and his troops could always negotiate their way back to England, or so it seemed to the Dutch. All the same, the ultimate cost in this policy of caution was quite enormous, for the outcome was a long war and, eventually, a less advantageous peace than might otherwise have been demanded.

Thwarted in wider enterprises, Marlborough was not idle. He was obliged to restrict himself to laying siege to French fortresses at Venlo, Ruremond, Liège and elsewhere. Boufflers, baffled by his opponent's subtle and patient skills, could not save them, and yet another success was therefore added to the Duke's credit.

In the campaign of 1703 Marlborough found the Dutch caution as maddening as ever, in their continued reluctance to allow him to go out and engage the French. Athlone was now dead, and the Duke missed his sound support, but he found a ready enough colleague in the Dutch Veld-Marshal Henry of Nassau, Count Overkirk. Still, he was obliged to open his campaign that year with the rather humdrum siege of the French-held town of Bonn on the Rhine, while Overkirk covered his operations from Maastricht. Despite a mishap at Tongres, where Boufflers surprised and overwhelmed an Allied detachment, Bonn fell to Marlborough on 15 May 1703. Three months later he seized the fortress of Huy near to Namur on the Meuse, and Limburg fell to his troops shortly afterwards.

Other plans miscarried badly. The Dutch generals, Opdham, Coehorn, Slangenberg, and even Overkirk on occasions, foiled and frustrated the Duke's attempts to engage Boufflers and his colleague, Marshal Villeroi, in open battle. A great project to seize Antwerp and Ostend descended into confusion, largely because of Dutch awkwardness. Often when the Dutch Field Deputies were agreed on action, their generals were not; in effect the Dutch would not let Marlborough fight, and they still hoped that victory was to be obtained without risk. Although the French commanders appeared to be unable to counter the Duke's adroit moves, the results from the Allied campaign in 1703 were disappointingly modest.

All this time, far away in central Europe, dramatic events were unfolding. The third main party to the Alliance, the Austrian Habsburg Empire, was deep in trouble. There was outright rebellion in Hungary, and the Imperial campaign in northern Italy progressed very slowly. The Elector of Bavaria, Maximilian Wittelsbach, although actually owing personal allegiance to the Emperor Leopold, concluded an alliance with France, partly to safeguard his role as Governor-General in the Spanish Netherlands, but also to take advantage of Vienna's present weakness. The major free city of Ulm on the River Danube was seized by Bavarian troops, and Leopold's armies, distracted by rebellion at their back and with treachery before them, rapidly lost ground in the campaign.

Although the Elector was for practical purposes quite isolated from his French ally by the formidable barrier of the Black Forest, this campaign opened exciting possibilities for Louis XIV. He could now exert even more pressure both on the Emperor and on the small German princely states that supported the Grand Alliance. In return for the payment of English and Dutch gold, these princelings, although very prone to external pressure from more powerful neighbours, were providing excellent troops for the Allied armies. A major blow at Austria, perhaps the capture of Vienna by French and Bavarian armies, and the subsequent detachment from the Alliance of the German princes, would be a prize of enormous worth to the French King. It might win the war for France, no matter what was going on in the Spanish Netherlands.

At the close of the year, Marlborough was despondent at the recent death from smallpox of his only son, and tormented by chronic migraine headaches. He looked gloomily forward to the prospects for a new campaign in 1704. The Dutch deputies, cautious, brave and obstinate, would always be at his side, and it seemed unlikely that he could achieve very much in their company. The thought of comfortable retirement as a private English gentleman attracted him, but Queen Anne was alarmed at such a notion. She wrote to her Captain-General in terms both bold and encouraging, asking that he continue in her service:

> Give me leave to say you should consider your faithful friends and poor country, which must be ruined if ever you should put your melancholy thoughts in execution . . . if ever you should forsake me, I would have nothing more to do with the world but would make another abdication; for what is a crown when the support of it is gone?[7]

Marlborough would never refuse such an appeal, and his fertile mind cast about for promising courses to pursue. It was apparent to the Duke that, if he were to achieve anything great, he had to be free from the confines of campaigning in the Low Countries. He considered plans for a wider war, perhaps he would take his army to campaign in the Moselle valley, or to attack the French in Alsace – he might even go to Spain or to Italy.

Meanwhile, the threat to Austria was growing. The French Marshal Villars had achieved a victory at Friedlingen over an Imperial army in late 1702, and the following spring he managed to march an army through the passes of the Black Forest to the support of the Elector of Bavaria. Falling out with that devious nobleman, the hot-tempered Villars left Marshal Marsin to continue the campaign in southern Germany and returned to Alsace. Marsin and the Elector then overwhelmed a smaller Imperial army at Höchstädt on the Danube in 1703; if matters went on in this way the Emperor might be forced to ask for terms. Then the Alliance must fall and France become triumphant.

On examination the threat to Austria was rather more apparent than real. Bavaria itself was open to attack on several fronts, and the brilliant but erratic Elector, as a result of his recent duplicity towards the Emperor, had few friends other than Louis XIV (and that shrewd monarch always watched his ally with care). The Bavarian army, tough and well trained though it was, was badly over-stretched, and required substantial reinforcement by the French before an attempt on Vienna could be made. Any French force would have to operate at a considerable distance from its supports, and would become dependent on the Elector for subsistence. This would give most commanders pause for thought. With the extensive commitments that already faced the armies of Louis XIV (not least in the Low Countries), and the sheer distances to be covered when campaigning in Bavaria, any advance on Vienna would have to take the form of a raid rather than anything grander. This would certainly be damaging enough and would threaten a dislocation of the Grand Alliance, but the occupation of Vienna would hardly bring the Emperor to his knees unless initial Franco-Bavarian successes were sustained in a wider campaign. However, the threat, in whatever degree, needed to be addressed seriously, and Marlborough astutely used this chance to get his army away from the restraining hand of the Dutch deputies.

NOTES

1. Martin, C, *Louis XIV*, 1975, p.77.
2. Provisions of the Treaty of Grand Alliance signed 7 September 1701:
   The Allies [at this time England, the United Provinces of Holland, and Austria] would seek to obtain, by negotiation or by war, that :
   (a) Binding guarantees be given that the thrones of France and Spain would remain separate (*not* that Philip of Anjou, the French claimant, would necessarily vacate the throne in Madrid);
   (b) Austria should receive the Milanese, Naples, Sicily, the Balearic Islands, the Spanish Netherlands, and Luxembourg;
   (c) Holland would regain her Barrier Fortresses, recently seized by the French;
   (d) The Elector of Brandenburg would become King of Prussia in return for his support of the Alliance;
   (e) Financial subsidies to German princes would be guaranteed in return for military support to the Alliance;
   (f) England and Holland should have a free hand to conduct trade in the West Indies.

   Clauses (b) and (c) are partly contradictory over the difficult issue of sovereignty of the Spanish Netherlands. While a prerequisite of an agreement to form an alliance, this would give rise to problems once the territory was in Allied hands, as happened after Ramillies. Almost inevitably, Holland and Austria would be at odds over this matter. Marlborough took care to see that the Treaty was drafted in terms sufficiently vague so as to be acceptable to the House of Commons in London. He resisted demands for guaranteed numbers of troops to be provided, even when William III would have conceded the point to get an agreement.

The intention of the Allies was to procure a division of the Spanish Empire, on equitable terms between the Habsburg and Bourbon claimants and this was eventually achieved. 'The objective of the war, which King William meditated, and Queen Anne waged, was a partition.' (Trevelyan, G M, *Blenheim*, 1948, p.146.) In April 1707 a subsequent clause was added, binding the Allies to strive for a Protestant (Hanoverian) succession to the throne of England. See Trevelyan p.149, for an interesting description of how Louis XIV got the news, and the details of the Treaty of Alliance against him.

3. Cowles, V, *The Great Marlborough and His Duchess*, 1983, p.172.
4. Trevelyan, p.238. Marlborough had no formal appointment to command Dutch troops but, in practice, he did so when on campaign with the Anglo-Dutch armies.
5. Green, D, *Sarah, Duchess of Marlborough*, 1967, p.86.
6. Trevelyan, p.239.
7. Churchill, W S, *Marlborough: His Life and Times*, Vol II, 1947, p.700.

CHAPTER III
To the Aid of Austria
The Long March to the Danube,
May–July 1704

To march where Britons never marched before.[1]

By the third year of the war, it was evident that the states in the Grand Alliance had no clear understanding of how to progress their diverse strategy against France to good effect. The campaign in northern Italy was producing few positive results and tied up large numbers of Imperial troops. Meanwhile, in Spain the nephew of the Duke of Marlborough, James Fitzjames, the Duke of Berwick, conducted a highly successful campaign against the Allies whose efforts, so expensive in money and men, held out little prospect of early success. All along the Rhine the French held strong fortresses and lines of defence, and the Allies had no serious plans for an offensive to shake their grip.

In the Spanish Netherlands, Marlborough had succeeded in capturing a string of important fortresses from the French during 1702 and 1703. Marshal Boufflers had been obliged to withdraw from the lower stretches of the Rhine and pull back deep into Brabant. Here complex lines of defence were under construction behind which he could manoeuvre to protect Brussels. In the Allied camp, the Dutch Field Deputies and their generals hampered the Duke in his desire to force a decisive battle on the French. 'Victorious without Slaughter' was the worthy inscription on a medal the States-General presented to Marlborough to commemorate his successes, but such a policy was unlikely to win a war. Marlborough felt the need to look farther afield, hoping to find an opportunity to operate away from the restraining hand of the Dutch, and the constricted positional warfare in which he was involved.

Danger for the Grand Alliance was growing in the south. General Bedmar held the Moselle Valley with 21,000 French troops, while Marshal Tallard had a firm grip on the Alsace region with an army 31,000 strong. From here he could maintain communications with the Elector of Bavaria on the Danube. The Elector could field about 45,000 troops, when

19

combined with those French soldiers under the command of Marshal Marsin; he posed a significant threat to Emperor Leopold in Vienna, who had also a revolt in Hungary on his hands. Leopold's field commander in Swabia, Louis Guillaume, the Margrave of Baden, had fewer than 35,000 soldiers and he was proving quite incapable of countering the Elector's moves. Should Louis XIV decide to reinforce his Bavarian ally still further, it seemed highly likely that Vienna would be in peril, with the most unfortunate consequences for the Allied cause.

After a certain amount of plotting with Marlborough, Count Wratislaw, the Imperial Envoy to England, persuaded Queen Anne to permit the Duke to shift the entire centre of gravity of the war. He would remove his army away from the Spanish Netherlands and go to southern Germany to aid the Austrian Emperor. The French forces were badly over-stretched on the Upper Rhine and the Danube, and the effort of maintaining a link between Alsace and Bavaria called for exhaustive and wasteful operations. Large numbers of French troops were tied down un-productively in this campaign, for the Elector was not a particularly reliable ally, being both devious and self-seeking. There was always the chance that he would want to switch his allegiance back to the Emperor once he thought it most advantageous to do so. However, in the spring of 1704, the danger to the Grand Alliance from this particular quarter seemed real, and Marlborough took the opportunity it offered to operate on a wider stage. This campaign was to be an enterprise of the most daring kind, fraught with major difficulties but offering the potential for enormous rewards.

The French threat to southern Holland once Marlborough's army marched away was also very real, and had to be weighed against the perceived danger to Vienna. Were the Dutch likely, with their dire memories of French invasions and devastation of their provinces, to permit this new far-off campaign? In addition, strong French armies lay along the route that the Duke's marching army must take – Bedmar and Tallard would hover on his right flank for long stretches of the march up the Rhine. It remained to be seen whether the Allied army could move with sufficient speed to elude them. If the French commanders recognised his intentions early enough to take action just once, their armies could combine to strike the Duke's columns at any sensitive point along the whole length of the Rhine from Maastricht to Colmar. Marlborough would be dreadfully vulnerable and out of position, forced to react to his opponent's initiatives, while simultaneously Vienna remained under threat and southern Holland in peril.

The keys to success for Marlborough were surprise and fast marching, and these required preparations of the most discreet and careful kind. He had a particular advantage in his ability to pay hard cash for the supplies and equipment to be gathered, and thus the Duke's agents were able to

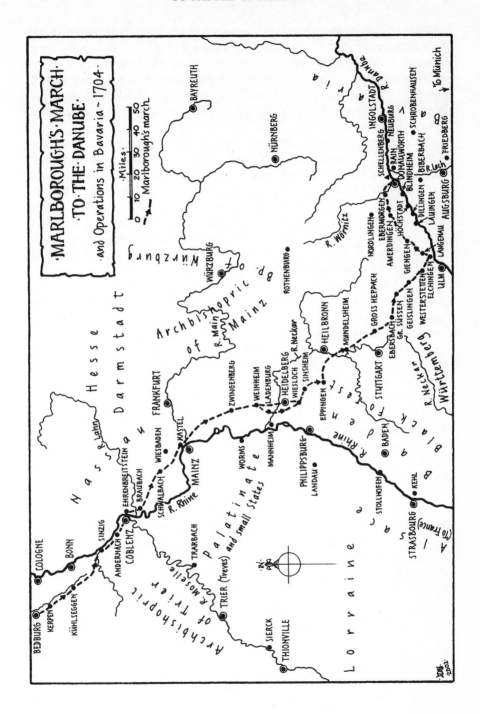

establish essential magazines and depots along the projected line of march well in advance. Davenport, Marlborough's agent in Frankfurt, had the capacity to dispense large sums to the rulers and populations of the districts through which his army must travel. Paying for supplies as they marched, the Allied soldiers would be welcomed, in stark contrast to the French who operated rather differently, and seized what they needed when they could.

Having received his commission from Queen Anne to go to southern Germany if he thought fit – 'to send a speedy succour to his Imperial Majesty and the Empire'[2], Marlborough crossed from Harwich to Holland on 19–21 April 1704. He sailed immediately after an appalling row with his fiery wife, the Duchess Sarah, over her unfounded suspicions that he was intriguing with another woman. Unsurprisingly, he was troubled with headaches. Once at the Hague, the Duke subtly hid the full truth from the Dutch, pressing the need to simply go and campaign in the Moselle valley against Bedmar, in preparation for a thrust into France. After a heated debate, the good reputation of the Duke in the eyes of the States-General, and their intrinsic confidence in him, asserted itself; they gave their consent to his proposed venture on 4 May 1704. The Dutch simply stipulated that those troops in Dutch pay should remain in the Low Countries to protect Holland, and they extracted a promise that Marlborough would return at once, should the French attempt an invasion. In particular, there was already a sizeable Dutch, Hessian and Prussian corps under General Johan Goor operating on the Upper Rhine with the Margrave of Baden's army, and the Duke was able to promise their speedy return, using barges on the Rhine, if they were needed.

Marlborough's first task was to disengage his army in the Low Countries, and to move so swiftly to the Middle Rhine that the nearest French commander, Marshal Villeroi, would have little time for proper reflection. The Duke let it be known, in an apparently indiscreet conversation, that he favoured a campaign in the Moselle valley, so his opening moves would fit that plan. Accordingly, the looming threat to Bedmar's French detachment in the Moselle would almost certainly draw Villeroi southwards away from the Dutch, and the fears of the States-General would be calmed. Once the march was in progress, and before Villeroi could combine with Bedmar and form a plan to strike at Marlborough's columns, the Duke would have moved on. The plan was simple, but the bewildering tempo of his operations along the Middle and Upper Rhine and over the hills of Swabia into the Danube valley, by exerting a fatal gravitational pull on the French armies, would keep Holland and the crossings of the Lower Rhine safe. Put at its most plain, Marlborough would strike in a quite unexpected way, and his opponents would have no time to consider what was to be done to regain the initiative.

The Duke arrived at Ruremond on 8 May, and he conducted a series of inspections of his troops gathered both there and also at Maastricht on 10 May. The troops put on a brave show, despite spring rain 'Not withstanding the rainey wether which happened at the same time [the army] made a most glorious appearance.'[3] His preparations were made with admirable capability, and on Monday 19 May 1704 the army began its march southwards from Bedburg. The force Marlborough took with him at this stage comprised about 19,000 troops, all of whom were in English pay.[4] With no hindrance, by 26 May, the Duke's army reached the confluence of the Moselle and the Rhine at Coblenz. Here they were joined by a contingent of 5,000 Hanoverian and Prussian troops, which the Duke had previously arranged should rendezvous with his army.

Marshal Villeroi, despite the forewarnings of an intended Allied operation in the Moselle valley, was puzzled by the speed of Marlborough's march, as it seemed to lay bare the Dutch frontier to attack. He appealed to Louis XIV in Versailles for advice, and the helpful reply was that if the Duke marched, then he too must march. So, Villeroi was drawn away to the south, just as Marlborough had expected. All the same, Count Overkirk soon asked the Duke to suspend his march, mistakenly fearing that the French were readying themselves to strike those Dutch forces that remained to watch the frontier. Marlborough, who understood far better than Overkirk that Villeroi's freedom of action was now snatched away, sent the stalwart Dutch Veld-Marshal a reassuring message, but nothing more.

On 27 May 1704 Marlborough began crossing his army over pontoon bridges to the east bank of the Rhine. This move made it plain to everyone that his intentions were not directed to the Moselle valley at all, but his line of march could still take his army, 'the Scarlet Caterpillar', to attack Tallard from the vicinity of Strasbourg in Alsace.[5] The French commanders remained in ignorance and indecision, and it was important for the Duke that this should be so. Once his likely intention to go the Danube was discovered, the Elector of Bavaria might move to defend the narrow passes through the Swabian hills. It was uncertain whether the 50-year-old Margrave of Baden had sufficient sense or energy to prevent such an operation. Before long, Marlborough might find the hills barred to him in his front, while Villeroi and Tallard closed threateningly up to the right flank of his line of march.

Marlborough's cavalry crossed the Main on 3 June and he had now openly flagged his intention to go to the Danube valley, rather than to strike at the French in Alsace. The Duke was simultaneously able to open new lines of communication and supply to central Germany, rather than all the way back to the Low Countries. These new routes were far less vulnerable to French interference, and must have been the source of considerable satisfaction to Marlborough. He had undoubtedly stolen a march on the French, and had neatly disentangled his army from the Low Countries and all the problems he found there. Now, wide horizons opened up before him; all he needed was the co-operation of his Imperial allies.

By 7 June 1704 the leading Allied soldiers crossed a bridge of boats over the Neckar at Ladenburg, where Hessian reinforcements joined the marching army. At this point Marlborough also cut loose from the Rhine and lost the ability to use barges to go swiftly back downstream to help the Dutch if their border was attacked. The Duke now admitted to the Dutch that his goal was, after all, the Danube and a vigorous campaign to assist Vienna. Seeing that, as he had predicted, the French armies were forced to march south in an effort to keep pace with his dazzling moves, the States-General took the news of the deception played on them with commendable calm. More than this, they confirmed that the Duke had the command of the Goor's corps on the Upper Rhine, whenever he saw fit to use them. With this increment, and with Danish troops marching to join him, Marlborough now had some 40,000 men under command. He could, on his own account and without reference to allies or field deputies, turn on and outmatch any of the different enemy columns slowly manoeuvering against him. However, he aimed at the destruction of the Elector of Bavaria's entire war-making capability, not that of isolated detachments.

The march to the Danube itself was a model of careful planning and well considered discipline. Frequent stockpiles of supplies – food, forage, clothes, boots, harness – had been arranged all along the route, courtesy of English gold. Day-to-day necessities were purchased by the commissaries of the army as it went along. Care was taken to pay for everything obtained, in stark contrast to the French way of campaigning, and farmers brought their produce to the line of march to sell to the Allies as they passed. The marching itself was in fairly easy stages, with strict march discipline being enforced. The troops were naturally quite used to this trudging labour and would readily appreciate the thought and care behind each well planned day. Starting before dawn each morning, the soldiers stepped out for six hours before stopping at a pre-arranged spot to bivouac for the remainder of the day. Ample rest was permitted, food was plentiful, beer was brewed, and frequent re-supplies of worn-out shoes and clothing were arranged.

Captain Robert Parker of the Royal Regiment of Ireland wrote: 'Surely never was such a march carried on with more order and regularity and with less fatigue both to man and horse.'[6] The result was that, despite the frequently wet and foul weather and the muddy roads they had to travel, when the army was reviewed by the Imperial commander, Prince Eugene of Savoy, shortly after its arrival in Swabia, he was enthusiastic in his praise of the excellent condition of the troops. His remarks illustrated the essential point very well, for only about 900 men fell out sick from the line of march despite the wet weather, and the rate of desertion was low. The soldiers even had time to comment on how pretty the German girls were.

These matters are not simple to arrange and they required a great deal of prior thought and preparation. Marlborough must have signalled his intention to march southwards, quite apart from the heavy hints he let drop before he took the road, intended to induce the French to think that either the Moselle or Alsace was his objective. However, his opponents had no way of knowing quite where the blow would fall. They had, by neglect, placed themselves outside the Duke's decision-making cycle, and were forced to await developments. This surrendering of the strategic initiative to Marlborough by the French commanders was a major success for the Allies before a blow was even struck.

While Marlborough's army pressed on southwards, Marshal Villeroi hurried after him, still on the west bank of the Rhine. Leaving Bedmar in place on the Moselle, he linked up with Tallard at Landau in Alsace early in June, well placed to shield Strasbourg but too late to attempt an interruption of the Allied march through the Swabian hills. It was now apparent that the Duke's real intention was to go to Bavaria, and in response to this the two Marshals debated whether they should make arrangements to reinforce the Elector and Marshal Marsin on the Danube. A significant complication was that they were now operating on exterior lines compared to the Duke (marching on the outer arc of a circle), with all the delay and extra labour that this imposed on their operations. They were particularly concerned about their own lines of supply and communications once they moved forward into the Black Forest, and the ability of the Elector to provision any major reinforcements. Torn as to the best course to take, they appealed to Louis XIV for advice. After consideration, the King sent instructions that Tallard should take his corps to Bavaria, while Villeroi manoeuvred to fix those Allied forces on the Upper Rhine and prevent any further increment to Marlborough's strength.

Emperor Leopold had sent the President of his War Council, the fiercely aggressive Prince Eugene, to take the field and work with Marlborough and the Margrave of Baden. In reality the 41-year-old Eugene out-ranked Baden, but he kept this fact quietly in his pocket and wisely treated that stiff nobleman as his colleague rather than a subordinate. On 10 June 1704 Marlborough and Eugene met for the first time. Four days later they joined Baden at the Inn of the Golden Fleece at Gross Heppach, near Stuttgart, and the three generals went into urgent conference. There was instant accord between Marlborough and Eugene, but relations with the Margrave were more reserved, for he was particularly sensitive to the seniority amongst them. Baden subtly suggested to Eugene that the operation to prevent French reinforcement of Bavaria was the most hazardous facing the Allies, suspecting that the Prince's pride would prompt him to assume that command. As he hoped, Eugene agreed to take command at the Lines of Stollhofen opposite Strasbourg.[7] Meanwhile, Marlborough and Baden would march with the rest of the Allied army to the Danube, and bring the Elector and Marsin either to the negotiating table or to battle.

As agreed at Gross Heppach, on 17 June Eugene began his march westwards. With admirable tact, Marlborough quietly watched his most effective colleague depart for the Rhine, and made the best of having to work with Baden. An added concern was that Eugene had told him of his suspicions that the Margrave was not only in contact with the Elector, but that he was passing to his old friend and comrade in arms information prejudicial to the Allied campaign. Marlborough knew that Eugene had full power to dismiss the Margrave and send him back to Vienna in disgrace if such suspicions should be proved true. In the event this was not necessary.

The Elector and Marsin, only able to field fewer than 40,000 men after detachments, were now obliged by the Allied advance to draw into a strongly entrenched camp at Dillingen on the north bank of the Danube. From here they could observe their opponents' moves in relative safety, while awaiting the arrival of the French reinforcements from Alsace. Five days after Eugene's departure, the armies of Marlborough and Baden met at Launsheim – their combined strength was about 60,000 troops, and they began to close up to the Danube, threading through the dangerous pass at Seislingen to cross the Jura hills.

With this march up the Rhine, Marlborough achieved a considerable strategic coup by switching the centre of gravity of the whole war in northern Europe away from the stifling conditions and narrow horizons of the Low Countries out onto the wider landscapes of the Danube. By dint of careful planning and preparation, he brought his army in fine condition over 250 miles of indifferent roads in poor weather. He crossed in front of two powerful French armies (those of Bedmar and Tallard) without interference from either, while a third army (that of Villeroi) was left toiling along in his wake, impotent and unable to interrupt his progress. The risk the Duke ran with this daring operation was daunting, not only in a military sense. The English parliament was not in session, and could not give expression to any opinion they might have of a general who took their only army off to campaign in central Europe without their knowledge or consent. They would be particularly severe if a mishap occurred, and there was a real danger here for Marlborough. One critic in London observed at the time that 'if he fails we will break him up as hounds upon a hare.'[8]

On the face of things, the Allied army was remarkably well balanced despite its various corps being widely separated. Prince Eugene was detached to keep the enemy armies apart, while the stronger portion, under Marlborough and Baden, went on to close with and destroy the main opposing army in the Danube valley. It was clear, however, that Eugene might not succeed and Marlborough was aware that French troops in considerable numbers could soon be marching through the Black Forest passes to bolster the Elector. Plainly, he had little time to spare.

NOTES

1. Churchill, W S, *Marlborough: His Life and Times*, Vol II, 1947, p.806.
2. Taylor, F, *The Wars of Marlborough 1702–9*, 1921, p.154.
3. Brereton, J, *History of the 4th/7th Dragoon Guards*, 1982, p.57. Quoting Captain Bonnell, an eye-witness to the review of the army prior to beginning the march.
4. The precise number of troops that began the march from Bedburg with Marlborough is not clear. Estimates range from 19,000 (Churchill) to 50,000 (Coxe). Given the scale of reinforcements that Marlborough received on the march (Danes, Hanoverians, etc.), and that, allowing for losses at the Schellenberg fight in July, he had about 32,000 troops to put in the line of battle alongside Eugene at Blenheim in August, it seems that Churchill's figure is the more precise. See Henderson, N, *Prince Eugen of Savoy*, 1964, p. 98.
5. Chandler, D, *Marlborough as Military Commander*, 1973, pp.132–3.
6. Chandler, D, *Captain Robert Parker and Comte de Mérode-Westerloo*, 1968, p. 31; Brereton p.58.
7. After receiving Prussian reinforcements, Eugene would have nearly 30,000 troops to hold the Lines of Stolhoffen, and to prevent further French reinforcement of Bavaria. It was a tall order. See Murray, G (ed.), *Letters and Dispatches of the Duke of Marlborough, 1845*, Vol. I, p. 319. A plan for Marlborough and Baden to form two distinct armies to operate against the Elector of Bavaria failed, as the Danish contingent was making slow time in marching to join the Allied army.
8. Churchill, Vol II, p. 780.

CHAPTER IV
The Hill of the Bell
The Storm of the Schellenberg,
Saturday 2 July 1704

Our success is owing to the unparalleled courage of your troops.[1]

The small town of Donauwörth in southern Germany is situated at the confluence of the River Donau (Danube) and the River Wörnitz which flows in from the north. The place is close to the boundary of Bavaria and Franconia, and is overlooked on the eastern edge by the long rounded mass of the Schellenberg. In the summer of 1704 the hill was laid to pasture with a crown of trees near the summit. An earthen fort constructed in the previous century by King Gustavus Adolphus of Sweden during the Thirty Years War stood near the trees. Although the 'Swedish' fort was semi-derelict and grassed over, it neatly illustrated the importance of the Schellenberg in dominating the river crossings at this place, and still provided a good starting point for any commander needing in a hurry to fortify the hill against an attacker. Colonel Jean De La Colonie, a French officer in the Bavarian service who fought at the Schellenberg, left vivid memoirs. He described the hill as follows:

> The Schellenberg height is oval in plan, with a gentle slope on the southern side, which affords very easy communication with Donauwert; whilst on the northern side the country is covered with very thick woods and undergrowth, reaching close up to the old entrenchments.[2]

With Marlborough's arrival in the Danube valley, the Elector of Bavaria was feeling increasingly vulnerable. On 22 June 1704 the French General Legalle, sent to Versailles with a plea for help, convinced Louis XIV that Marlborough's strategic intention really was the defeat of his ally. More aid must be sent to Bavaria, or the Elector would be defeated with dire results for the entire French war effort. The matter was plain and the necessary orders were sent by the King to his two Marshals in Alsace the following day.[3]

Also on 22 June the armies of Prince Louis, the Margrave of Baden, and the Duke of Marlborough linked up on the northern approaches to Bavaria. The combined Allied total (excluding Prince Eugene's detachment on the Rhine) was about 60,000 men. Command of the army on the Danube had to be shared between Marlborough and Baden, at least in theory, due to the diplomatic niceties of alliance warfare. In practice this meant little more than the Margrave being permitted to set the password on alternate days and the field command was firmly in Marlborough's hands. Still, the Duke had to contend with Baden's rather dull and impractical schemes for manoeuvring to draw out the Elector of Bavaria from his entrenched camp at Dillingen on the north bank of the Danube. He also had doubts whether the Margrave really wanted to close with and engage the man with whom he had shared many a past campaign.

Marlborough's worries were heightened by his anxiety for Eugene, who was relatively isolated in the Lines of Stollhofen, watching for the approach of new French armies. Additionally, there was a pressing need to establish a secure forward base for the coming campaign in Bavaria; the Duke's present supply depots at Nordlingen were too small and distant from the Danube to be of real use once that river was crossed. Still, Marlborough's greatest difficulty was how and where to force that river crossing and engage the Elector before (in broadly equal importance) either autumn or the French should come. The Elector was a seasoned soldier, if rather erratic, and he was perfectly able to comprehend the choices open to his adversary. He could be counted on to manoeuvre with all his considerable skill to dispute any attempt to cross the Danube, and all the likely crossing places would be held by his troops and barricaded against the Allies.

The sheltered river crossings over the Danube at Donauwörth were ideal for Marlborough's purposes, and the small town would provide the secure forward base he needed for his campaign. Furthermore, it was within easy striking distance of the present Allied encampment at Amerdingen. However, the Elector could also see the value of Donau-wörth, and on 30 June 1704 he sent a corps of veteran troops, under the command of Count D'Arco, a Piedmontese officer and the foremost general in the Bavarian service, to garrison the Schellenberg and the town. D'Arco had at his disposal sixteen Bavarian and five French battalions, nine squadrons of French dragoons, and two batteries, each of eight heavy guns. In all, this detachment comprised about 12,000 men, but four battalions of French infantry were immediately sent in to garrison the town itself.[4] The remaining soldiers were immediately employed to put the hill in a better state of defence, and peasants were conscripted locally to serve in labour gangs throwing up earth and timber defences, and clearing fields of fire across the lower slopes. As Marlborough's troops trudged along roads made muddy and slow by heavy rain, the defences

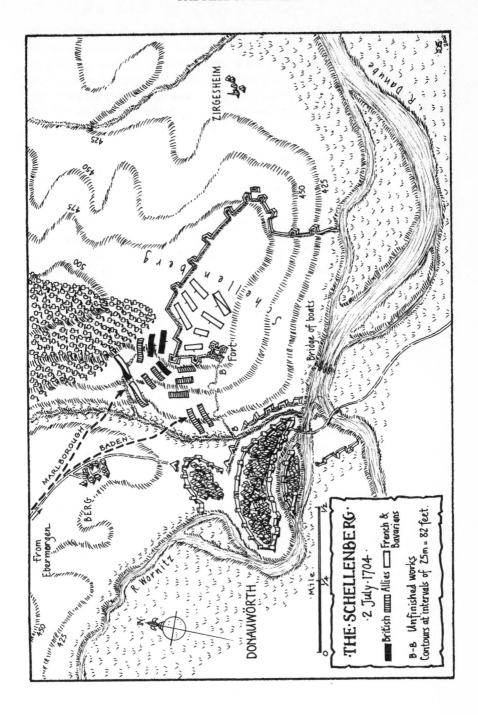

ZIRGESHEIM

R. Danube

Bridge of boats

Schellenberg

B Fort

MARLBOROUGH

BADEN

From Ebermorgen

BERG

R. Wornitz

DONAUWÖRTH

N.

·THE·SCHELLENBERG·
·2·July·1704·

British ▨▨▨ Allies ☐ French & Bavarians

B—B Unfinished works
Contours at intervals of 25 m = 82 feet.

Mile
½   ¼
0

450
475
500
450
425
425
450
475
500

on the hill before them gradually took shape as a formidable obstacle.

Although time was short in which to complete the preparations, D'Arco was an energetic and seasoned commander, and he got into position in reasonably good time. He had plentiful men and guns, he was well supplied and could expect reinforcement and support from the Bavarian main army, once Marlborough's intentions became clear. His task in occupying the Schellenberg, and by doing so securing the river crossings, seemed quite simple.

Nonetheless the Count was in something of a quandary. If he simply held the hill and waited for the Allies to attack, he neglected the natural advantages that the terrain to the north of Donauwörth offered, and would surrender all initiative to his opponent. In particular, the line of the fast flowing Wörnitz ran right across the route that Marlborough must take to approach Donauwörth from the camp at Amerdingen. There were few fords and still fewer bridges for the Allies to use and it was therefore a significant obstacle in itself. D'Arco could choose to mount an aggressive forward defence on this line. With a good mix of infantry, dragoons and guns he might expect to force the Allies to pay a heavy price for the passage of those river crossings – the Duke's soldiers, struggling waist deep in the turbulent water, would be at a significant disadvantage. D'Arco might well turn Marlborough back – at the very least he could expect to delay the Allied advance while the Elector's army closed up. However, by pushing forward in this way, D'Arco would risk distancing himself from his supports – he would chance defeat in detail, isolated and outnumbered in the open country to the north of Donauwörth.

A safer course for D'Arco was to level the Schellenberg defences entirely and fire the town of Donauwörth with its valuable magazines and depots. He could then fall back onto the southern bank of the Danube, tearing up the bridges behind him, before combining with the Elector's main army. This would place the immense obstacle of the river between himself and the Allies, and conserve the strength of his corps, picked from amongst the best troops the Elector had. However, this would meekly surrender ground, supplies and fortifications with no corresponding price demanded. So, he held the Schellenberg, and no doubt felt that he would receive reinforcement before Marlborough could mount a major attack. This was in many respects the correct course, but took no account of the daring of his opponent. By the military norms of the day Marlborough's forthcoming actions were quite reckless and unexpected.

Marlborough was acutely aware that time was pressing. His scouts reported the movement of Bavarian and French troops into the neighbourhood of Donauwörth almost as soon as they began to arrive. Local peasants who feared impressment into the labour gangs working on the Schellenberg also came to the Allied camp with information. Not only that, Colonel De La Colonie on the hill had particular suspicions that paid

32

spies of Marlborough and Baden were active in the area, and he knew of a corporal from the Bavarian Prince Elector's Regiment, who gave the Allies a full account of the defensive arrangements.[5] All the timely information on D'Arco's activities coming in to his headquarters tent at Amerdingen confirmed to the Duke the need to mount a speedy attack.

The Margrave of Baden was horrified at the notion, and protested bluntly to the Duke about the plan for an outright assault. He was a soldier brought up in an older and altogether more cautious school of tactics than Marlborough, and preferred nicely planned manoeuvres and stately set piece sieges before direct attack. To be fair, he was an experienced general (who had known considerable success in past campaigns) and he rightly foresaw heavy losses amongst the attacking troops. Marlborough was in no doubt, however, and there was no questioning his authority in the argument, for he was the appointed representative of the paymaster of the Grand Alliance, England. The Margrave gave way, and preparations for the attack went forward rapidly, despite his misgivings.

The avenues of approach available to the Allies were quite restricted. A thickly wooded ridge, known at that time as the Boschberg, ran past the left of the Schellenberg as Marlborough approached from the west. This prevented a rapid move around the northern edge of the hill, which might have led the Allied troops to Zirgesheim village on the rearwards slopes. From there D'Arco could probably have been manoeuvred out of position and been obliged to fall back across the Danube, at little cost to the Duke's army. On Marlborough's right hand side, the Wörnitz ran down to its confluence with the Danube under the walls of Donauwörth itself, and this constricted his ability to manoeuvre in that direction. His own close reconnaissance, early on 2 July 1704, confirmed the necessity for a frontal attack and the Duke was rightly concerned that D'Arco would soon be reinforced. His scouts reported that Bavarian quartermasters were laying out the neat tent lines for a fresh encampment across the river from Donauwörth; the Elector and his main army were plainly expected before long.

Marlborough then employed precisely the same labour in a ruse to mislead D'Arco. He had his own quartermasters, under William Cadogan, his Irish Quartermaster-General, begin to mark out a camp near to the crossings of the Wörnitz. This gave the clear signal to any observers that he would not attack until his troops had rested the night, and were fresh for a great effort the following day.

The rather dated walled fortifications of Donauwörth (contemporary maps also show some rather sketchy Vauban-type earthworks) were linked to the Schellenberg by a hastily constructed and only partially complete line of wicker baskets filled with earth and stones known as gabions. These had been put in place as there was insufficient time to complete the earthen and timber breastwork defence across the breadth of the hill. Most of D'Arco's efforts were concentrated on the northern and eastern sides, presumably because he anticipated that the threatened attack would come from that quarter. De La Colonie comments that no one really expected the Allies to attempt an assault from the direction from which it eventually came, in part because of the cover given by the defences and guns of Donauwörth itself. However, despite what De La Colonie has to say, the Bavarian artillery was in place in good time and this indicates some intelligent anticipation by D'Arco of the actual line of the impending threat.

Along the line of gabions linking Donauwörth with the hill the Count placed the two battalions of the French Nectancourt Régiment, both to protect his left flank and provide a supporting connection with the defenders in the town. D'Arco understandably kept most of his strength on the hill itself, massing the Bavarian Liselbourg Regiment and the Prince Elector's Regiment, under the command of Count Maffei, along the breastwork on the upper slopes facing to the north and north-west. A strong detachment of Bavarian Electoral Guards, under Major Ranowski, was kept back on the right flank near the trees, probably in case the Allies should unexpectedly try and force their way through the Boschberg woods onto the ridge. This particular terrain was poor for the rapid movement of troops, but it was as well to be sure.

As a main reserve D'Arco kept the French Béarn and Nivernois Régiments (one battalion each) under the Marquis de Montandre, and a battalion of the Grenadiers Rouge, under De La Colonie himself, on the higher ground away from the firing line, in the general area of the old earthen fort. As it turned out, these troops were in a rather exposed position due to the curvature of the hill. Eight of the Bavarian guns were placed in the breastwork angle closest to the woods, from where they could enfilade any attackers, while the other eight guns were kept in a central battery near the old fort. The guns in Donauwörth would add weight to their bombardment.

Marlborough's arrangements for what would be a very difficult assault were made with great care. Parties of stormers to lead the assault, 130 strong, were selected from each battalion in the Allied army. Ten soldiers for the task were detailed to be drawn from each of the grenadier companies. These particular soldiers were usually tall and well built men, often in distinctive conical grenadier caps tipped with fur, and armed additionally with long-handled hatchets to help clear away obstacles. The remainder of the stormers were volunteers and picked men from the line companies. The common practice of bounty pay, the total of which was paid out to the survivors of an assault, would serve to induce otherwise reluctant men to volunteer for a hazardous operation, for the survivors of the action would each receive an equal share of the total bounty money.[6] As each of the forty-five Allied battalions present provided troops for the attack, these stormers totalled 5,850 men, to which was added a forlorn hope of eighty picked men of the 1st English Foot Guards, who volunteered to spearhead the attack under Lord John Mordaunt.[7]

The main attacking force behind the stormers comprised two infantry echelons each of eight battalions with a total strength of about 12,000 British, Dutch and German troops commanded by Major-General Henry Withers and Count Horn. The third attacking echelon was made up of eighteen squadrons of dragoons and seventeen squadrons of cavalry under Generals Lumley and Hompesch. The dragoons remained mounted in the initial stages of the attack, but they had been busy with others collecting bundles of sticks known as fascines in the local copses, for the stormers to carry to fill in any obstructing ditches as they advanced. All these troops, added to three battalions of Baden's Imperial grenadiers (two Swabian and one Austrian) and squads of pioneers to clear obstacles and break down the defences, totalled about 22,000 men. Baden's troops, the right Wing of the Allied army, would approach as a reserve force. They would not initially close up to the Schellenberg due to lack of frontage in which to properly deploy in the constricted area between the Kaiback Stream at the foot of the hill and the walls of Donauwörth. It may fairly be said that this whole attacking force was the cream of the Allied army on the Danube – the steel tip at the end of Marlborough's strategic thrust from the Low Countries to the Danube.[8]

Leaving their camp at Amerdingen, fifteen miles north-west from Donauwörth, early on 2 July 1704, the Allied troops trudged along roads thickly mired in mud. Four hundred pioneers laboured to clear the way forward. The army reached the undefended Wörnitz at the small hamlet of Ebermorgen at 3.00 o'clock that afternoon. Marlborough and his staff officers awaited them, and the troops were directed to an ancient stone bridge and three additional pontoon bridges laid by engineers in adjacent water meadows earlier in the day. The approach was soon detected by D'Arco's outposts, who were stationed not far from the Wörnitz, on the wooded Boschberg ridge that so hampered Marlborough's line of approach. These troops, three squadrons of dragoons, were initially misled by the Duke's ruse of having his quartermasters begin to lay out the ground to the west of the Wörnitz. The dragoons prudently pulled back past the hamlet of Berg as soon as the Allied advanced guard began to pour across the river. D'Arco, who had received news of the Allied march as early as 9.00 am, had spent the day strengthening the threatened side of the hill, but plainly expected the actual assault to be delayed until the following morning. He sent fresh messages to the Elector at Dillingen asking for support, and then went to dinner with the town commander, Colonel DuBordet. Marlborough's true intentions were soon plain enough, for he was observed making his own personal reconnaissance of the Schellenberg with a small mounted party, and was fired on from the hill.

Mrs Christian Davies, a redoubtable woman who served as a soldier in Marlborough's army while searching for her absent husband, took part with Hay's (Royal Scots) Dragoons in the assault on the hill. She remembered afterwards:

> ... our vanguard did not come in sight of the enemy's intrenchments til the afternoon; however, not to give the Bavarians time to make themselves yet stronger, the duke ordered the Dutch General Goor, who commanded the right Wing, composed of English and Dutch, with some auxiliary troops, to attack, as soon as possible; thus we did not stay for the coming up of the Imperialists.[9]

This was not the entire reason for the Duke's haste. The pace of the whole campaign was quickening, for the French were also moving to concentrate on the Danube. As the leading Allied soldiers swung across the Wörnitz at the Ebermorgen bridges, Marlborough was handed a note by Baron Moltenburg, Prince Eugene's Adjutant-General, who had just then ridden in with important news. Marshal Tallard, covered by Villeroi, had evaded Eugene's forces on the Rhine, and was even now pressing through the Black Forest with a fresh French army to the support of the Elector and Marsin.

The village of Berg stands on a small hill just to the north of Donauwörth, and it lay firmly on the Allied line of approach. The Bavarian pickets in the place set the cottages and barns ablaze, hoping to obstruct the Duke's progress, and once this was accomplished they withdrew to help man the breastworks on the hill. Count D'Arco was still at dinner in Donauwörth when the news of Marlborough's advance was brought. As flames and smoke engulfed Berg, and made smudgy the early evening sky to the north, it was very apparent to the Count that Marlborough had stolen a march on him. Against all reasonable expectations the hill would be under attack before nightfall, and D'Arco hurried to join his troops on the slopes. He impressed on Colonel DuBordet the necessity of maintaining the link between the town and the Schellenberg, where the makeshift line of gabions was held by the Nectancourt Régiment.

Led by their dragoons, who fanned out to clear the way, the Allied stormers moved easily past Berg and deployed into three ranks in the fold of dead ground where the Kaiback Stream ran away southwards between the village and the Schellenberg. They were not troubled by the guns either of the town or of the batteries on the hill, for the depression of barrels was too great to allow the Bavarian artillery to properly reach into the forming up point in the dip. Henry Withers and James Ferguson had command of the English and Scots battalions just behind the stormers, while Count Horn's Dutch soldiers and the Hanoverian and Hessian battalions under Berensdorf formed to their rear. The cavalry and dragoons in their turn drew up as the reserve echelon in rear of the infantry, having first delivered their fascines to the stormers, each officer and foot soldier carrying a bundle into the assault.

An Allied battery of ten guns, under Colonel Holcroft Blood, had been dragged through the muddy tracks past the village of Harburg to free the direct route from Amerdingen for the Allied infantry. By this roundabout path the guns were brought into place on the hill near to the smouldering remains of Berg just as the stormers moved into place. This battery very effectively engaged the temporarily impotent Bavarian guns but, because of the extreme angle of elevation required to reach the breastwork on the hill, the cannon balls skimmed the parapet leaving the forward infantry relatively unscathed. The French troops, standing in the open on higher ground to the rear, suffered severely from Blood's fire. To add to their troubles, an Imperial battery was soon also in place to give weight to the Allied barrage. Colonel De La Colonie, whose Grenadiers Rouge were badly mauled at this time, wrote afterwards that he was splattered with the blood and brains of one of his officers, the Comte de la Bastide, with almost the first shot. He afterwards estimated that he lost over eighty men to Blood's accurate fire before the Allied infantry assault even began: 'The enemy's battery opened fire upon us, and raked us through and through.'[10]

In the smoky early evening light of summer, nearly 6,000 storm troops were formed up in three ranks in the fold of ground facing the Schellenberg hill – lean and formidable men, all picked out especially for the gruesome task ahead. To their right ran the small marshy stream of the Kaiback, beyond which were the neglected fortifications of the walled town of Donauwörth. These walls were lined with alert French soldiers, but they were well out of musket shot. Behind the stormers stood rank upon rank of formed infantry, English, Scots and Hanoverians in their red-coats, and Hessians and Dutch in Blue and Grey. Farther back still, in the lee of the hill on which stood the burning cottages of Berg, the massed squadrons of cavalry and dragoons were in position, and grey-coated Imperial grenadiers were filing into place beyond the hamlet. The grassy domed hill to their front was struck with the evening sun, and crossed just below the crest with the fresh earthwork scar of the enemy breastwork. As Blood's battery fired at the hill, the veterans amongst the stormers measured by eye the distance to be crossed before they could get at the Bavarian defenders – there were about 400 yards of open slope before them.

Observers near Berg noted that the time was 6.00 pm when the Allied stormers were given the order to step off. Marlborough's close friend and confidante, the 57-year-old Dutch engineer officer, Johan Goor, was in command of the stormers and he took the three dense leading ranks forward up the grassy slopes. Mordaunt led the way with his forlorn hope; the men were shouting and cheering with all their might but very soon they were in difficulties. They had undertaken a hard march, now the steepness of the ground slowed their paces and the fascines they clutched across their breasts were cumbersome and heavy. When the leading companies came upon a partially sunken lane running across the lower slopes, this was mistaken for a ditch obstacle, and many of the soldiers tossed their fascine bundles into the dip, thereby wasting them. They were relieved to lose the burden, but at this early stage, in the rush and noise of the approach, control of the assault was already becoming a little ragged.

The defenders awaited the onslaught in tight silence, broken only by the tapping of De La Colonie's French drummers, ordered to try and drown out the intimidating shouts of the approaching masses. Allowing the Allied soldiers to come well out of the dead ground in which they formed up, the Bavarians waited until their adversaries were well exposed on the open slopes, and then unleashed a storm of close range musketry and canister fire upon them. Fizzing hand-grenades, bowled under-arm, showered easily down the slopes into the ranks of the Allied stormers:

> An increasing fire swept their line of advance with a torrent of bullets, accompanied by numberless grenades, of which we had several wagon loads in rear of our position. These, owing to the slope of the ground fell right amongst the enemy's ranks, causing great annoyance.[11]

Scores of men were tumbled down in the terrible fire, and the leading ranks appeared to melt away in the storm from above. Those soldiers following had to stumble and scramble over the torn bodies of their stricken comrades. The wasted fascines were now badly missed, for the Bavarian breastwork lay behind a ditch that was excavated to help form the parapet, and the attackers faced a dangerous impasse. The confusion and crowding rapidly grew worse, with great congestion on the narrow frontage in front of the Bavarian defences. Samuel Noyes, a chaplain who went forward with Orkney's Regiment that day, wrote afterwards that the attacking ranks at some points were stood twenty men deep. Those at the front were in danger from the fire of their comrades at the rear who, in turn, were desperate to quell the fearsome musketry of the Bavarians. However, despite their losses, which were particularly severe amongst the officers, conspicuous as they were in their laced hats and coats, the Allied soldiers stood their ground and began to reform for another attempt.[12]

Before this, with the stormers halted and reeling under the dreadful fire, hundreds of Bavarian grenadiers came pouring out from behind the breastwork to drive the Allies back down the slope. They were too impetuous for the fight was not yet won. The grenadiers were met with steady volleys from the English 1st Foot Guards and Orkney's and Ingoldsby's Regiment of the second attacking echelon, which in timely fashion were toiling up the slope into place nearby. The Bavarians were promptly forced to scramble back behind cover by the weight of this fire, leaving their own dead and wounded scattered on the grass as they went. The sturdy Allied soldiers pressed upwards once again through the smoke to the parapet, where fierce hand-to-hand fighting took place wherever they could cross the ditch to reach the defenders. Sword, hatchet, musket butt and bayonet were freely used and no quarter was given.

Goor was now dead, bleeding to death from a wound to his eye, and Count von Styrum took over the command, dismounting from his horse to encourage forward the infantry. He was soon shot down also and the Allied soldiers, many now with no officers to command them, fought on bravely in the face of the awful Bavarian fire the like of which, it was subsequently told, had not before been seen on a European battlefield. Despite all their gallantry, nothing the attackers could do moved the steadfast Bavarian infantrymen at this point, and the storming troops began to fall back once again to recover their order. They left the ground in front of the ditch and breastwork grotesquely choked with the bodies of their dead and injured.

Marlborough was close at hand, anxious that his troops maintained the momentum of the attack, but to have exposed himself to the direct fire of the defenders would have been pointless.[13] This was not necessary, his aides and running footmen came to him with news of what they saw. The Duke ordered the dragoons of the third attacking echelon to dismount and close up to the infantry, to add weight to the assault, and to put fresh heart into the battered soldiers clinging to their slim gains on the ghastly slopes. The men of Ross's (Royal Irish) Dragoons and Hay's Dragoons fixed bayonets and, hampered by their long boots, began the deadly climb. Lord John Hay dismounted to lead his regiment forward in person, while at the same time the mounted squadrons of cavalry closed right up to the foot of hill. This effectively, and rather ruthlessly, made it difficult for any wavering soldier to make off to the rear. Marlborough's Chaplain, Dr Francis Hare, diplomatically wrote: 'The Horse and Dragoons stood so close and animated the Foot so much by their brave example that they rallied and went on again.'[14]

All this while (in a space of about an hour according to Dr Hare, who was one of those watching the action on the smoking hillside from the safety of the ruins of Berg), the three battalions of Imperial grenadiers from Baden's Wing of the army were held back from the battle. They still stood at the edge of the Kaiback Stream near Berg. Whatever the original intentions for this potent force may have been, there was no space on the slopes immediately ahead for them to deploy and join the attack. To throw them into the fighting would merely add to the crowding and confusion, and leave the Duke with no uncommitted troops, except those of the mounted squadrons of cavalry at the foot of the hill. It is also likely, given the tactics that Marlborough was to employ on other occasions, that these excellent troops were deliberately held back until D'Arco had been forced to commit all his available troops to holding the main attack and a vulnerable spot had appeared elsewhere.

Shortly after 7.00 pm a messenger came to Marlborough with news that some of his soldiers, who had drifted off to the right of the assault, had found the gabion breastwork linking the town and the hill to be poorly manned, even empty, in places. The French soldiers posted there to maintain the link with the town, had apparently been drawn into the fighting on the hill, although DuBordet may have brought some of them back into Donauwörth for shelter. D'Arco's left flank as a result was quite unguarded, and due to the dead ground formed by the course of the Kaiback Stream, and the distance from the walls of Donauwörth, this area was now not covered by effective fire at all.

Marlborough sent an officer to check the report and, once reassured, he promptly asked Baden to take advantage of this terrible lapse. The Margrave, who also seems to have spotted the opportunity, responded rapidly, pushing his grenadier battalions along the marshy shallows of the Kaiback Stream. A Bavarian deserter (perhaps the infamous corporal of the Prince Elector's Regiment mentioned by De la Colonie) actually led Baden into position. Quickly realising that the centre of gravity of his attack had shifted, the Duke soon afterwards directed Horn to disengage his own Dutch and German battalions from the main assault, and to move down to the right and support Baden's thrust. Meanwhile, untroubled by a rather ineffective musketry fire from the walls of the town, the Imperial grenadiers were able to form up at the foot of the Schellenberg. By about 7.30 pm they were facing the open flank of the Franco-Bavarian position above them on the hill.

The approach of Baden's soldiers did not go entirely unnoticed by D'Arco, despite the pressing demands on his attention of the vicious Allied assaults on his main breastwork. Aware of the movement to his left, he went to the dismounted French dragoon squadrons drawn up in reserve on the rear slope of the Schellenberg, and formed them for a quick counter-attack. There was no real punch in the effort and Baden had little difficulty in deploying a few companies of grenadiers to drive these dragoons off, and in pressing his main attack upwards to the crest of the hill. Once brushed aside, D'Arco found himself out of position, unable to communicate with his main body as this new and dangerous attack went in.

D'Arco's second in command, Count Maffei, plainly saw fresh lines of troops climbing the steep slopes of the hill towards the battle. At first proper identification was impossible; the field emblems of foliage worn in the hats and garnishing the regimental colours of the Imperial grenadiers could not be clearly seen, and their faded light grey uniforms must have looked suspiciously like the white uniforms of the French army. Bavarian officers on the hill shouted to their soldiers not to fire on the advancing ranks, for they must be reinforcements sent by Colonel DuBordet from the garrison in the town. The drifting smoke of battle would have added to the problem. The mistake was soon realised as the Imperial grenadiers formed their ranks, actually in rear of the Franco-Bavarian defence, and Maffei had to frantically re-deploy his battalions under a growing weight of musketry to meet this new threat. In the confusion and the noise, the weary Allied storming troops found that their opponents were melting away into the smoke. At last they were able to clamber their way across the ditch and breastwork so long denied to them, and pour into the Bavarian position.

The defence rapidly fell apart, and command and control was lost as the disordered French and Bavarians were hustled back towards the reverse slope of the Schellenberg and the deep waters of the Danube. To fight a battle with a water obstacle at the back is always an immense risk, and so it proved at the Schellenberg. Although Berensdorf and Ferguson pushed their troops forward impetuously, Marlborough halted the infantry near the crest to consolidate the hold on the hill. He remounted his dragoons though, and these were let loose, together with the cavalry, into a relentless pursuit over the brow of the hill.

De La Colonie attempted to stem the rout of fleeing soldiers, taking a firm stand with the Grenadiers Rouge. His battalion managed to maintain its ranks for a time, and withdrew with measured pace across the crown of the hill. The Allied soldiers were kept at bay with the steady fire, but the ranks of the French were badly torn by the returning volleys which poured into them. At last, as the grenadiers clambered the parapet at the rear of the position, a sudden storm of musketry struck them and their composure snapped. The French soldiers bolted and joined the fleeing throng, while De La Colonie was struck on the jaw with a ball and momentarily stunned. Once recovered, the gallant colonel, whose coat was drenched with blood, took to his heels to avoid the cavalry pursuit. Hampered by his gear, he found it impossible to get away and persuaded the wife of a Bavarian soldier: '... so distracted with weeping that she travelled no faster than I did' to pull his boots off so that he could swim the Danube to safety. A hail of musket balls were directed at him by those vengeful Allied dragoons who had not turned aside to plunder the Colonel's effects that had been abandoned at the water's edge, but he got away.[15]

The Franco-Bavarian wagons had made off early in the assault, and their weight caused one of the pontoon bridges over the Danube at the rear of the Schellenberg to collapse. This would certainly hamper the flight of the fugitives after the defence was broken, and quite a number of soldiers were reportedly drowned. However, it is also certain that many of D'Arco's men were refused quarter and were simply cut down in the pursuit. Mrs Christian Davies remembered the enemy's flight from the hill very well:

> We began about six o'clock, and were twice repulsed, with very great loss; but this did not abate anything of our courage; our men, rather, were animated by this resistance, gave a third assault, at the time the Prince of Baden arrived with the German troops, who attacked on his side. The slaughter, which was very great, had lasted about one hour. The Bavarians were now soon routed, and a cruel slaughter made of them, and the bridge over the Danube breaking down, a great number were drowned, or taken prisoners.[16]

Such a merciless pursuit was the ruthless custom after a bloody assault, but those of the defenders who could keep to their ordered ranks were able to fall back to the shelter of Donauwörth town, or to the remaining bridges over the Danube. Colonel DuBordet, whose efforts this day are sometimes forgotten, attempted a sally from the town with part of his garrison, hoping to assist the broken battalions, but Marlborough's cavalry were able to fend them off without great difficulty. Gathering together those fugitives closest at hand, including Count D'Arco, the Colonel prudently withdrew inside the town walls. The time was about 8.00 pm and all was smoke, noise and death on the dusky hill. D'Arco's army was smashed and in flight – the Allied horsemen were off the leash and would continue their bloody work while the light lasted. Meanwhile, the gates of Donauwörth were now firmly shut, and Marlborough had not time or strength enough to attempt to storm the walls, obsolete though they might be.

Count D'Arco took himself off to find the Elector to make his sorry report, although the din of battle must have carried plainly enough to the Bavarian camp at Dillingen, and would have told its own tale. DuBordet gathered together those troops in the town and, as the night passed, set off to re-unite this force with the Elector's main army. Before he left he attempted to destroy the stockpiled munitions in Donauwörth, but the fires failed to take hold, partly because townspeople rushed to quench the flames. A vast quantity of valuable stores, including 200 tons of gunpowder and 3,000 sacks of flour, fell into Marlborough's hands when Donauwörth opened its gates to him the following day.[17] The Bavarian engineer train, including all their pontoon bridges, was abandoned at the river's edge.

That night it rained heavily, tormenting the scores of stricken men littering the slopes of the Schellenberg. The Allied wounded were to be cared for in Nordlingen thirty miles away to the north, and they faced a grim wait while transport was provided. Despite Marlborough's careful preparations, the sheer numbers of casualties inevitably overwhelmed his good intentions. Francis Hare wrote: 'All his Grace's care was now employed about sending the wounded away to hospital.'[18] On 8 July 1704 the Duke wrote to the Mayor of Nordlingen with his thanks for the attention shown to the Allied wounded, and asked that the more lightly wounded be sent to outlying villages to relieve the pressure on the doctors in Nordlingen itself. Little is said of the care offered to the fallen French and Bavarian defenders, and it may be assumed that their fate was generally an unhappy one. It was a rough age.

D'Arco's corps was so shattered at the Schellenberg that it is not possible to get a clear estimate of the extent of his losses. All his guns and regimental colours but one were lost (that of De La Colonie's Grenadiers Rouge), and the Allies seized about 2,000 prisoners. The Count's own silver plate-ware was left in his tents, and fell as booty to the Allies. Few of the fugitives who successfully fled from the Schellenberg rallied to their regiments in the weeks that followed, and it seems that no more than 3,000 troops made their way to rejoin the main army. This had serious consequences for the coming campaign, as D'Arco had been given command of the very best troops in the Bavarian service. The Elector, who had been on the march with his army, arrived a day too late to help the Count. He had now lost the line of the Danube, and would soon be manoeuvred out of his entrenched camp at Dillingen as a result. Together with Marsin's French corps he fell back towards Augsburg, where their outnumbered forces would at least have the shelter of the River Lech.

Marlborough, pleasantly surprised that DuBordet made no attempt to fight for the town, now had his forward base, pretty well intact and provisioned, and the important secure river crossings. However, the cost of storming the Schellenberg was very heavy for the Duke's army. Five thousand and forty one of their soldiers were killed and wounded, amongst them 1,287 Britons. The fallen included seventeen officers of the rank of Colonel and above, and the Margrave of Baden was wounded by a musket ball in the foot (an injury sometimes referred to afterwards, rather facetiously, as 'the Margrave's toe'). The loss of excellent general officers and close confidants like Goor and von Styrum was a sore blow to Marlborough, who had made good use of their efficient services in the running of his small headquarters.

The victory at the Schellenberg caused quite a stir throughout Europe and the Imperial Court at Vienna was agog with the daring of the enterprise, rejoicing that salvation was at hand. In their camps beside the Danube, Marlborough's soldiers had few doubts about the magnitude of their achievement. They had stormed the enemy stronghold on that hill, sword in hand under the watchful eye and firm command of the Duke. The troops knew a victory when they saw one, and were well aware that these things, so precious to each soldier's heart, are not to be had cheaply. Hompesch wrote:

> The Duke of Marlborough gave orders throughout the action, with the greatest prudence and presence of mind. The Prince of Baden, everybody must own, has done all that could be expected from a great and brave general.

However, not all the soldiers were convinced of the benefit of the assault. Lieutenant Richard Pope of Schomberg's Regiment of Horse, whose mount was shot and killed under him that day, wrote to his brother: 'It appeared to us with a different face to what it did all over Europe, it being in my opinion a considerable advantage purchased at a dear rate.'[19]

There was, inevitably, wide comment on the scale of the losses suffered by the Allied army, and some critics wondered whether Marlborough would fight such a bloody battle for every hill in Germany. Perversely, the Dutch minted a coin in celebration of the victory, but it featured Baden not Marlborough. This all points to a complete misunderstanding of his achievement. The Duke had boldly side-stepped the Elector's competent dispositions to defend the Danube; the whole of the line of the river had now to be abandoned to the Allies, except for the fortress at Ingolstadt downstream from Donauwörth. The Elector himself had to leave his strong camp at Dillingen because of Marlborough's success, and until French reinforcements came he was forced back deep into Bavaria, unable to defend his own lands. He was forced to meekly rely on the dubious protection of what secondary river lines he could find. Most importantly, Marlborough had interposed his own troops between Vienna and the Franco-Bavarian army, and there was little to prevent him from making an advance on Munich itself if he so chose. His opponents were badly outgunned and off balance, and the Duke could next go pretty well wherever he pleased. Marlborough wrote in his despatch to Queen Anne:

> I must humbly presume to inform your Majesty that the success of our first attack on the enemy has been equal to the justice of the cause your Majesty has so generously and zealously espoused. Mr Secretary Harley will have the honour to lay the relation of yesterday's action before your Majesty, to which I shall crave humbly to add that our success is in great measure owing to the particular blessing of God on the unparalleled courage of your troops. I shall endeavour to improve this happy beginning to your Majesty's glory, and the benefit of your allies, being with the greatest zeal and

submission, Madam, Your Majesty's most dutiful and most obedient subject and servant.[20]

Fine and stirring words, fairly announcing a significant success, but the Duke now had to take the war into Bavaria and force either peace or battle on the Elector before Marshal Tallard could arrive.

The Schellenberg Battlefield Today

The Schellenberg hill is now shady with trees and partly built over with residential flats and villas. The municipal swimming pool sits on the site of Gustavus Adolphus's old fort, and a by-pass for the town of Donauwörth crosses the lower slopes. A German army base occupies the rear part of the hill, and this area is closed to the public. Despite all this the mass of the hill dominates the town, amply demonstrating its importance to a commander wishing to deny any opponent the vital river crossings. The small hamlet of Berg, through which Marlborough's army passed to go into the attack, is now a suburb of Donauwörth itself, but the town is still very attractive, having been rebuilt after World War II. The medieval street pattern was maintained, but there are now few traces of the old town walls.

The building of the by-pass across the Schellenberg, in a curious and fortunate way, has preserved much of the lower part of the hill, the very part over which Marlborough's army advanced to make their desperate assault on the Franco-Bavarians. Without the road Donauwörth town might have spread its suburbs out over the whole feature. The breastwork and entrenchments used in the battle were levelled in the 1740s, but the wide grassy verges left by the road-builders are indented still with the marks of D'Arco's defensive ditch. Near the crest, in the woods next to the pool, is a bronze plaque in commemoration of the battle, etched with a representation of the old Swedish fort. There is also a Kalverie memorial, showing the Stations of the Cross, at the foot of the slope at about the spot where the Margrave of Baden's Imperial grenadiers turned up the hill to hit the defenders' open flank.

A few miles to the north of Donauwörth lies the small village of Ebermorgen, luckily by-passed by the modern main road to Nordlingen. The River Wörnitz flows swiftly past the village and is spanned by an old stone bridge. This is not the bridge used by Marlborough and his troops, but a replacement built in the mid–18th century, although it is very much in keeping as the supporting piers are original. The scene along the lush water-meadows, from which the Allied pioneers launched their tin-boat pontoons, seems to have changed little over the years – the Duke would recognise the place today.

NOTES

1. Murray, G (ed.), *Letters and Dispatches of the Duke of Marlborough,* Vol 1, 1845, p. 330.
2. De La Colonie, J (ed. W Horsley), *Chronicles of an Old Campaigner,* 1904, p. 176. De La Colonie was a provincial dragoon officer without influence or powerful friends. He was seconded to command the Grenadiers Rouge, a regiment of French and Italian deserters from the Venetian service. They were rather a polyglot outfit, but the soldiers fought well all the same and acquired a fine reputation.
3. Churchill, W S, *Marlborough: His Life and Times,* Vol II, 1947, p. 767.
4. D'Arco's army at the Schellenberg comprised:
   The Prince Elector's Regiment (Bavarian)
   The Electoral Guards (Bavarian)
   The Liselbourg Regiment (Bavarian)
   The Nivernois Régiment (French)
   The Nectancourt Régiment (French)
   The Béarn Régiment (French)
   The Grenadiers Rouge (French and Italian troops in Bavarian service)
   Sixteen Squadrons of French Dragoons
   Two batteries of guns (sixteen in total) plus the guns in Donauwörth.
   Herr Gerald Lang of Harburg kindly made his very detailed notes on the order of battle of both armies at the Schellenberg fight available to me.
5. De La Colonie, p. 178.
6. Bounty pay, which was sometimes offered for hazardous or meritorious service, is not to be confused with the 'Dead Man's Wage' which referred to the compassionate practice in the British Army at that time of holding an extra 'dead-man' on the company strength and drawing pay for that non-existent soldier. This money was allocated to the dependant widows and orphaned children of men of the battalion. Although occasionally open to abuse, this custom was officially sanctioned, and Queen Anne took a keen interest in the effectiveness of the measure. 'Elizabeth Rowlands, widow of Reginald Rowlands, killed Blenheim, praying for a pension [£24 Blenheim Bounty was paid]. The Secretary at War requested that the pension fund was exhausted, but the Queen has directed that a man per troop should be mustered under a fictitious name, whereby the fund for the Flanders widows would be enlarged, and the pensions paid more regularly.' (See Dalton, C, *English Army Commission Lists and Registers,* Vol. IV, *1702–6* p.62 for the Blenheim Roll, referring to Treasury Papers Volume CLI No. 3 for 5 September 1712. See also Burn, W, *A Scots Fusilier and Dragoon under Marlborough,* JSAHR, 1936, p. 58.)
7. Lord John Mordaunt survived the carnage on the Schellenberg and fought at Blenheim six weeks later. Here he was wounded and lost an arm, but subsequently went on to the colonelcy of a regiment.
8. Armies at this time were divided into a right and a left Wing, which were similar to modern army corps. Each commander of a Wing would report to the general commanding the army, and this aided tactical control and flexibility. Sometimes, as with Marlborough and Baden, the generals were of broadly equal rank and the command had to be shared, at least in theory. The terms right and left Wing are apt to cause confusion, as they were tactical divisions named regardless of the nature of their employment. Accordingly, the left Wing could be holding the right flank while the right Wing put in an attack on the left.

46

9. Defoe, D (ed. J Fortescue), *Life and Adventures of Mrs Christian Davies*, 1929, p. 55.

10. De La Colonie, p. 182. Colonel Blood's father had infamously tried to steal the Crown Jewels from the Tower of London during the reign of King Charles II.

11. See De La Colonie p.182. Canister-shot is composed of cans of musket balls which are fired by artillery at close range like a massive shotgun. It is not grape-shot, which comprises larger pebble or grape sized balls, and was less commonly seen on battlefields (although it is often described as being used). Canister was not only used in defence; attacking soldiers, if they could manhandle their guns forward into the firing line, could often blast a path using canister through defending troops, even those sheltering behind light cover. The effect of canister upon troops massed in square was quite awful. The use of grenades was fairly widespread at this time, the round bombs being hurled under-arm. Their effect was quite unpredictable as the burning fuse was prone to go out, or to be snuffed out by an alert enemy. The bombs might also be tossed back to their owners before they went off. Additionally, the iron casings of the bombs fractured into quite large pieces and their destructive physical effect could be small, particularly in the open. As with modern grenades, they were most effective in confined areas like trenches or houses.

12. Johnston, S (ed.), *Letters of Samuel Noyes*, JSAHR 1959. Noyes was the chaplain in Orkney's Regiment.

13. Marlborough took particular care to keep himself informed of developments on the battlefield, not only by riding close to the fighting (at considerable personal risk) but by employing fit and able young men as 'running footmen' to scour the battlefield, observing with practised eyes what was taking place, and then returning to make their report. Mounted aides were also used, as was customary with all commanders, but these officers were conspicuous and vulnerable – being in the personal service of a general officer was no peaceful sinecure. The Virginia born rake and plantation owner, Dan Parke, who served as a volunteer on the Danube with Marlborough, was shot through both ankles at the Schellenberg while engaged on this kind of duty. (See Miller, H, *Colonel Parke of Virginia*, 1989 p. 127.)

14. Dragoons at this time were armed, like the infantry, with musket and bayonet, not carbines. Although they normally wore long boots like the cavalry, sometime these were replaced with stout laced shoes and gaiters. If employed on foot, one dragoon in ten would be detailed as a horse-handler and would take the mounts to the rear. (See Brereton, J, *History of the 4th/7th Dragoon Guards*, 1982, p. 60.)

15. De La Colonie, p. 194.

16. Defoe, p.55. A rather lurid contemporary print exists in the Donauwörth Stadt archives showing the hectic scene at the water's edge, with fleeing troops being thrown helpless into the River Danube from the broken bridge.

17. Defoe, p.57. The account of the battle in the Donauwörth Stadt archives also refers to Allied troops entering the town to help quench the flames. See *Die Schlacht am Schellenberg*, 1974.

18. From the journal of Dr Hare, quoted in Green, D, *Blenheim*, London, 1974, pp, 50–1. Marlborough had arranged for hospitals and medical supplies to be prepared at both Amerdingen and Nordlingen. Despite this the lot of the wounded on the battlefield was rather grim. Prompt attention and recovery was very much a matter of chance, and depended largely on whether friends were able to find where a stricken man lay. Still, the marching soldiers of the

time were a tough lot – Mrs Christian Davies, who fought on the hill as a
dragoon, was shot and wounded yet lived to recount her memoirs to Daniel
Defoe. Chaplain Samuel Noyes wrote of the suffering of the wounded as they
lay in the rain that night. However, it seems that the rain would have been
refreshing after the exertions of the hot day, and the shock of gunshot
wounds often brings on a terrible thirst. Sabine's Regiment lost 71 killed and
173 wounded, about a quarter of their strength, in the assault. This seems to
have been a typical cost in casualties amongst the attacking battalions,
although the worst affected unit, the Hessian Baden regiment, lost 320
officers and men, the worst tally in the Allied army that day. Marlborough's
military secretary, Adam Cardonnel, wrote that the 'widows' of the Allied
army were ordered to report for duty as nurses. It was thought that too many
would be available to use – an interesting comment on both the size of the
domestic and administrative tail of the army, and of the scale of the Allied
losses at the Schellenberg. A considerable number of the Allied wounded,
taken to hospitals in Nordlingen, did not survive the ordeal. There are several
memorial plaques in the Evangelische Lutheran Church in the town. One of
these is inscribed to the memory of Marlborough's great friend, Johan
Wigand Goor, General of Infantry of Dutch troops, aged 57 years. The bodies
were interred in mass graves at the foot of the hill. For many years
afterwards, visitors to the site found caps and military accoutrements lying
about. (See also Chandler, D, *Marlborough as Military Commander*, 1973, p. 137;
Tipping, C, *The Story of the Royal Welsh Fusiliers*, 1915, p. 74; Edwards, H, *A
Life of Marlborough*, 1926, p. 141 for comment on the Duke's thanks to the
Mayor of the town.)

19. Edwards, p.144; Brereton p. 60.
20. *Letters and Dispatches*, Vol I, p.330.

CHAPTER V

Marshal Tallard is in My Coach
The Battle of Blenheim,
Sunday 13 August 1704

We made a great slaughter of them and took all their tents and cannon.[1]

After the storming of the Schellenberg and the occupation of Donauwörth on 2 July 1704 Marlborough hoped that Maximilian Wittelsbach, the devious Elector of Bavaria, would agree to terms. Alarmed at the recent disastrous turn of events, with the corps of his best troops under Count D'Arco destroyed, the Elector held out hopes that this would be his choice, and that he would abandon his alliance with France. However, despite the urgings of his wife, who rather perceptively foresaw disaster in his chosen course, the Elector decided to trust to the safe arrival of Camille d'Houtun, Marquis de Tallard, who was by now heading through the tangled passes of the Black Forest with a fresh French army. The news of Tallard's approach march reached the Elector by messenger on 14 July and he suspended talks with Marlborough's emissaries soon afterwards.

Meanwhile, the long awaited Danish contingent, comprising twenty-one squadrons of cavalry and seven infantry battalions, reached Donauwörth on 5 July 1704, camping that night on the Schellenberg hill. Marlborough declared the following day to be one of Thanksgiving for the recent victory, but a pressing operational problem had arisen. He had been unable to bring heavy guns on the march from the Low Countries, and promises that the Margrave of Baden would provide a decent siege train proved empty. This serious deficiency now prevented a proper exploitation of the Schellenberg victory, for even the reduction of such a small town as Rain took four precious days (12–16 July) as breaches in the defences could not be easily made with the artillery to hand. Any Allied attempt on greater targets such as Augsburg or Munich would be almost certain to fail.

Exasperated at this lack of heavy guns, and by the evasions of the Elector who, after prevarication, had now declared that he could not desert his French allies, Marlborough let loose his cavalry on 23 July, on a

49

campaign of destruction of the Bavarian countryside. The troopers burned and looted freely, and raided to the outskirts of Munich itself. The Elector, snugly encamped behind the River Lech at Augsburg, could do little but wait for Tallard to arrive, and watch the skyline as Bavaria burned. He protested loudly at the extent of what he described as Marlborough's outrages, but this had a hollow and hypocritical ring. He would have been quite content to see Donauwörth in flames if he could only have destroyed the depots and magazines there, rather than allow them to fall into his enemy's hands.

Such ruthless operations had been a common feature of the wars of the previous century, and a French army had only a few years before devastated the Palatinate with considerable zeal. Marlborough's ravaging operations at this time, however, were against the supposedly more enlightened spirit of the age, and attracted comment and criticism. 'With fire and sword the country round was wasted far and wide, and many a childing mother then and suckling baby died, but things like that, you know, must be, at every famous victory.'[2]

In his letters to Sarah, Duchess of Marlborough, the Duke said that 3,000 cavalry had been sent towards Munich, to raid and destroy, and he claimed that English troops had no part in these depredations, but this must be doubted. The entire Allied army had been actively gathering supplies in the region ever since the Schellenberg fight. Those crops that could not be gathered were systematically destroyed, and so were the barns in which the harvest would soon be stored. The burning barns adjoined the cottages and inevitably the homes went up in flames too. Soldiers are notoriously careless about such matters when in enemy territory.

Although the damage varied in extent (Colonel De La Colonie claimed that the reports of destruction were greatly exaggerated), Adam Cardonnel, the Duke's military secretary, wrote ruefully on 7 August 1704 'We have made no progress since our success at Schellenberg, except that it be burning and destroying the Elector's country, wherein we have not been sparing.' He went on: 'I wish to God it were all over that I might get safe out of this country.' Others also had their doubts. The Hanoverian soldier Hans Bellingh wrote that: 'The villages were prosperous and thickly populated and it distressed every officer to see over 40 or 50 more villages go up in smoke in an hour.'[3] The Margrave of Baden also protested at Marlborough's ruthless campaign, saying that he intended to fight like a general and not a hussar (those particular troops having a reputation, at this time, of being mere bandits). The Duke would not have this squeamishness and the latter forays were conducted almost entirely by the Margrave's own Imperial soldiers. The dragoon, Mrs Christian Davies, was also in more robust mood, and related with some relish her parts in the looting forays in Bavaria 'We spared nothing, killing, burning or otherwise destroying.'[4]

The military benefit of the wasting of large areas of the Bavarian countryside should not be under-estimated, cruel necessity though it was. The Elector was obliged to disperse his already weakened army to protect his far-flung estates, and this seriously hampered his ability to concentrate his forces to fight a pitched battle. When the time came, he had only five infantry battalions at full strength and twenty squadrons of cavalry to put in line of battle alongside his French allies, and De La Colonie estimated that some 15,000 veteran Bavarian soldiers were absent from the main army on these secondary guard duties.[5] Ironically, the Allied troops had strict orders to avoid the Elector's personal property, but the wide dispersal of many of these troops was heavily criticised by his French colleagues, who perhaps saw what Marlborough's campaign of raids was intended to achieve rather more clearly than he did.

There was a wider strategic factor. Had Marlborough not succeeded in his campaign in 1704 and been obliged to withdraw from the Danube before the onset of winter, the Elector's ability to pursue him, or to renew the attack on Vienna, would be seriously hampered by having no well provisioned base from which to operate. He would be unable to properly supply either his own army or that of his French allies, and the Bavarians already relied on the arrival of Tallard, whose very soldiers could not easily be fed from their own depots. In the meantime, Tallard reluctantly continued his march through the passes of the Black Forest. He entertained serious doubts about the wisdom of the whole operation, complaining that his army had insufficient strength to be truly effective, either alone or as strategic reinforcement in Bavaria. Tallard was particularly concerned to be at the end of such a tenuous supply chain, and had lively and valid doubts about the assurances given that depots and magazines of supplies awaited him in the Danube valley.

The French had decoyed Eugene's vigilant watch at the Lines of Stolhoffen, by employing Marshal Villeroi to engage the Prince's attention with a skilful diversion. Tallard's enormous column, which included 2,000 laden wagons (some reports, rather improbably, suggest 8,000 supply wagons), struggled gamely through the difficult wooded valleys. After wasting six days on a futile siege of Villingen (16–22 July 1704), Tallard drew off on learning of Eugene's approach. The Prince, in the face of Villeroi's manoeuvrings at Stolhoffen, had split his army, not thinking it wise to bring with him more than a corps of 20,000 troops. Tallard, who had 34,000 men, was not aware, at this point, of his opponent's lack of numbers, so he pressed on, hoping to leave Eugene well behind. At last, on 3 August 1704, the Marshal safely delivered his precious supply column to Ulm, and then moved southwards across the Danube to combine with the Elector and Marsin, who marched to meet him.

Tallard's progress was ponderously slow when compared to the smart pace that Marlborough set while marching up the Rhine to challenge

Bavaria. His whole vast operation, although ultimately successful, had consumed thirty-six days and took place in the face of the implacable hatred of the inhabitants of the country through which the army passed. Many villages were barricaded against the column and the French soldiers had to force each road in order to proceed. They behaved in their customary fashion and pillaged and looted continually. Tallard's cavalry, in particular, suffered from the rigours of the road and glanders, known as 'the German Sickness', took a heavy toll of his horses, drastically weakening his tactical capability. About one third of his horses were left lying beside the road.

The veteran Swiss regiments in French service had refused to go to Bavaria, and Louis XIV ordered that they should not be pressed to go beyond their usual terms of service. Partly in consequence, less experienced regiments were sent on the campaign, and many of the French infantry marching with Tallard were relatively raw. However, his army was generally well equipped and in good heart on its arrival in the Danube valley. Tallard was perplexed to find that the depots in Bavaria were, as he suspected, nowhere near as well stocked as he had been led to believe. On 6 August 1704 he joined Marsin and the Elector at Biberbach on the River Lech not far from Augsburg. With so much of the Bavarian army elsewhere, their combined strength was now some 56,000 troops. Despite concerns at the provisioning of the army, and some discord amongst the three commanders as to the best course of action to adopt, the full response to Marlborough's strategic offensive could begin in earnest. In the meantime, orders were sent to the dispersed Bavarian detachments, calling in thirteen infantry battalions and twenty squadrons of cavalry and dragoons to join the main army.

Eugene, whose army was nearing the north bank of the Danube, had shadowed Tallard's march with considerable skill. Hanging malevolently around the flank of the French column, he kept near enough to be sure of the route taken, but was never so close that the French commander could turn and savage his smaller force. The combined strength of the armies of Marlborough, Baden and Eugene was 67,000 men, and they could out-match that of the Elector and the French Marshals if encountered in open battle. The best course for the French and Bavarians, accordingly, was to catch Eugene before he could be supported, and overwhelm his small army on the line of march. Marlborough was concerned that Tallard intended this.[6] Should such a French move fail, then an alternative policy of delay and avoiding battle would frustrate the Duke's plans to gain a clear decision before winter, and might oblige him to abandon the campaign on the Danube altogether.

The night that saw the junction of Tallard with the Elector and Marsin, also saw Marlborough, Baden and Eugene in fresh conference at Schrobenhausen, to the south of Donauwörth. The Prince had just ridden in from the west with only a single trooper in attendance. There was now an intriguing twist in the Allied campaign. Baden was keen to free himself of the other two, quite correctly feeling cast rather into the shade and irked by the obvious rapport between the Duke and Eugene. He suggested a perfectly sound scheme to go and besiege the Bavarian stronghold at Ingolstadt down the Danube, while the main Allied army covered his operations from Donauwörth. This was agreed, and Baden went off on that mission with a detachment of 15,000 troops, including nearly 2,000 cavalry. It would certainly be useful to secure another good crossing over the Danube, and to seize a fortress of the rank of Ingolstadt would be a prize of some value. However, this apparently rash dividing of the Allied army, giving up a precious numerical advantage in the face of a powerful and active enemy, is interesting and requires explanation.

The Allied army's lines of communication and routes of supply into central Germany were well covered from the area of Donauwörth. The chances of a sudden Franco-Bavarian raid to interrupt these routes were very limited, and any attempt to by-pass the position at Donauwörth in order to do so would lay their flank open to Allied attack. However, such a threat could not be entirely discounted, and would be an embarrassing distraction if the Allied army was operating some distance to the south of the Danube, possibly deep in Bavaria. An additional river crossing at Ingolstadt would protect against that eventuality. Also, even allowing for the detachment of the Margrave's troops to the siege, Marlborough and Eugene had quite enough strength to counter any attempt by Tallard to operate effectively to the north of the Danube. This broadly defensive posture, blocking the French and Bavarian army, was what Baden expected when he marched away, but his colleagues undoubtedly had something more adventurous in mind when they let him go.

Most importantly, Marlborough and Eugene plainly felt it worthwhile to have the cautious and obstructive Margrave out of their way during the series of bold operations about to commence. Baden never forgave the two friends for what he considered to be a trick, slyly employed to deny him his place in the field on the fateful day of battle:

> His military epitaph for all time must be that the two greatest captains of the age, pre-eminent and renowned in all the annals of war, rated, by actions more expressive than words, his absence from a decisive battlefield well worth 15,000 men.[7]

This is all valid, and there is no obvious urgent reason otherwise for a siege against Ingolstadt to be pressed at this time; unless, of course, it was convenient to have Baden somewhere he would not be a nuisance, or be able to communicate with his old comrade, the Elector. Still, the Margrave was no coward and his military career had been long and generally successful. He was even then suffering the effects of his injured foot, and this poisonous wound would fester and eventually kill him, so the episode is not without a certain sadness.

By 10 August 1704 Eugene's army was camped on the Plain of Höchstädt on the northern bank of the Danube, only about eight miles west of Donauwörth. His position was exposed as Marlborough's army still lay between Exheim and Rain to the south of the river, a good day's march away. Eugene's scouts reported that Tallard's forces were beginning to pour across the pontoon bridges over the river near Dillingen and Lauingen a few miles farther west, apparently intending to catch and destroy his small army before he could manage to combine with the Duke. The Prince sent an urgent despatch to his friend: 'The Plain of Dillingen is crowded with [enemy] troops. I have held on here all day, but with 18 battalions I dare not risk staying the night . . . Everything Milord, consists in speed.'[8] As he began to fall back eastwards, the Prince sent squads of pioneers on ahead to repair the battered defences on the Schellenberg in case he should need them in a hurry.

On receipt of Eugene's message, at 11.00 pm that evening, Marlborough sent twenty-seven squadrons of Imperial cavalry under the Prince of Württemberg from Rain to support him. A substantial force of infantry, under Marlborough's younger brother, Charles Churchill, was warned off to follow. Marlborough remembered:

> We thought it advisable that he [Eugene] should be reinforced, and that the whole army should advance nearer the Danube in order to join him if the enemy passed [the river]; upon which I ordered the Duke-Regent of Wirtemburg to march early this morning to reinforce the prince with 27 squadrons of Imperial Horse, and at the same time sent my brother Churchill with 20 battalions over the Danube, so as to be at hand to join him.[8]

As Eugene's army fell back through the small village of Münster towards Donauwörth and the security that a combination with Marlborough would provide, his eastward march drew Tallard onwards away from the river crossings at Lauingen and Dillingen. This fixed him firmly in position on the north of the Danube, and may be seen, with the valuable gift of hindsight, as conveniently setting the French and Bavarians up for a sudden Allied attack. However, it seems that Tallard considered his own position the stronger of the two, once he had taken up a firm position on the recently vacated and eminently defensible Plain of Höchstädt. Tallard, Marsin and the Elector were becoming careless and over-confident.

Despite their respective tactical achievements, each admirable in their own way, the failure to isolate and destroy any one of the several detachments of their opponents was a failing in the commanders on both

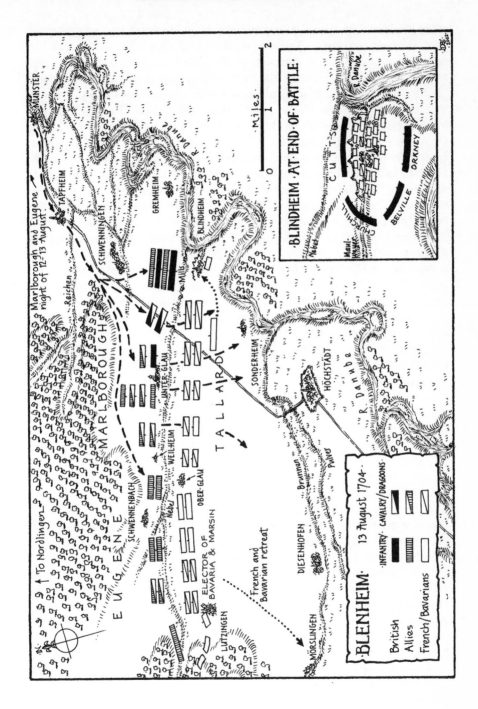

sides. Each had managed to combine their main forces, but had failed to prevent their opponents from doing the same. Once the junction of the opposing armies was accomplished, the Allied army comprised 52,000 troops while, in comparison, the Franco-Bavarian army had 56,000 men. Neither side now had a significant advantage of numbers (although Tallard did not know this, not appreciating that Baden had left Marlborough). It seemed unlikely that either army could now achieve a tactical mass superior enough to overpower the other, and this whole campaign could soon become a stalemate, greatly to the benefit of the Elector and the French, unless something radical was attempted. Marlborough's strategic concentration of the combined Allied armies in southern Germany, so cleverly contrived and long and laborious in the achieving, could evaporate in the damp mists of autumn. Without a real substantial victory he would not be permitted, even if he could feed his soldiers, to stay and pass the winter on the Danube

As soon as Marlborough was assured that his opponents had indeed crossed to the north bank of the Danube with their main force, he moved towards Eugene's army with all speed. The junction of the Allied armies was achieved without mishap on the afternoon of 11 August 1704, on the River Kessel just to the west of Donauwörth. A very dangerous twenty-four hours had passed safely, and the artillery train closed up at daybreak the following day. The Duke needed a speedy victory, and he was keen to force the pace now that he and Eugene were acting together, acutely aware of the great distances between his own army and their home depots, and that the Dutch could, at any time, demand the return of their troops.

The plan quietly hatched between the Duke and the Prince now came into effect. On the morning of 12 August 1704 the Allied army began a stealthy westwards movement, with the Schellenberg at its back – most of the soldiers would never see that dark hill more. Led by an advanced guard of twenty-eight squadrons of cavalry they crossed the River Wörnitz, marching through the low wooded hills past Ebermorgen, and on up the Danube, to halt for the night between the villages of Münster and Tapfheim. From Tapfheim village church tower Marlborough and Eugene were able to observe the Franco-Bavarian encampments near Höchstädt earlier that afternoon. They also moved to a spot on the Huhnersberg hill near the village of Wolperstetten to obtain a better view with their 'perspective glasses' (their cavalry escort attracted the unwelcome attention of French patrols). To their satisfaction they saw that the Elector and the Marshals had come forward from the vicinity of the difficult marshy ground near Höchstädt. The Bavarian and French quartermasters were busily marking out the site, and they had moved out onto the more open plain beside the Nebel Stream. This may have been a drier and more pleasant camping ground, but it was also good cavalry country. 'Here was a fine plain without a hedge or ditch, for the cavalry on both sides to show their bravery.'[9]

Squads of Marlborough's pioneers were busy removing obstacles along the Reichen Stream beyond Tapfheim, and improving tracks through the woods to ease the forward passage of the army. It was to be expected that this activity would attract the attention of Tallard, and the French commander sent forward the Marquis de Silly with twenty squadrons of French cavalry, which had been covering their front, towards the Reichen to find out what was going on. Archibald Rowe's English brigade moved forward as this French threat developed, and de Silly's troopers drew off after a sharp skirmish, but Rowe was obliged to call forward the 1st English Foot Guards to support his own four battalions before he could achieve this small and important success.

Despite the ample evidence of an Allied approach towards Höchstädt, the real significance was not recognised by Tallard and his comrades, for their thoughts seemed to lie exclusively with plans of their own. Meanwhile, they neglected to hold the relatively narrow defile (or opening) around the village of Schwenningen, where the wooded hills and the marshy meadows along the Danube came close together. This place was occupied by Rowe's brigade and a brigade of Hessians under the overall command of Major-General Wilkes, later in the evening of 12 August. Had the French and Bavarians only held this village, the frontage that they had to cover would have been little more than a mile in width, instead of the more than four miles on the Plain of Höchstädt.

The uncontested passage of such an easily defended gap was a prize of very great worth to Marlborough, who had brought off a considerable tactical surprise on his opponents. The Elector and the Marshals remained in neglectful complacency of the dramatic events unfolding about them; they lay snugly encamped nearby with all their baggage and impedimenta. Despite the fairly widespread cavalry contacts in the area, particularly along the Reichen Stream near Schwenningen, they remained in ignorance of the imminence of the Allied attack. Engrossed in their own plans and their gleeful anticipation of success now they had combined their forces, they fondly believed that their firm moves and bold approach must make their opponents retire along their supply lines. This would surely take Marlborough steadily away from Bavaria and out of the campaign altogether.

It seems likely that Tallard would have been content to let the Allies go; stagnation in southern Franconia during the winter months would deplete the Allied army soon enough, especially as the Dutch grew impatient at the Duke's absence with their troops. Ultimately Marlborough would be left with little to do to aid the Emperor in Vienna. However, it seems that the more adventurous Elector and the darkly ambitious Marshal Marsin were inclined to force a battle, especially as reports, yet to be confirmed, were now being received of the detaching of Baden's corps to attack Ingolstadt. In the event, such choices were made irrelevant as Marlborough's dynamic plan took hold. The French and Bavarian commanders had badly underestimated their opponent, with all the dreadful risk that this entailed, and the penalty was severe. In its ignorance, their camp was a merry, convivial place that Saturday evening, and the senior officers relaxed in their canopied tents, exchanged toasts and enjoyed a good bowl of campaign soup together. All that time the Allied army was lying under brilliant stars in the wooded hills nearby, readying itself to attack.

Across the wooded spur of low hills from the Plain of Höchstädt, the Allied soldiers were roused from their brief slumbers shortly after midnight on 13 August 1704. Slow and sleepy, the soldiers were chivvied into marching columns by their sergeants in the darkness, without beat of drum. They gradually began to move forward along the dark paths that led westwards through the trees and into more open country. At 6.00 am Marlborough held a last roadside conference with his senior commanders on a small hill to the south-east of Schwenningen. Ghostly columns of many thousands of men tramped past in the early morning mist, while the Duke sought the advice, in particular, of Dubislaw Natzmer, a Prussian cavalryman, now in the Dutch service. He had been defeated by the Elector of Bavaria at the Battle of Höchstädt the previous year, and with grim certainty knew the terrain well.

Soon afterwards, the Allied army began to move out from the defile of Schwenningen onto the Plain of Höchstädt. Forty squadrons of cavalry fanned out onto the open ground as an advanced guard for the eight great columns of marching infantry that followed. Ahead lay the marshy Nebel Stream, running protectively from north to south across the front of the sleeping enemy encampment. The two brigades under Wilkes closed up to the left of the army after it cleared the village of Schwenningen and formed a ninth column of march. The British brigades of Ferguson and Hamilton, and six Hanoverian battalions under Hulsen joined them, as did fifteen squadrons of English and Scots cavalry and dragoons commanded by Henry Lumley.

Just before the awful realisation of an impending Allied attack, Tallard penned a remarkable letter to Louis XIV in Versailles, in which he wrote that it was expected that the enemy army would soon withdraw and head for Nordlingen. At about 6.00 am the approach of Marlborough's army was detected by his pickets, and frantic preparations ensued to put the Franco-Bavarian army in what state of battle could be managed. Signal guns were fired to bring in pickets and foragers, and those French batteries able to bear opened fire on the advancing columns, hoping to slow the Allied deployment. The sound of these guns was plainly heard by the Margrave of Baden at his headquarters near to Ingolstadt, forty miles away. He was also writing a letter, to the Emperor, and he now added that Marlborough and Eugene were being attacked at Donauwörth, and he hoped for good fortune for them, in the battle that lay ahead.[10]

The Comte de Mérode-Westerloo, a distinguished and shrewdly observant Walloon brigade commander serving with Tallard (he held the command of the cavalry of the second line of the right Wing that day), left an entertaining account of how he was raised from his curtained camp bed that morning by his head-groom, LeFranc. He was given, not the accustomed cup of morning chocolate which the sleepy Count pleasantly expected, but the alarming news that the Allied army was pouring forth onto the plain beside them. 'I rubbed my eyes in disbelief' Flinging on some clothes, Mérode-Westerloo scurried about his brigade lines getting his sleepy troopers to saddle their mounts and draw up in order, while the remainder of the camp was still awakening to the boom of signal guns being fired to recall foraging parties.[11]

Amongst the first of Tallard's actions was to set on fire the small village of Unterglau in the centre of the field, close to the eastern bank of the Nebel Stream, which comfortingly separated the French and Bavarians from Marlborough. It was hoped in this way to further hamper the Allied arrangements, and two watermills on the stream, near to the village of Blindheim (Blenheim), were also set alight for the same purpose. Tallard deployed his thirty-six battalions of infantry and twelve squadrons of dismounted dragoons (who had left their horses dead of glanders in the Black Forest) of the right Wing of the army, in an arc stretching from the marshy slopes of the Danube northwards to the open cornfields beyond Blindheim. He had already detached two battalions to support the centre where taciturn Marshal Marsin stationed his own fourteen battalions of French and émigré Irish infantry around the village of Oberglau, just to the west of the Nebel Stream. Twelve more battalions extended the French line leftwards towards the Elector's troops. The sole five blue-clad battalions of sturdy Bavarian infantry in their distinctive red stockings that were present with the army that day were put in place near to the village of Lutzingen on the left of the army. Count D'Arco, veteran of the Schellenberg fight, commanded them. Beyond Lutzingen Marsin sent eleven French battalions to bolster the far left flank of the army, and these troops took up position in the wooded hills beyond the village.

The villages of Blindheim, Oberglau and Lutzingen were each barricaded and packed with infantry. The Franco-Bavarian army had ninety guns, and their batteries were placed swiftly but with great care. The French artillery commander, the Marquis de Frequelière, gained considerable praise for his adroit handling of the guns that day but, except for a great battery of sixteen heavy Bavarian guns near Lutzingen, the fields of fire were not very good, particularly on the right of the army.

Additionally, the guns emplaced around the villages could not provide effective overlapping fire to entirely cover the intervening cornfields.

The 143 squadrons of French, Bavarian and Walloon cavalry drew up in the cornfields between the villages (except the dismounted dragoons building barricades beside the River Danube). Sixty-four of these squadrons deployed under Tallard, and Marsin detached sixteen of his squadrons to join them. The remaining sixty-seven squadrons of cavalry, under Marsin and the Elector, formed on the open fields between Oberglau and Lutzingen. The ground on which the squadrons took position was gently sloping downwards to the Nebel Stream, and was in many places thick with the corn of the coming harvest; through necessity the farmers had left much of it lying to be spoiled in the fields. It presented an ideal setting for a cavalry battle.[12]

Although they had to cover a wide front, the position in which the Marshals and the Elector had to fight possessed a certain natural strength. Both flanks were secure, with the Danube protecting the right flank of the army and the wooded hills, thronging with French infantry, covering the left. The marshy Nebel Stream, divided into several boggy rivulets in places, crossed the entire front and this was a significant obstacle requiring time and effort to cross. However, their army was obliged, by the time pressure imposed on them by Marlborough's daring approach, to draw up in battle array in the same overall positions in which they had gone into camp the previous day. These dispositions were not necessarily the best from which to fight a pitched battle against skilful opponents. Still, the best was made of a flawed situation, and the French and Bavarian commanders made a competent enough job of forming their troops to meet the Allied attack.

One particular weakness was that, as the horses in Tallard's army had suffered from sickness, Marsin was keen to keep most of his own cavalry well away from potential infection. Apart from sending some of his squadrons across the Höchstädt road to support Tallard, Marsin kept the left Wing of the Franco-Bavarian army more distinctly separated from Tallard than might otherwise have been the case, even with such a divided command. (Although the French Marshals deferred to the Elector by virtue of his rank, and agreed to his particular request not to disturb the standing crops by preparing entrenchments, there was a general equality of rank between them.) The tactical shortcomings of this arrangement would become very apparent as the day wore on.

In the event, the dispositions for battle that they adopted allowed Marlborough to mass one third more cavalry than did Tallard on the beautifully open fields between Blindheim and Oberglau. The numerically stronger French and Bavarians would very soon find themselves badly wrong-footed and allowed no time to recover – with their excellent cavalry off balance in the face of the vibrant Allied attack, while their numerous infantry were wastefully devoted to holding the barricaded villages as fixed points.

At 9.00 am the Elector and the Marshals held a hasty council of war in Blindheim village. From the churchtower they were able to view the progress of the Allied army, whose confident approach seemed to indicate a real superiority in numbers; they must have thought that Baden's troops were still with Marlborough and Eugene. After discussion, Marsin and the Elector opted to fight for the line of the Nebel Stream, to force their opponents to pay for each foot of ground obtained. Tallard, however, decided to hold his troops back from the stream, on the gently rising ground some hundreds of yards from the water's edge. This ground was ideal for his cavalry, and in this way he hoped to lure his opponent on to defeat with a water obstacle at his back. Any forced withdrawal by the attackers would tend to lead to disaster as the disordered Allied troops struggled to re-cross the boggy stream to safety.

Benefiting enormously from hindsight, both Marsin and the Elector subsequently claimed to have questioned the wisdom of Tallard's decision in keeping his troops back from the stream. Mérode-Westerloo, who had an opinion on most matters, also felt that the two lines of French cavalry were spaced too far apart to be fully effective. Tactically, however, the arrangements were sound enough in the circumstances, as long as the cavalry on that Wing were well handled and properly supported by infantry and artillery.

On the other side of the Nebel Stream, Marlborough's plan was quite simple, although enormously demanding in execution. Prince Eugene, with the smaller Wing of the Allied army (about 20,000 Imperial, German and Danish troops – eighteen Infantry battalions and seventy-nine cavalry squadrons) would attack on the right and fix the 30,000 Bavarian and French troops under the Elector and Marsin in position between Lutzingen and Oberglau. If he deployed promptly, they could not drive his army against the wooded hills behind him, nor would they send reinforcements southwards to Tallard in good time. In the meanwhile, Marlborough would attack with the 32,000 men of the left Wing (British, Dutch and Germans – forty-four infantry battalions and eighty-two squadrons) and engage and destroy Tallard's army (about 26,000 troops strong) on the ideal cavalry country of the Plain of Höchstädt. The pace set by the Duke needed to be dynamic, so that the initiative was rigorously kept away from his numerically superior opponents.

To achieve all this Marlborough had first to neutralise the French infantry and dragoons in Blindheim Village, and so remove the threat they posed to his left flank as he moved forward from the Nebel. His infantry had to force the line of the stream and hold the far bank long enough for the cavalry to struggle across the obstacle and join them. All this was to be achieved in the face of the forty-eight squadrons of French and Walloon cavalry, under the command of the veteran Swiss General Beat-Jacques von Zurlauben, standing only a few hundred yards away with powerful batteries in support.

Marlborough's infantry were commanded by his brother, Charles Churchill, and by 10.00 am these troops were in line stretching between Unterglau and the Danube. The French batteries hammered away, and at one point a round-shot struck the ground beneath Marlborough's grey horse, covering both rider and mount with dust. Unperturbed, he calmly gave directions to Colonel Holcroft Blood regarding counter-battery fire. Looking around at the soldiers leaning stoically on their muskets, he suggested that they should lie down to gain shelter both from the French fire and from the warm sun. He then completed his unhurried inspection of the line of battle, before dismounting to take some refreshment with his aides. Meanwhile, the musicians in the opposing armies engaged in their own duel across the stream, exchanging drum rolls and flams, and trumpet fanfares.

It was a Sunday, and the Duke ordered that the regimental chaplains should now offer divine service at the head of each Allied regiment. The men knelt in the trampled cornfields while the French guns thundered above them; the chaplains stood at the piled drums and gave their blessings, and the soldiers heads were bowed in perhaps more fervent devotion than was usually the case.

The actual severity of this cannonade is difficult to judge, for the forming up points for Churchill's troops were in many parts in dead ground to the French gun-line on the slope beyond the Nebel Stream. Additionally, in places the corn was still uncut, and obscured the view. The artillery tactics of the day allowed for no forward observers and the gunners were unlikely to have been permitted to fire off much of the expensive ammunition blindly. A little later, a six-gun French battery near Blindheim did subject the British troops to a harassing fire during their advance on the village, but the field of view there is better. It is possible that this battery was the cause of the fire which gave rise to the expedient of the Allied soldiers lying down, and a number of eye-witnesses refer to the difficulties that de Frequilière's boldly efficient gunners caused to the Allies during this part of the operation. Still, the damage was not all on one side, and Mérode-Westerloo wrote afterwards that an Allied round-shot decapitated one of his favourite horses, and injured another, during the gunnery duel.

Hay's Scots Dragoons were there, and Mrs Christian Davies does not make much of the French bombardment in her reminiscences, but remembered that:

At six o'clock in the morning on 13th August 1704 we came in sight of the enemy, and, at about 11.00, were drawn up in order of battle;

62

we then threw five bridges, made of fascines and tin pontoons, over the rivulet before the forces of the enemy, posted behind it.[13]

Meanwhile, Prince Eugene had difficulty during his tedious march to get into position opposite the Bavarian army, for the ground he had to cross was marshy and choked with scrub. He also felt the need to throw out strong detachments of troops to his left, to guard against a French thrust against this exposed flank. This was a wise precaution, but it certainly delayed his progress, and time was at a premium for Marlborough. It has been suggested that Eugene was intended by Marlborough to deceive the French and Bavarian commanders into thinking that his line of march was actually the route for Nordlingen, and that the Prince rather overdid this deception and had to double back to a greater extent than intended. This is unlikely, for the Duke's Wing of the army was deploying for battle in plain sight of Tallard and any such intended deception would have been rather feeble. The difficult country over which Eugene had to march is the reason for the length of time and the labour required getting into place. This also had serious consequences for the deployment of Eugene's artillery, which was unable to get properly into place until well after the battle began. The power of his initial attack was lessened accordingly. Dr Hare, Marlborough's chaplain, wrote:

> All this while both armies continued to cannonade each other very briskly, but the fire of the enemy's artillery was not so well answered by the cannon of Prince Eugene as it was by that in the left wing [Marlborough's]; for his highness was obliged to sustain the fire of the enemy's artillery all the while he was drawing up his troops, but could not bring his own field-pieces to bear against them on account of many ditches and other impediments from one extremity of his wing to the other. His Highness was obliged therefore to order fascines to be prepared for the more easy passage of these ditches, and his cannon were kept in the meantime at too great a distance to reach those of the enemy with effect.[14]

At mid-day the Duke felt obliged to send his Quartermaster-General, William Cadogan, to enquire after Eugene's progress. It was a tense time, as the troops of the left Wing stood in anticipation before the Nebel Stream. There was a very real danger that the advantages Marlborough had seized so audaciously early in the day would slip away, and that his opponents would stir themselves and attack. At last, at about 12.30 pm, Marlborough received a message that Eugene's troops were in place. He sent back word requesting that the attack on that flank commence immediately, and, mounting his horse, gave Churchill the order to move forward in the centre and force the line of the Nebel. Simultaneously, the young Prince of Hesse (who would one day become the King of Sweden, by marriage) was sent to Lord John Cutts of Gowan on the extreme left of the Allied line to request that he take the powerful infantry column gathered there against Blindheim village.[15] By 1.30 pm on 13 August 1704, a good six hours after the passage of the Schwenningen defile, and more than eighteen hours since the French cavalry first came forward to investigate Marlborough's approach, the Battle of Blenheim (Höchstädt) began in earnest along the marshy length of the Nebel Stream.

Churchill's infantry began to pour across the stream, where parties of pioneers had laboured to level the banks and constructed the walkways with fascines and wood salvaged from the ruined cottages of Unterglau and the two watermills. An old stone bridge had been hastily demolished by French engineers, and this was partly rebuilt. The less fortunate soldiers floundered across the stream thigh deep in marshy water, but the crossing was not actively opposed, in accordance with Tallard's plan. Cutts was able without much difficulty to form his infantry into line of battle on the far bank, and to move up the short gentle incline away from the stream course and towards Blindheim. Rowe's brigade of English and Scots troops had been the first to cross, and his soldiers briefly lay down in the boggy grass only about 300 yards from the French barricades around the village. Meanwhile, a brace of guns was manhandled to the edge of the stream, and opened fire, sending their round-shot cleanly towards the nearest French breastworks.

At his word of command Rowe's troops rose from the sodden ground and moved steadily towards the village, hurriedly dressing their ranks as they went. At first, the fire from the French battery to their right was the only opposition, the gunners switching to canister shot as the range closed. Rowe's right-hand companies wilted under the blasts, but kept trudging doggedly on through the enveloping smoke. The French infantry were well disciplined, and held their fire, but as Rowe's attackers neared the village, their ranks were suddenly torn by heavy and accurate volleys of musketry from the defenders. Blinded in the smoke, and reeling under the fire, the soldiers valiantly tried to force their way to the barricades, but were everywhere driven back with heavy loss. Rowe, who led his men forward on foot, was mortally wounded, shot through the thigh as he defiantly struck the barricade with his sword. Lieutenant Colonel Dalyell and Major Campbell of Rowe's own regiment, the Scots Fuziliers, were also killed as they ran to recover his body.

At the same time as Rowe's attack, Cutts' second brigade, that of James Ferguson, advanced towards the left of the village. Here, squadrons of dismounted French dragoons had erected improvised breastworks of overturned carts and branches, leading down to the marshes of the River Danube. Despite a hard-pressed attack, which saw the 1st English Foot Guards (who had been attached to the brigade since the skirmishing the previous afternoon) and the French exchanging bayonet thrusts across the carts, the dragoons were not to be driven out. The Guards' commanding officer, Lieutenant-Colonel Philip Dormer, was killed in the exchange and Ferguson was obliged to withdraw his battered battalions back towards the Nebel Stream to re-form. The well disciplined French soldiers bit fresh cartridges, re-loaded their muskets, and calmly awaited the likely renewal of the attack.

Cutts' leading brigades were recoiling in some disarray at such a robust repulse. Now, an adroit counter-attack was launched by von Zurlauben, who led forward three squadrons (six companies) of the elite Gens d'Armes of the French Household cavalry, resplendent in their laced red coats. These charging squadrons, making full use of the slope, cut sharply in at the flank of Rowe's brigade as it fell back towards the Nebel Stream. Rowe's Regiment was caught off balance as the soldiers tried desperately to form square, and it was thrown into confusion by the mass of sword swinging horsemen. The colour ensign was hacked down and the regimental colour seized by a triumphant gendarme.

Fortunately for Cutts, Wilkes' brigade had just crossed the Nebel Stream and was close at hand but not yet committed to action. These sturdy Hessian soldiers rose from the marshy grass and moved smartly forward to assist the stricken English regiment. They drove off the milling French horsemen and recovered the lost colour, and von Zurlauben had to hurry his squadrons back out of range of their deadly musketry, and re-form them on the neighbouring cornfield, overlooking the stream. He called forward more squadrons of Gens D'Armes from the first line cavalry, ready for a fresh effort.

The casualties amongst the attacking infantry were already heavy and many officers had fallen. The huge regimental colour of the 1st English Foot Guards was all shot to pieces. These were mostly the regiments that had been badly depleted at the Schellenberg, and Cutts' task was starting to seem impossible. The real purpose of his attacks was well achieved however, for the numerous French troops in the village were at once entirely committed to its defence. The commander in Blindheim, the Marquis de Clerambault, originally had just nine battalions of infantry, and the dismounted dragoons, and he grew increasingly concerned at the pressure his troops had to endure as Cutts came into the attack once more. The Marquis began to bolster his defence by drawing into the village every infantry battalion and dismounted dragoon squadron within reach. Clerambault was justifiably concerned about the security of the village, but he was stripping the cavalry on the right Wing of its supports. Tallard can hardly have been entirely unaware of this and his lack of grip on the situation at this early stage of the battle is damning.

Clerambault's ill-considered actions increasingly left Tallard's cavalry weakened and without the infantry support so necessary against a concerted all arms attack. Marlborough was close at hand, just across the Nebel Stream, viewing the fighting from near one of the smouldering watermills. He could see that his aim in fixing the French right Wing in Blindheim and neutralising the troops in that place was more than adequately achieved. At about 2.00 pm the Duke sent word to Cutts that no more of the bloody attacks should be attempted; but just to keep the French garrison occupied and contained in the village.

The full measure of Cutts's accomplishment was that, with only sixteen under-strength battalions of infantry (perhaps 6,000 men), and fifteen squadrons of cavalry and dragoons who were soon deployed elsewhere, he held twenty-seven French infantry battalions and twelve squadrons of dismounted dragoons in and around the village of Blindheim. This garrison must have totalled well over 12,000 good troops, who could, if properly used, have influenced to great effect the main battle on the Plain of Höchstädt. As it was, the congested streets of the village were soon packed with French infantry, mostly impotently unable to use their weapons or deploy properly through the narrow exits between the cottages to fight. This was a considerable tactical success for Marlborough with very far reaching effects.

Soon after Cutts pressed forward against Blindheim, Prince Eugene's army advanced on the far right of the Allied line to attack the Elector. The rump of the Bavarian army lay 600 yards to their front in the area of Lutzingen, with French infantry on either flank. The Imperial cavalry under the Duke of Württemberg and Prince Maximilian of Hanover picked its way across the many rivulets of the Nebel Stream in this area, and advanced to the left of Eugene's infantry. Despite artillery fire from Marsin's batteries near Oberglau on their left, Württemberg's cavalry closed with and broke the first line of the Bavarian cavalry. His troopers were then too disordered to withstand the shock of a smart counter-attack by the Elector's second line squadrons, assisted by Marsin's cavalry, who then rode forward. Threatened in front and from the flank, the Allied cavalry were forced to retire behind the Nebel Stream to re-form.

Simultaneously, Eugene's infantry, comprising seven Danish and eleven Prussian battalions under the command of Prince Leopold of Anhalt-Dessau, advanced to attack Lutzingen. The plain was open and even, and the Bavarian and French gunners had excellent fields of fire; they worked their field pieces with feverish efficiency and to good effect. As the lines of Allied infantry struggled gamely through the smoke, the bombardment tore great gaps in their ranks and the Danes, in particular, took a heavy battering. However, they were now supported by the fire of fourteen of Eugene's guns (all he had got into place at this time) emplaced on rising ground near to the wood line between Schwennenbach and the Weilheim Farm. The Prussians and Danes forced their way forward at bayonet point towards the great battery near Lutzingen. The five Bavarian battalions there, under the command of Count D'Arco, were tough veterans, the best the Elector could muster. Fighting with great gallantry they launched a devastating counter-attack, led by two battalions of the elite Bavarian Life Guards, and drove the Prussians back in disorder. This, in turn, perilously exposed the left flank of the Danish infantry who were hotly engaged with the French troops in the woods behind Lutzingen.

Faced with a dangerous out-flanking threat of the Elector's cavalry, Anhalt-Dessau's infantry hastily fell back from the Bavarian battery, and sullenly walked to the Nebel. Hard pressed by the French and Bavarians at the water's edge, the troops got across the stream, but it was rather a scramble. In the awful confusion, scores of Prussian prisoners were taken and ten regimental colours were lost. Order too was lost for a time, particularly amongst the less experienced battalions, and it required energetic efforts by their commanders to rally the Danes and Prussians at the wood-line, farther back than their original starting point. They were shocked and dispirited, and the Allied right Wing badly needed time in which to recover.

This was a severe rebuff for Eugene, and there was the danger that the initiative would now pass to the Elector and Marsin. The Prince and his commanders were active, however, encouraging and exhorting their men for a fresh effort. Considering the scale of the initial repulse, the soldiers regained their composure with admirable speed, and a second attack against the Elector's position was attempted by the Imperial cavalry at about 3.30 pm, although Eugene's infantry were not yet really up to another attempt. Rather inevitably this attack lacked the enthusiasm and fire of the first attack. Once again the artillery fire the Allies faced was brutally efficient, and they suffered terribly for lack of support from their own gunners. The cavalry, with Eugene riding at its head, was caught in a deadly cross-fire and failed to drive the French and Bavarian first line squadrons very far this time. As before that afternoon, a hasty withdrawal beyond the stream was necessary.

By about 4.00 pm the opposing troops on the northern half of the battlefield were left watching each other warily across the Nebel. The opposing commanders, Eugene and the Elector, both exerted themselves unceasingly to hearten their tiring troops, riding amongst their men with words and shouts of praise and encouragement. Dr Hare was an interested observer: 'The Elector of Bavaria was seen riding up and down, and inspiring the men also with fresh courage.'[16] Anhalt-Dessau now persuaded his shaken infantry to undertake another attack. Their advance was harried by the French infantry who poured in a heavy musketry from the woods to their right, while canister from the guns in the great battery scythed through the Prussian and Danish ranks, tumbling scores of men down. Eugene had guns brought forward on the extreme right to try to suppress the French infantry in the wood-line, and this is clearly shown in contemporary maps. With fine courage the Allied soldiers stormed the great battery and drove out the gunners, but a bloody battle through the cottages and gardens of the village of Lutzingen followed. Unsupported by the Imperial cavalry, which was all fought out, and most of whose squadrons hung back, the Prince's infantry could not sustain their advance, and had to withdraw towards the Nebel Stream once more.

From this point onwards however, the disheartened and unenthusiastic efforts of Württemberg's squadrons became increasingly ineffective. Eugene, beside himself with frustration and rage at their failing efforts, threatened to shoot troopers with his own hand if they would not face their front and form for fresh attacks. (Anecdotes that he did, indeed, pistol some of his own troopers for hanging back are rather unconvincing.) At last the Prince took himself off to fight with Anhalt-Dessau's infantry, muttering that he would rather die amongst brave men; his wish was almost granted, as he was nearly dragged off his horse by Bavarian soldiers in one mêlée. After four hours of grim combat he had done little more than capture and hold the Elector's attention, and to partly divert Marshal Marsin at Oberglau from the greater battle to the south. However, this was an achievement of considerable value for, as with the French infantry in Blindheim, the enemy were pinned in position by the remorseless and expensive attacks, and the chance of taking the initiative was ruthlessly kept away from them.

While Eugene's attacks foundered on the Allied right, in the centre of the battlefield, Churchill's troops clambered with difficulty across the boggy expanse of the Nebel Stream. They comprised two lines of cavalry (seventy-two squadrons at this point) interspersed with two lines of infantry (seven battalions in the front line, whose principal task had been to be first across the Nebel and secure the far bank, and eleven battalions in the rearmost line). This powerful force was able to form up in battle array on the slope to the west of the stream, although the French artillery made fairly good practice against the knots of struggling men and horses as they scrambled up onto drier ground. Steadily the Allied numbers on the Plain of Höchstädt grew. Churchill's infantry commanders were instructed to leave generous gaps between their battalions, so that the cavalry could pass through and re-form when under pressure, and both Marlborough and his brother took particular care to ensure that this was done.

As this deployment proceeded, a fresh sudden and bold thrust by eight squadrons (sixteen companies) of von Zurlauben's Gens d'Armes threatened to force a wedge between Churchill's infantry and Cutts' infantry, still held outside Blindheim. Cutts' troops had already been roughly handled once by the French cavalry and the moment was tense. Opposing the French horsemen were five squadrons of English cavalry, drawn from the regiments of Wyndham, Wood and Schomberg, deployed onto this flank to cover the infantry as they attacked the village. These troopers were amongst the first to cross the Nebel Stream and, under the command of Colonel Frances Palmes, they moved promptly forward to blunt von Zurlauben's thrust. Audaciously sending the squadrons of Majors Creed and Oldfield out onto either flank, Palmes was able to envelop the Gens d'Armes as the Frenchmen halted to discharge their carbines (a tactic very outmoded in 1704 and guaranteed to surrender the initiative to a bold and mobile foe). Palmes' squadrons overthrew their more numerous opponents, who found their flanks over-ridden. The Gens d'Armes fell back in considerable disorder, their headlong flight taking them ingloriously through the formed ranks of Tallard's cavalry, drawn up on the slope behind them.

Colonel Palmes then rather over-did his success, and his pursuit of the Gens d'Armes was pressed too far. Overwhelmed by fresh French squadrons, who came teeming forward to oppose him, the Colonel's slender force was promptly chased back towards the Nebel Stream and the shelter of the Allied infantry. Creed was killed and Palmes' second in command, Colonel Charles Sybourg, was tumbled from his horse and trampled and injured, but managed to get away after being ridden over by two whole squadrons. Once again, Wilkes' Hessians were on hand and their steady volleys enabled Palmes' squadrons to extricate themselves. Still, this minor success over the elite cavalry of the French army, with perhaps no more than a couple of dozen casualties inflicted by either side, had vivid and unexpected consequences.

The Elector, on hearing the incredible news of the almost impudent repulse of such a notable body as the Gens d'Armes, exclaimed: 'What, the Gentlemen of France fleeing? Go, tell them that that I am here in person. Rally them and lead them to the charge.'[17] These heartening words did little to stem the flight as the unfortunate messenger was taken prisoner by Allied cavalry soon afterwards. More significantly, the effect of this reverse upon Tallard's nerves seems to have been quite dramatic. Dismayed at the inexplicable repulse of such fine cavalry, alarmed at the unceasing clamour about Blindheim (and coincidentally distracted by his own physical short-sightedness), Tallard went urgently to find Marsin, in the saddle near to Oberglau, to ask for support. Marsin refused the request, as Eugene's second series of attacks were only just ebbing towards the Nebel Stream, and he would spare no troops for the relief of the right Wing of the army. Unavoidably, Tallard must fight on alone.

While the Marshals were in hurried conversation, the increasingly nervous Clerambault was drawing Tallard's supporting infantry (most particularly the eleven battalions deployed along the Höchstädt road, and seven battalions standing in rear of Blindheim) into the village. Although soon aware of this, Tallard then failed to correct the folly of his subordinate, and his cavalry were left unduly exposed to the force of the impending Allied attack. He was left with only nine raw battalions of French infantry to assist in the cavalry battle on the Plain of Höchstädt. By contrast, Marlborough quietly withdrew Hulsen's Hanoverian brigade and Hamilton's English brigade from Cutts' effort against Blindheim (leaving only the brigades of Rowe, Ferguson and Wilkes in place). Lumley's British cavalry squadrons had already moved to engage the French Gens d'Armes, and the Duke now brought Hulsen and Hamilton, together with the dismounted dragoon regiments of Hay and Ross, to the centre of his line where they could support Churchill's infantry.[18]

Charles Churchill still had to secure the right flank of his infantry against possible attack from the French troops in the vicinity of Oberglau. The Danish cavalry had already been roughly handled here by the musketry and cannon fire from Marsin's troops around the village. At about 3.00 pm, as Eugene's army surged towards Lutzingen, the Prince of Holstein-Beck moved forward from Unterglau with Count Berensdorf's column of ten Dutch battalions. Crossing the Nebel Stream on yet more fascine walkways (Marlborough's pioneers had spent a hectic morning), the Dutch fanned out to deploy in readiness for the attack on Oberglau.

The French commander in that village was the Marquis de Blainville (Marsin's senior infantry commander, and the son of the great French naval reformer, Colbert). He immediately replied to this dangerous move by the Dutch with a very well handled counter-attack by the Irish regiments of O'Brien (Clare's Dragoons), Dorrington and Lee. These émigré Catholic troops, conspicuous in the red coats, came on in fine style, driving forward in well ordered ranks at the Dutch as they clambered away from the cloying bogs along the Nebel Stream. Holstein-Beck was ill supported by his artillery, who seem also to have been emplaced too far back to be effective, and he sent an aide hurrying to some Imperial cavalry standing close to the Weilheim Farm with a plea for assistance. The Imperial officers, rather obtusely, refused to move without authority from Prince Eugene. The two leading Dutch battalions (those of Beynheim and Goor) were soon routed and put to flight; the regimental colours were lost and Holstein-Beck was himself wounded and left for dead. Carried away by the Irish on a handcart, Holstein-Beck was released soon afterwards, but his wounds proved fatal.[19]

Marsin's own cavalry had already played an effective part in the repulse of the Imperial cavalry in the cornfields between Oberglau and Lutzingen. The Marshal had his squadrons nicely in hand and their strength had been well conserved. At this critical moment, he saw an opportunity to strike and sent his horsemen teeming in towards the stricken Dutch infantry, the troopers galloping excitedly past the barricaded village of Oberglau, and on through the émigré Irish battalions, who opened ranks to allow them to go past. The French veered to the right, intending to strike at the open flank of Churchill's infantry, the fault line between the two Wings of the Allied army, which was suddenly exposed and vulnerable. This was the one really good chance to present itself that day for the French and Bavarians to break up the marginally smaller Allied army and defeat it in detail. However, because of the rapid pace of their advance and the close proximity of the Nebel Stream, boggy and treacherous at this point, Marsin had to pause and realign his squadrons to make his thrust against Churchill really effective. Precious moments were thus, of necessity, allowed to his opponents.

The Duke of Marlborough was alert to the unfolding danger, and had ridden to near the critical point, having observed the onset of the disaster to the Dutch column. Brigadier-General Averock was already in action beyond the Nebel Stream with some squadrons of Hompesch's Dutch cavalry, but these too were in danger of being overwhelmed by Marsin's counter-attack. The Duke ordered forward the newly arrived three battalions of Hulsen's Hanoverian brigade, together with three Hessian battalions from his reserves. He also directed Blood to re-deploy one of his batteries to engage Marsin's squadrons, personally showing the gunners just where to put their pieces. In the perilous moments that followed, while the success of the Allies hung very much in the balance, Marlborough sent to Eugene for help. Hard pressed though he was, the Prince immediately sent orders to Count Fugger (whose brigade of Imperial cuirassiers had refused to assist Holstein-Beck) to swing to the left and advance. In this way he would threaten the flank of Marsin's squadrons on the bridle arm (the weak side away from the sabre) as they resumed their advance. Very soon, the French troopers were forced to change front yet again to meet the dangerous new threat from the cuirassiers, the chance for Marsin to strike with any effect at Churchill faded, and the crisis passed.

Marlborough, calmly surveying the hectic scene, ordered Hulsen and Berensdorf to thrust ahead with their infantry against Oberglau. He then sent an aide, Lord Tunbridge, to Eugene with an encouraging message that all was well with his Wing of the army, and that the decisive phase of the battle was about to commence. The Prince just needed to hold fast the attention of the enemy on the Allied right. Severe hand-to-hand fighting around Oberglau followed as the Dutch and German infantry forced de Blainville's troops back from the Nebel Stream. The French and Irish soldiers, flushed with their initial success over the Dutch, fought bitterly hard to regain the initiative. De Blainville exposed himself devotedly as he encouraged his soldiers into attack after attack, but at last he was shot down and mortally wounded while reforming the shattered ranks of the Poitou Régiment for a fresh effort. Steadily his troops were penned into Oberglau, where they could have little impact on the wider battle, just like their embattled comrades across the fields in Blindheim.

In the centre of Tallard's army meanwhile, the first line French

71

squadrons darted forward across the sloping cornfields to challenge the growing lines of Allied cavalry. At first the British and Hanoverian cavalry were forced back., and in many places the action was hectic and fierce; the Marquis de la Vallière remembered that he took part in the repulse of seven Allied attacks, and was cut about the head repeatedly. Gradually, the numerically superior Allied squadrons were able to thread through the thinner ranks of the French, repeatedly turning their flanks. Then, whenever they pressed the Allied horsemen these fell back through the gaps in their infantry supports to recover. The French, without adequate infantry, could not do this.

Von Zurlauben charged with the Gens d'Armes once again, but the rebuff they received was as prompt and firm as before, and the veteran Swiss general was mortally wounded in the mêlée. Von Bulow's Prussian squadrons, who had not taken the initial shock of the Gens d'Armes attack, then pursued them back beyond the small Maulweyer Stream that meanders down from the low ridge of the Plain of Höchstädt to Blindheim village. The enthusiastic Prussians rather over-extended themselves and had to fall back hurriedly towards the Nebel Stream to avoid being routed by the French Régiment du Roi who, at this point, were still deployed on the outskirts of Blindheim, and could offer some support to the cavalry.

Despite the breathless Allied recovery at Oberglau, Tallard, Marsin and the Elector could have felt that, all things considered, they had fought rather a good battle so far. Their flanks remained secure, and they were in the process of holding and throwing back the attacks against Lutzingen and Blindheim; the Allied effort had been ruthlessly met in every quarter that it came. The three strong-point villages remained firmly in French and Bavarian hands, with the enemy dead and wounded lying in thick droves on the approaches to each. Above all, their massed squadrons of cavalry, although a little ragged and tired after the scrambling fights along the Nebel Stream, were still in position and in good order. However, and importantly, it seems likely that they entirely failed to see the crucial battle-winning point. Everywhere the Elector and his colleagues were responding to Marlborough's moves; they were quite unable to make effective use of their overall superiority in men, horses and guns, and their cavalry on the right, in particular, was seriously devoid of adequate support. Tallard had not repulsed Churchill's foot and cavalry when crossing the Nebel marshes, and this powerful force, in very good order despite the best efforts of the French cavalry, was poised to strike. In effect, Marlborough was dictating the battle with fast-paced multiple attacks, to which they were reacting, nothing more.

Mérode-Westerloo, as recounted in his colourful memoirs, was almost alone amongst Tallard's officers in appreciating the peril in which his army stood. The Count, still with the second-line French cavalry on the right, went and attempted to draw out of Blindheim the battalions of the

St Second and Montfort Régiments, and to deploy them in the open next to the village. For his interference he was roundly abused by Clerambault and had to withdraw with what good grace he could muster. The unlucky French infantry had to stay where they were, contained between the cottages by the volleys of Cutts' soldiers, who swept the narrow exits to the village with devastating efficiency.

At about 4.30 pm Anhalt-Dessau took his infantry forward once again towards the Bavarian defences of Lutzingen, the pugnacious general waving a shot-torn regimental colour over his head as he cheered his men on. The Prussian battalions, with a sublime disregard for their losses as Bavarian canister fire tore their ranks, stormed into the great battery for a final time that afternoon. They took possession of the big guns in a desperate struggle with their crews who, scorning to run, fought the Prussians with hanger and handspike and, mostly, died on the position. The Danish infantry meanwhile were working their way through the woods to the north of the village, clearing out the French troops posted there, and edging behind the left flank of the Elector's position. With enormous effort and at heavy cost, Eugene was valiantly holding the Elector and Marsin in place while Marlborough struck elsewhere.

With Marsin distracted by Eugene's attacks, and the French and Irish infantry in Oberglau fully engaged, the threat to Charles Churchill's right flank was now contained. The infantry in Blindheim on the Allied left were neutralised also, unless Tallard could suddenly shake off his inability to grip his stubborn infantry commander there. Unhindered, Marlborough was able to draw up his main force of eighty-one squadrons of cavalry (Danes, Dutch, English, Scots and Germans) to face the sixty rather ragged squadrons of French and Walloon cavalry. The Allied horsemen were well supported by the infantry, and by Holcroft Blood's field batteries, many of which were manhandled across the boggy stream and onto the cornfields of the plain.

At this significant point, the Duke's opponents were all fixed in position by the pressure so skilfully exerted on them by the multiple Allied attacks. Tallard's cavalry, the centre of gravity of the whole Franco-Bavarian army, was now exposed to direct assault by significantly greater numbers. They could expect no assistance from their left Wing. Frustratingly unable to make good use of their superiority in men, guns and horses, or to benefit from the natural strength of their position, they could only wait for what would be delivered to them. Marlborough alone retained freedom of action that afternoon, and this was the culminating point of the entire Danube campaign. At about 5.00 pm Marlborough ordered the advance of the Allied left Wing. Over 8,000 cavalrymen, backed by 14,000 infantry, advanced at a vigorously enforced steady pace up the gentle slope. There was no urgent or hectic charge, for that would have blown the horses too soon; the troopers had been taught to approach at a steady walking speed, slowly increasing to a trot, before pitching into their opponents at the last moment.

Tallard's first-line cavalry, commanded by the Marquis d'Humières since the wounding of von Zurlauben, was badly shaken by this grand advance, but the troopers rallied quickly and pushed back the Allied first-line squadrons upon their infantry supports. A tired attempt to follow up this initial success was thwarted as the Allied horsemen once again sought cover behind the lines of bayonets of Churchill's infantry as they stepped boldly forward. The French squadrons had only nine raw battalions of young soldiers (the Régiments de Robecq, de Beuil and de Bellisle) standing there to help them, as Marlborough's cavalry came on to the attack again. The French infantry did their work manfully enough, and their fire caused some scattering amongst the Allied troopers nearest to them – the Duke had to gently direct at least one of his officers not to quit the field. A fleeting opportunity for Tallard did now occur, as the Allied squadrons recoiled towards their infantry supports. The three battalions of the Régiment de Robecq moved forward in pursuit, and might have done great damage had they been supported. The battered French cavalry, however, did not move to assist them and the chance was lost, the small battalions having to withdraw over their own fallen comrades.

Control amongst Tallard's cavalry was fast disappearing as a second effort to overthrow the Allied advance was again blunted by the fire of Churchill's infantry. The Marquis d'Humières and his officers galloped frantically amongst their men encouraging and cajoling the troopers, but the ranks were disordered and horses tired. Mérode-Westerloo pithily commented:

> . . . they [the Allies] had brought their infantry well forward and they killed and wounded many of our horses at 30 paces. This was promptly followed by a definite but unauthorized movement to the rear by my men.[20]

The Count had his horse shot under him at this time (he lost thirteen mounts in all that day), and he marvelled that no Allied infantryman had the grace to step forward and help him to his feet! He was, perhaps, lucky not to have his brains dashed out before his purse was plundered.

Marlborough's second-line squadrons now rode forward through the gaps between their infantry battalions, in a determined effort to end matters. Their horses were fresh and their dressing and order was impeccable as, standing in his stirrups, the Duke urged his commanders on. The tired French squadrons could not face the attack and, as De La Colonie mentions, they began to break ranks before the Allied cavalry, who rode forward in splendid and disciplined style. Tallard's cavalry was simply worn out, while Marlborough had fresh and vigorous squadrons to put into the battle.

In the ensuing cavalry mêlée, the devoted efforts of the French officers were to no effect. All rapidly became confusion as their troopers broke ranks and fled in disarray. Shouted commands were disregarded, and the tracks leading to Höchstädt and Diesenhofen were instantly choked with mounted fugitives, all desperate to escape the rampaging Allied troopers who pursued so close behind. The press of horses in the flight was awful, and Mérode-Westerloo recalled that his fresh mount's hooves did not touch the ground for several hundred yards as the beast was borne up by others crowding in on either side. He was then thrown down a steep bank near the Danube, along with many other riders, several of whose horses then rolled on the unhappy Count. Mérode-Westerloo was helped to his feet by his faithful groom, LeFranc, only to see him casually shot down by a passing Allied dragoon. Nearby, the rout continued unabated, with a large number of the fleeing French troopers attempting to swim their horses across the river. Many who did so were drowned in the swift flowing waters. Marlborough wrote afterwards:

> We have cut off great numbers of them, as well in the action as in the retreat, besides upwards of 30 squadrons of the French, which we pushed into the Danube, where we saw the greatest part of them perish.[21]

Meanwhile, the nine small battalions of young French soldiers (perhaps 3,000 men) remained standing loyally and grimly in position, exposed on the open plain before Höchstädt. The Marquis d'Humières commendably attempted to go to their aid with some squadrons of cavalry, previously held in reserve beyond the Höchstädt road, but the troopers refused the order to move forward and soon took themselves off the field. The Royal Irish Dragoons saw the youngsters die: 'For a long time the young French infantry stood the storm of shot. To relieve them, Tallard ordered the squadrons on their left to charge, but they refused.'[22]

The French infantry were too brave to run away, and their faithful officers either had no inclination to surrender or were too inexpert in the ways of the battlefield to recognise the right moment to do so. These things can be left too late, and the attacker becomes no longer inclined to take prisoners. The French officers managed to form the troops into square, and they maintained a musketry fire against the Allied cavalry surging around them. Soon, a brigade comprising three battalions of Hanoverian Zelle infantry under Colonel Belville were ordered forward by Charles Churchill to engage them, as were a nine-gun battery of Blood's artillery, brought up from the Nebel Stream. The young men were taken in a devastating storm of canister fire and musketry. They died where they stood, closing up the gaps in the ranks and huddling about their regimental colours. France had some fine infantrymen on this sad corner of the Plain of Höchstädt that hot August afternoon, and George

Orkney wrote that they stood '. . . in battalion square in the best order I ever saw, till they were cut to pieces almost in rank and file.'[23] Colonel De La Colonie icily compared the stout conduct of these brave but inexperienced troops with that of other veteran regiments on the field:

> It was said that personages of rank and distinction took upon themselves to surrender their colours so that [they] should escape the fate of the other two brigades which had been surrounded in the centre of the front line. These, however, stood firm, in and around the camp and amongst the tents, with all possible valour; but overcome at last by numbers, their defeat became inevitable.[24]

Few of the boys managed to escape the carnage. Marlborough's chaplain, Dr Hare, saw the broken battalions the following day as he rode past, and recalled that the white-coated youngsters lay in their ranks as if on parade, but asleep. He wrote: 'They stood firm for a time, closing their ranks as fast as they were broken, til they were cut down in entire ranks.'

As his infantry was being destroyed, Tallard attempted to make a stand near Sonderheim, and he gathered about him some unbroken squadrons. There was insufficient room to form a line and too few troops to heed his commands, but the Marshal sent the Marquis de Maisonelle to Blindheim to seek infantry support. This was far too late to achieve anything worthwhile. In any case, Maisonelle was never seen again, and was presumably killed. As his remaining troopers took to their heels, Tallard was taken prisoner by a Hessian trooper from Bothmar's Dragoons, between Sonderheim and Höchstädt, just after 5.30 pm. The Marshal was recognised by the Order of St Esprit he wore (which marked him as someone of importance and may have saved his life). He was conducted to where the Duke of Marlborough sat astride his horse, directing the pursuit of the broken enemy.

The Duke chivalrously greeted the Marshal who murmured, 'I congratulate you, Sir, on beating the best soldiers in the world', to which the Duke, with crushing yet exquisite courtesy, drily replied, 'Your lordship, I presume, excepts those who had the honour to beat them?'[25] The Marshal was packed away into the privacy of Marlborough's own coach, where he could grieve for his young son, pistolled at his side that afternoon as he sought to surrender. Several other of his senior officers soon joined him as the scooping up of prisoners proceeded.

While all this was going on between Blindheim and Höchstädt, away to the north Marsin and the Elector could plainly see that Tallard's army had gone. Gradually forced back by Eugene's persistent pressure, the two commanders prudently began to draw their armies away from their positions, sometime about 7.00 pm. Their well ordered withdrawal (they commanded battered but largely unbeaten troops) was largely uncontested, for Eugene's own army was worn out with the efforts of the terrible afternoon. Any fear they might have had of an envelopment by Marlborough's triumphant forces, swinging in behind their right flank, was alleviated by events on the other side of the battlefield. Hompesch led some Danish and Dutch cavalry across the Höchstädt road to intercept Marsin's retreat, but in the failing light he mistook some of Eugene's cavalry for the enemy, and halted. In fact, the Duke could not push on vigorously with the unconquered village of Blindheim at his back, and his victorious cavalry were also, in their turn, disordered and tired. It was essential to re-form and rally for a fresh effort.

The French troops in Blindheim, now twenty-seven battalions of infantry and twelve squadrons of dismounted dragoons, were crammed into the narrow, smoking streets and alleys with little room to deploy. Many of the cottages were on fire, and some of the wounded who had sought shelter inside were in danger. However, French numbers were such that Cutts' troops could make no headway against them on the eastern edge of the village. Marlborough, viewing his triumph over Tallard's cavalry, now directed Churchill to use Orkney's infantry to seize the place. Hamilton's English brigade and Hulsen's Hanoverians turned from the plain towards the village. Then Belville's Zelle battalions and the dismounted dragoons regiments of Hay and Ross moved from the centre of the field to cut off the garrison and banish any lingering hopes they may have cherished of a fighting retreat.

Orkney's soldiers advanced on Blindheim across the open plain, and were met with fresh volleys of French musketry. Undaunted, the British and German troops pressed forward. Heads down and bayonets levelled, they crowded over the barricades and drove the defenders back along the wreckage-strewn streets of the village. At the walled churchyard the French made a resolute stand and, as the firing raged on, Tallard sent a message to the Duke offering to give orders for the French troops to retire from the field. Marlborough, pausing in the ordering of a fresh effort to disrupt Marsin's withdrawal towards Diesenhofen, sent a rather haughty rebuke to his prisoner for presuming to think that he could still give orders while sitting in the coach of his captor: 'Inform Monsieur de Tallard that in the position in which he is now in, he has no command.'[26]

Accordingly, the house-to-house struggle must go on, but at least one attempt to break out of Blindheim was attempted by Colonel de la Silvière with the battalions of the Provence and Artois Régiments. The soldiers were driven back pell-mell in the face of the crumbling effects of the Allied fire, which remained highly effective despite the weariness and excitement of Orkney's soldiers, and the fouled and red-hot barrels of their muskets. Steadily the French soldiers were pressed towards the centre of the village and around the church they fought with desperate gallantry. Orkney's men were beaten back along the narrow street again and again.

North and Grey's Regiment and Webb's Regiment, both of Hamilton's brigade, fought a particularly savage battle with the Régiment du Roi here, the men grappling together in the deepening twilight. At last, Orkney, frustrated and tired, sent Colonel Belville forward by beat of drum with word that he wished to parley. No French officer could immediately be found to undertake the task for Clerambault was nowhere to be seen, and was thought to have drowned himself in the muddy waters of the Danube.[27]

There was now an anxious discussion between the French regimental commanders over the propriety of talking surrender terms at all, given the secure hold they still had on the village. However, it was apparent that the garrison had been abandoned, and the Allied infantry seemed to be gathered in overwhelming strength. At length, the Marquis de Blanzac unhappily shouldered the burden that others meanly dodged, and he was conducted past the grimy soldiers kneeling and lying at the barricades in the rubble-strewn street, to where Orkney stood. The evening sky was smudgy with drifting smoke and the dead and wounded, clad both in redcoats and white, lay thickly scattered around them in the dust.

Playing a feeble hand very well indeed, Orkney urged de Blanzac of the necessity to avoid further bloodshed. There was no escape he insisted; Tallard was taken prisoner; the French army had broken and fled. No man of honour would sacrifice his soldiers needlessly. The Marquis was persuaded and so, shortly after 9.00 pm nearly 10,000 of France's best infantry were told to laid down their arms. Sir James Abercromby, an aide to Orkney, rather rashly spurred his horse forward into the village square and tried to grab the regimental colour of the Régiment du Roi. The outraged French colour ensign promptly cut him across the forearm with his sword, and it briefly seemed that the battle would erupt once again, but the disturbance subsided and Abercromby withdrew. Nearby, in plain violation of the terms of capitulation, the proud veterans of the Navarre Régiment, all of whose three battalions surrendered in the village, burned the colours rather than surrender them to the Allies, while their officers wept bitter tears of desperation, frustration and disgrace.[28]

On the eastern edge of Blindheim stood Lord Cutts, whose infantry had battered themselves against the seemingly impregnable barricades of the village for much of the day. The 'Salamander' expressed himself amazed at the French capitulation, so strong did their position seem to him right up to the last moment. In actual fact the Allies had not won the battle for Blindheim at all, the village was still firmly in French hands when they surrendered it and it is not easy to see how a night-long battle for the place would have turned out. The garrison suffered a collapse of command and control more than anything, and a more robust commander might have negotiated terms and been allowed to march off the field, to fight another day.

The left Wing of the Franco-Bavarian army managed its withdrawal rather well, as did those few of Tallard's own troops able to keep in disciplined bodies. Mérode-Westerloo, although grazed and bruised after his adventures, arranged a series of rearguard actions on the road to Diesenhofen with what scattered squadrons of the cavalry of the right Wing he could draw together. These slowed the pursuit of the tired Allied army, for any successful commander really needs a second echelon, or wave, of troops to move through the tired victors and exploit to the utmost the gains achieved. Marlborough, victorious as he was, was operating at full stretch, and did not have that second echelon to hand. The Duke wrote of this phase of the battle:

> The Elector and M. Marsin were so advantageously posted that Prince Eugene could make no impression on them til the third attack at or near 7.00 o'clock at night, when he made a great slaughter of them, but being near a wood side, a good body of Bavarians retired into it, and the rest of the army retreated towards Lauingen, it being too late and the troops too much tired to pursue them far.[29]

Although Marsin and the Elector of Bavaria were able to retire with their armies in good order, their own losses, when put together with the devastating destruction of Tallard's army, gave an astonishing and overwhelming victory to Marlborough and Eugene. The 54-year-old Duke, who spent eighteen hours in the saddle that hot day, scribbled a note of the day's events on the back of a hotel bill that he borrowed from an aide. This note was handed to the raffish Virginia born Colonel Dan Parke to carry to Duchess Sarah in London, and it read:

> I have not time to say more but to beg you will give my duty to the Queen and let her know that her Army has had a glorious victory. M. Tallard and two other generals are in my coach and I am following the rest. The bearer, Colonel Parke, will give her an account of what has passed. I shall doe it in a day or two by another more at large.[30]

Eight days later, on 21 August 1704, a travel-weary Parke ran the length of the long gallery at Windsor and dropped to his knee before Queen Anne who was reportedly just then playing dominoes with her Danish husband, Prince George. The Colonel handed his sovereign the grubby note, sent on by the Duchess of Marlborough to her good friend. In this dramatic way, Anne learned that, nearly six months after giving her Captain-General an instruction to go to the aid of Austria, months which were filled with anxious anticipation, Marlborough had destroyed a major French army on the River Danube. Here was projection of English power on an unbelievably grand and unprecedented scale, with the acknowledged military balance of many generations turned quite upside down.[31] Parke was requested by Anne to name his reward, and he politely asked only for her likeness. Delighted with such gallantry, the Queen gave him a jewelled miniature of herself (which he always wore thereafter), and a purse of £1,000 in gold coin as well. A few days later Lord Tunbridge followed hard on Parke's heels with a rather more full account of the battle. These were tumultuous days, when unbelievable news of glorious victory was brought to London by dusty messengers on sweat-lathered horses. It was afterwards remembered that the news was so glorious, so exciting, that no one could sleep.

In Bavaria meanwhile, on the night of the fatal conflict, Marlborough sought shelter in an abandoned watermill on the outskirts of Höchstädt. The place had apparently been used by the French as a powder magazine and much of the stuff was still lying around, but no harm came to him. In the brilliantly starry night outside, unexpectedly cold, the mass of prisoners on the battlefield were watched over by the weary Allied infantry, leaning sleepily on their muskets. Mrs Christian Davies wrote of the aftermath:

> After the battle of Höchstädt in which I received no hurt, though often in the hottest of the fire, I was one of those detached to guard the prisoners; and surely, of all I ever saw, none were more miserable; some having no shirts, some without shoes or stockings, and others naked as from the womb.[32]

French and Bavarian losses at Blenheim (as the battle rapidly became known in Britain) amounted to over 34,000 men, including the astonishing total of some 14,000 prisoners. Staggeringly large numbers of senior officers surrendered, including ten general officers, apparently caught in a kind of daze at the day's awful events. Almost all of those taken fell into Marlborough's hands in the débâcle around Blindheim. (The severity of the fighting that faced Eugene on the right Wing gave little opportunity for quarter to be offered, and he had few prisoners to show.) In addition, over 100 guns and smaller mortars, 129 regimental colours, 110 cavalry standards, 5,400 loaded wagons, 3,600 tents, 4,000 horses and 3,000 loaded mules were taken by the victorious Allies. Uncounted amounts of baggage, stores, ammunition, tackle, fodder and camp impedimenta were seized. Amongst the most exotic items taken by the victors were thirty-four coaches containing officers' 'ladies' whose duties with the army were not precisely specified, but were fairly well understood. The sheer scale of the booty imposed a considerable strain on the ability of the Allied quartermasters detailed to superintend its collection, and distribution amongst the victors.

The Allied losses were some 14,000 killed and wounded (9,000 men from Marlborough's Wing of the army). The Danes, whose infantry fought with such out-and-out gallantry for Lutzingen, alone lost 2,400 men; the Dutch casualties were 2,200 troops, almost exactly the same number as that of the British (2,234). These simple figures are sure evidence of the severity of the fighting along the entire line of battle, and of the devotion of the soldiers of both armies. One army collapsed and ran, but not before making a fight of it.

The bad news of defeat travelled comparatively slowly to Versailles. Louis XIV was aware that numbers of his officers were in Marlborough's hands, for they were writing home to France, courtesy of their captors, setting their affairs in order. Undoubtedly something had gone wrong on the Danube, but the King was unaware of the dreadful magnitude of the disaster for the French army. When he heard the terrible news of the defeat at Blenheim (ironically enough, shortly after watching a masque to celebrate the triumph of the River Seine over the other rivers of Europe), he could not believe what he heard. Such a catastrophe for one of his main armies was quite unprecedented, and would have the most severe consequences for his war effort. A major part of France's overall strategy was shattered; ruined too was one of his principal allies, for the Elector of Bavaria was now almost a fugitive. The threat to Austria, so long a cherished French war aim, was gone and the lustre of French military prestige was tarnished for all time.

Tallard went to England in the entourage of Marlborough when he eventually returned to London. He was kept a prisoner for eight years in Nottingham Castle where he taught his gaolers to embroider lace and make French bread. The veteran Marshal's campaigning was over for good, but Louis XIV appeared to bear his old friend no grudge for the dreadful disaster to French arms at Blenheim. On his eventual return to Versailles in 1713, the broken old Marshal was kindly received, and shown every mark of Royal favour.[33]

On this extraordinary Sunday, when Marlborough afterwards said that he never prayed harder in all his life, the Duke became the first captain of the age. All eyes turned to him to see what he would do next. The tide of war, hitherto so favourable to the fortunes of France, now ran strongly for the Allies, and this was the true extent of Marlborough's achievement that day.

The weeks that followed the disaster at Blenheim were of unmitigated misery for the French and their allies. Bavaria itself was entirely over-run by Imperial forces, and the Elector was made a fugitive with all his estates forfeit; his wife had to beg a peace for her family in his absence. In the field, Marshal Marsin brought most of his army away from the Plain of Höchstädt, and with the remnant of the Bavarian army got across the Danube at Ulm. Their troops fell back towards Strasbourg in great despair, while desertions and attacks by vengeful peasants further weakened their ravaged numbers. Downstream, the fortress of Ingolstadt fell to Imperial troops under the Margrave of Baden on 21 August 1704. A week earlier the victorious Allied army of Marlborough and Eugene halted at Steinheim and the division of the haul of prisoners from Blenheim was arranged. The march was then continued to Philipsburg on the Rhine, as the Duke pressed his campaign once again up towards the frontiers of France.[34]

The Blenheim Battlefield Today

The countryside around the villages of Höchstädt and Blindheim is largely unchanged from 1704. The modern development of the area has altered the size and shape of the villages only slightly, although the modern houses are larger and much smarter than those of the 18th century. In Blindheim in particular there are numbers of cottages and barns dating from the time of the battle around the churchyard, scene of a bitter battle at the close of the day. These give a very good idea of the place in 1704. The cornfields and orchards round about are still open and attractive, the wide landscape stretches from the Danube (now straighter and better drained than in Marlborough's time), to the far wooded hills leading northwards past Lutzingen to Swabia and Franconia.

The wide open Plain of Höchstädt, still given over to arable farming, is so very obviously excellent cavalry country – really the only obstacle anywhere is the Nebel Stream. The gentle rolling terrain leading down to the water indicates very well the practical advantage that the French cavalry would have enjoyed, cantering forward with the assistance of the slope, to engage Marlborough's cavalry as they scrambled breathlessly across the stream. Less easy to see is where the French batteries would have got a good field of fire over the crossing points of the Nebel Stream.

The Nebel Stream is also straighter and less boggy, but obviously still a formidable obstacle after rain – there remain only a few bridges across the water. Apart from the main Ulm-Donauwörth road and the railway line (both unobtrusive enough not to spoil the view), these crossing places are opposite the villages of Oberglau(heim), Unterglau(heim), Lutzingen and Blindheim. Weilheim Farm, where Eugene belatedly placed his guns, is easily identified, standing on a slight rise and offering a decent, if rather long, field of fire towards the Bavarian position. Direction finding in this stupendous four-mile wide plain is difficult at first, but the onion-shaped church towers in the villages are very prominent, and assist identification. There is surprisingly little on the Plain of Höchstädt to mark the great battle that once took place here. However, set into the wall of the churchyard at Blindheim (the church interior is particularly attractive in a baroque style) is a small plaque in commemoration of the tumultuous events all those years ago.

NOTES

1. Murray, G (ed.), *Letters and Dispatches of the Duke of Marlborough*, Vol I, 1845, p.394.
2. Southey, R, *The Battle of Blenheim*, London, 1794.
3. Green, D, *Blenheim*, 1974, p.58; McKay, D, *Prince Eugene of Savoy*, 1977, p.83.
4. Defoe, D (ed. J Fortescue), *Life and Adventures of Mrs Christian Davies*, 1929, p.61.
5. De La Colonie, J (ed. W Horsley), *Chronicles of an Old Campaigner*, 1904, p.224.
6. *Letters and Dispatches*, p.385 – the Duke's letter to Robert Harley, Secretary of State, dated 3 August 1704.
7. Churchill, W S, *Marlborough: His Life and Times*, Vol II, 1947, p. 836.
8. Ibid., p.837. This strongly indicates some loose ends in the Allied plan, for Eugene apparently expected a concentration with Marlborough at Höchstädt on 10 August 1704. He was rather out on a limb if Tallard moved against him quickly. Marlborough may have felt unable to commit himself north of the Danube until he was sure that Tallard had done the same and was marching against Eugene. The decision was finely balanced, for if the Franco-Bavarian army moved fast enough it could catch and destroy Eugene's detachment while the two Wings of the Allied army were apart. See *Letters and Dispatches*, pp 387–8 for the Duke's letter to Harley, dated 10 August 1704.
9. Chandler, D (ed.), *Captain Robert Parker and Comte de Mérode-Westerloo*, 1968 p. 41.
10. Churchill, p. 836.
11. Mérode-Westerloo's Walloon brigade comprised the Caetano, Acosta and Heider Regiments of cavalry. He had to leave some of his troops on the Rhine due to illness. See Chandler, p.166.
12. Accounts differ whether the harvest had been gathered before the battle, but it is known that the Elector was unwilling to allow Tallard to entrench his camp on 12 August 1704, because that would damage standing crops.
13. Defoe, p.58.
14. Dr Hare's Journal, quoted in *Letters and Dispatches*, p.401.
15. Lord John Cutts, nicknamed 'the Salamander' for his liking of being in the hottest fire, was described by Jonathan Swift as being as brave and as brainless as the sword at his side – in essence, just the sort of bluff commander that this blunt, frontal attack on the fortified village of Blindheim required. Samuel Noyes, Chaplain of the Royal Scots (Orkney's) wrote that his battalion was across the Nebel Stream by 1.30 pm that Sunday. See Johnston, S, *Letters of Samuel Noyes*, JSAHR 1959. Accounts of Major-General Wilkes' precise involvement vary, but it seems that he acted as Cutts' second in command during the assault. The *Stadtarkiv Donauwörth* papers plainly show him commanding the Hessian brigade during the battle (although mis-spelt Wilkens).
16. Dr Hare's Journal, quoted in *Letters and Dispatches*, p.405.
17. Churchill, p. 856.
18. Chandler, D (ed.), *Journal of John Deane*, JSAHR, 1984, p.13. Hay's Dragoons, the Royal Scots Dragoons, or 'Our Gray Draggoons' as John Deane describes them, became the Royal Scots Greys. Ross's Dragoons, also known at this time as the 'Royal Dragoons of Ireland', eventually became the 5th Royal Irish Lancers.
19. Churchill, p. 857. Colonel Goor (not to be confused with General Johan Goor who died on the slopes of the Schellenberg) was left with only fifty men standing in the ranks of his regiment at the end of the battle. This was

probably the greatest individual loss by a unit in the Allied army that day, a fact that Goor bitterly drew to Marlborough's attention.

20. *Captain Robert Parker and Comte de Mérode-Westerloo*, p.172.
21. *Letters and Dispatches*, p.391 – Marlborough's letter to Harley, dated 14 August 1704.
22. Willcox, W T, *Historical Records of the 5th Lancers*, 1908, p.94.
23. Trevelyan, G M, *Blenheim*, 1948, p. 387.
24. *Letters and Dispatches*, pp. 394–409. See also De La Colonie, p. 229.
25. Some accounts refer to the young French battalions being killed to a man at Blenheim, but this is rather unlikely. The dust, smoke and confusion of the battlefield, and the hectic pace of events, would permit soldiers to slip away, or to hide amongst the fallen bodies of comrades, as all went to pieces around them. However, there are enough contemporary accounts of the catastrophe which overtook these soldiers, to acknowledge that most of the youngsters did, indeed, die that day. Their courage is not in doubt. See Verney, P, *The Battle of Blenheim*, 1975, p. 143.
26. Churchill, p. 875.
27. Ibid., p.865.
28. Verney, pp.155–6. The Marquis de Blanzac became something of a scapegoat for France's disgrace, but in truth the blame for the debacle in Blindheim lay firmly between Tallard and Clerambault. The misguided actions of Clerambault are puzzling, as his military career had been long and distinguished. Tallard picked well when he chose the man to defend Blindheim and there is really no accounting for why this veteran officer lost his head so spectacularly that day. See also Chandler, D, *Marlborough as Military Commander*, 1973, p.148.
29. Chandler, *Captain Robert Parker and Comte de Mérode-Westerloo*, p.176; *Letters and Dispatches*, p. 391.
30. The famous 'Blenheim Dispatch', now a proud but fairly ragged piece of paper, is on display in a cabinet at Blenheim Palace. The bearer, Colonel Parke, had apparently recovered from the wounds received at the Schellenberg.
31. A contemporary commentator said that the world looked on Marlborough with a sort of amazement. This incredible month of August 1704 also saw the capture by an Anglo-Dutch amphibious force, under the command of Admiral George Rooke, of the fortress of Gibraltar in southern Spain.
32. Defoe, p.62.
33. Broken in fame, reputation and fortune, Marshal Tallard returned from Nottingham to meet a chilly reception in Versailles at the hands of one-time friends and sycophants, while he tremulously awaited an audience with the monarch he had so dramatically failed. However, the King's warm reception of his old friend, even to the extent of taking a few steps towards the elderly Marshal (unheard of in that proud monarch), instantly restored him. Tallard afterwards gave the following as the reasons for failure at Blenheim:
    (a) the Gendarmerie had failed to repulse the English cavalry
    (b) Marsin's right and his (Tallard's) left were unable to crush their opponents before they were reinforced
    (c) the second line cavalry, both on the left and the right, were unsuccessful, and the second line infantry were abandoned.

    Rather strangely, when considering the reasons for defeat, Tallard put little emphasis on the obvious folly of allowing his best infantry to be crammed into Blindheim. To the three listed could also be added over-confidence, contempt towards an opponent's abilities and daring, and an unwillingness amongst senior commanders to cooperate effectively. Finally, quite a number of Tallard's infantry, although they fought well overall, were inexperienced, and not really up to a full-tilt battle.

34. Cowles, V, *The Great Marlborough and His Duchess*, 1983, p. 33.

CHAPTER VI
The Toils of War
Marlborough's Campaigns from the
Danube to Ramillies

Our friends could not be persuaded to attack them.[1]

The Allied cause was enormously boosted by the success of Marlborough's army at Blenheim, and the whole of France was rocked in disbelief at such a catastrophe. The prestige of both the Grand Alliance and of the Captain-General was the talk of the capitals of Europe; many German princely states, hitherto wavering before French political pressure, became more firmly bound to the common cause against Louis XIV. In the same way, the resolve of vulnerable allies such as Portugal and Savoy was made stronger.

Marlborough now needed to press home the advantage so dearly gained; as little breathing space as possible should be granted to Louis XIV's Marshals. The Duke handed large numbers of the French and Bavarian prisoners over to Prince Eugene, as a fair share of the spoils of the day and a compliment to his valour on the day of battle (Marshal Marsin and the Elector of Bavaria had yielded few captives in their stout defence of Lutzingen and Oberglau). Many of these soldiers were pressed into Imperial service against the rebels in Hungary, but no one seemed to find this odd.[2]

Hampering all immediate plans were the enormous logistical and organisational problems facing the Duke. His lines of supply were ill-suited to an immediate autumn campaign on the Rhine, for they ran at present through a land horribly devastated by war. Fresh arrangements had to be made. The more battered battalions, including almost all the English and Scots, also needed to be sent down the Rhine to rest and reconstitute themselves with new recruits before further service. The same barges were used that would have sent aid to the Dutch in other less happy circumstances. The burden all this placed on Marlborough and his small staff was enormous, as some of the officers slain in Bavaria had been of considerable assistance to the Duke in administrative matters. (Johan Goor, in particular, was sadly missed.)

Despite all this Marlborough moved with reasonable speed considering the circumstances. He detached the Margrave of Baden to besiege Landau (the place was taken on 25 November) and his own army was soon in place before Trier on the Moselle. The town fell on 26 October 1704, but efforts to seize Trarbach were only successful after muddled operations against a competent French defence in worsening weather, on 20 December. This was long after the troops felt that they should be in warmer quarters. By now Marlborough had gone to England to receive his triumph for Blenheim, and the campaign had to close for the winter.[3]

On the way to London, the Duke conducted a series of highly successful diplomatic visits in the princely courts of northern Germany. He was received as the conquering hero fresh from the banks of the Danube and in this subtle and effective way Hanover and Prussia were secured to the Allied cause. The Dutch Deputies were included in the warm afterglow of great victory, and Marlborough received the acclamation of the States-General at the Hague on 9 December 1704. On 14 December Marlborough arrived quietly in England at Greenwich, but in the days that followed he was greeted with tremendous acclaim wherever he went. Marshal Tallard and thirty-five senior French officer prisoners of war accompanied the Duke to London. A solemn and eulogistic address, which Marlborough received from the House of Lords, ran:

> Your Grace has not overthrown young, unskilful generals, raw and undisciplined troops, but . . . has conquered the French and Bavarian armies that were fully instructed in all the arts of war, select veteran troops, flushed with former victories and commanded by generals of great experience and bravery.[4]

On 14 January 1705 the captured standards and regimental colours of the defeated French army were carried to Westminster Hall in triumph. There, over time, they were permitted to rot away to nothing.

Amongst the rewards that came to Marlborough were an annuity of £5,000 from the Queen during her lifetime, and the colonelcy of the 1st English Foot Guards, in whose service he had begun his military career as an Ensign, forty years earlier. At the special request of a grateful House of Commons, he also received the gift of the Royal manor at Woodstock, together with the money to build there a magnificent palace suitable for England's greatest soldier. Before long the Emperor, in grateful thanks for the Blenheim campaign, would also make him Prince of Mindleheim, taken from amongst the Elector of Bavaria's forfeited estates. Furthermore, in March 1705 Queen Anne approved the payment to her victorious army of 'the Blenheim Bounty' in recognition of the extreme nature of their triumph. These sums ranged from £600 to Marlborough, to £1 for each private soldier. Staff officers and the wounded got a double sum –

John Ligonier for example, as a Major in North and Grey's Regiment, was granted a total of £30.

As a result of their reverses on the Danube and elsewhere, the French were obliged to stand on the defensive in the spring of 1705. Louis XIV had three great armies in northern Europe – Marshal Villeroi, together with the now dispossessed Elector of Bavaria, had over 60,000 men to hold the line in the Spanish Netherlands; Marshal Villars with another 60,000 troops watched the Moselle Valley and the Middle Rhine frontier; Marshal Marsin's reconstituted army of 30,000 men guarded Alsace and the Upper Rhine. Great efforts had been made to refill the depleted ranks of France's regiments, but for the time being Louis XIV must surrender the initiative and watch for his opponents' moves. As an aid to this necessity, extensive lines of defence in Brabant and other locations were improved and refined. Behind these comforting works, which assumed a greater importance than before, the French Marshals could manoeuvre to foil their enemies.

The Allied campaign got off to a poor start in 1705. The overall plan was for Veld-Marshal Overkirk to occupy Villeroi in the Low Countries, and for Eugene to campaign in northern Italy to aid the hard-pressed Duke of Savoy. Marlborough, meanwhile, would combine with the Margrave of Baden to force the passage of the Middle Rhine and undertake an invasion of France through the Moselle valley. Everything was delayed by squabbles amongst the Dutch and German allies, and matters were greatly complicated by the death, in May 1705, of Emperor Leopold of Austria. His son, Joseph I (who was a great admirer of Marlborough), ascended the Imperial throne in his stead, but there was inevitable delay and inconvenience to the campaign plans.

Marlborough's army moved to Treves on the Moselle by relatively easy stages, only to find on arrival that the army contractor there had both embezzled the stores and defected to the French. Also, Baden now sent his excuses, claiming that he could not provide the troops agreed upon for the joint campaign. He pleaded his own sickness as reason for not attending at the rendezvous in person (his injured foot, 'the Margrave's toe' of the Schellenberg fight, apparently still gave trouble). Many thought at the time that this was Baden's mean revenge for being excluded from the day of glory at Blenheim the previous year.[5]

Forced to abandon the project in the Moselle valley, Marlborough neatly extricated his troops from in front of Villars' reinforced army, and fell back from the town of Sierck, moving closer to depots of supplies and forage. At this point, on 10 June 1705, the French pounced on the Allied fortress of Huy in Brabant, and moved on to threaten Liège. The Dutch were immediately in a state of alarm, and Overkirk sent an express appeal to Marlborough to bring his army back to Brabant. The march was begun on 17 June, and the Duke's prompt return caused Villeroi to fall back towards Tongres from in front of Liège without achieving its capture.

The frustrations of coalition warfare thus thwarted Marlborough's efforts to maintain the tempo of the victory achieved at Blenheim. By a series of competent manoeuvres, both on a strategic and tactical level, the French had regained much ground and bought valuable time in which to refill their ranks. The Duke was reluctantly drawn back into the congested country of the Spanish Netherlands, with the constrictions on manoeuvre imposed by the great fortified towns and the greater still rivers of the area. A lingering desire to take his army back to the Moselle was thwarted when the Duke's rearguard commander in the valley took alarm, burned the stores left there for future need, and abandoned Treves on 27 June 1705.

Despite the generally gloomy beginning to the year's campaign season, Marlborough acted decisively and sharply on his return from the Moselle. He achieved a concentration of his army with the Dutch at Hanette in Brabant on 2 July 1705, and Overkirk retook Huy nine days later. The Duke now prepared an ambitious plan to pierce the seventy-mile-long defensive Lines of Brabant, stretching in a great arc from Antwerp past Brussels and Louvain to Namur. Once past this obstacle he could, perhaps, force another pitched battle on the French.

The Lines of Brabant were not continuous entrenchments in the modern sense, but a series of flooded meadows, dammed streams, earthen redoubts and fortified farms and hamlets, all of which could be quickly occupied once the approach of an enemy was detected. Wherever possible, the Lines followed the course of the rivers, and this added considerably to their strength. Well provisioned detachments of troops were held ready at intervals to man the defences at any threatened point; the army able to make use of such pre-prepared positions would be at a distinct advantage over its opponents. Marlborough's attention was drawn to the stretch of Lines in the area of Taviers, to the south-east of Louvain. Here, the lie of the land obliged the French engineers to construct the works forward of the local streams, thereby making them less formidable than elsewhere. Although care had been taken by the engineers to disguise this fact, local scouts revealed the deficiencies to the Duke.

On Saturday 17 July 1705 Marlborough directed Overkirk with his Dutch corps to march to the southwards across the Mehaigne river as if to threaten Namur. The French commander, Marshal Villeroi, took the bait and edged his army southwards towards Merdorp. As soon as it was dark, the Duke led his English, Scots, Danish and German troops northwards. Major John Blackadder, serving with Cranstoun's Cameronians, wrote in his journal: 'When I came home I found that the whole army had orders to attack the French line; accordingly we marched at nine o'clock, and marched all night.' After a difficult tramp through the misty night, Marlborough's pioneers and grenadiers broke across the Lines near the villages of Elixheim and Wanghe, just as dawn came up. The infantry commander, George Orkney remembered: 'Though the passages were very bad, people scrambled over them.'[6] The Allied grenadiers hacked away the palisades at the crossing points with their hatchets, and the few troops of French dragoons in the area could offer no real resistance to the thrust, and took off to raise the alarm.

No sooner had Marlborough formed up his breathless troops on the far side of the obstacle belt, than a strong column of Bavarian, French and Walloon troops, under Count Caraman and the Marquis d'Alègre, were seen fast approaching from the south to challenge them. The blackened armour of the Bavarian cuirassiers could be plainly seen in the morning sunlight. The time was about 7.00 am on 18 July 1705 and Marlborough's corps had to stand and take the shock, for Overkirk was still many miles distant, having been recalled from his march towards the Mehaigne river during the night. The Dutch troops were stepping out manfully, but they were toiling wearily along the lanes to the south and would be some hours in their coming. Fighting alone, Marlborough had twenty battalions of infantry, thirty-eight cavalry squadrons, and a battery of six guns – in all about 16,000 troops immediately to hand.[7]

Caraman and d'Alègre were actually rather outnumbered by the Duke, for they were just an advanced guard and brought with them only twenty infantry battalions and fifty rather weak squadrons of cavalry (probably about 10,000 soldiers) – all that were immediately available after Villeroi moved south to shadow Overkirk. Still, they were valiant commanders and unhesitatingly pitched their veterans into Marlborough's hastily assembled line of battle, not far from the village of Elixheim. A furious mêlée of horse and foot along the sunken lanes in the area ensued. Marlborough was well forward and was hotly engaged, crossings swords repeatedly as the fighting swirled around him. He was nearly sabred by a Bavarian horse grenadier, but the trooper lost his balance and fell to the ground where the Duke's trumpeter killed him. Before long the superior numbers began to tell and d'Alègre's cavalry broke and withdrew. Although abandoned to their fate, Caraman's Bavarian infantry quickly formed a great square, at about 8.00 am, and they fell back with superb discipline westwards towards the sheltering river crossings over the Gheete. Their steady volleys kept the pursuing Allies at bay.[8]

Ten guns fell into Marlborough's hands, together with numerous prisoners, amongst whom was the wounded Marquis d'Alègre. Allied losses were very light (some reports, rather optimistically, put the cost at no more than about 200 killed and wounded). Aware of the audaciousness of their achievement, the British, Danish and German soldiers crowded around Marlborough shouting their cheers, which he smilingly acknowledged. These were his Blenheim battalions, and his delight at their success could not have been greater.

Overkirk's Dutch troops were now arriving on the scene, but these soldiers were hot and weary from their long march, and reluctant to undertake a pursuit. Overkirk, usually so cooperative, was tired and short-tempered. Although this success at forcing the Lines must oblige Villeroi to retire behind the Gheete and, probably, the larger Dyle river, Marlborough felt it best not to press Overkirk to undertake an advance against his wishes. He reluctantly let Caraman go. The Duke's English cavalry did savage the French baggage trains as they struggled to reach the river crossings, and then went on to take the town of Tirlemont, where the Montluc Régiment was forced to surrender. This was small change however – the far greater prize of Louvain might have been had, and the French perhaps brought to a major battle, if the Dutch had felt so inclined.

With this neat operation, and at modest cost, Marlborough completely turned the whole French strategic posture in Brabant. Villeroi had no option but to fall back to cover Brussels and Louvain. Towns to the south-west, such as Oudenarde and Mons, were uncovered and vulnerable to an Allied offensive and Villeroi's difficulties were greatly increased as a result. In the meantime, Marlborough had his troops level extensive stretches of the now abandoned Lines of Brabant, preventing their ever being of use again. He also took this chance to thoroughly scout the district all around, storing away the information gained for future use.

Marlborough advanced again on 15 August 1705 heading towards the Dyle at Genappe. The Allied troops were provisioned with their customary four days' supply of bread, with four days' more supply on the battalion carts. The Duke felt able to cut free of his supply trains for a spell – an innovation at this time, and rather a rude shock to the slower moving French commanders. Alert to the need to cover the southern approaches to Brussels, Villeroi concentrated his army at the Yssche river to the south of that city. On 18 August 1705 Marlborough was in place to attack him there, and was confident of success as the French position was not very well chosen. The Dutch field deputies would have none of it, fearing a bloody battle for their soldiers. General Slangenberg was at his most obstructive, even demanding precedence for his own private baggage wagons over the artillery trains, and Marlborough had to call the promising operation off.

This apparent fumbling by the Allied generals inevitably put heart into their French counterparts. For once Marlborough could not curb his anger, and he sent blunt letters to the States-General at the Hague. He had, he wrote on 18 August 1705, less authority than the previous year when in Germany, and he would not go on in this way. The Duke looked forward again to retiring to private life, and they must find another general. Thoroughly alarmed, the States recalled Slangenberg and the more awkward of the field deputies from the army, and assured Marlborough that their generals would cooperate with him in every way in the operations to come.

As this campaigning season came to a close with the rapid onset of colder weather, Marlborough undertook another round of diplomatic visits to bolster the Alliance. He travelled to Vienna to calm tensions between Emperor Joseph and the Prussians and the Dutch, and he accomplished this tedious task with patient skill. The Duke also arranged for troops to be sent by the Elector of the Palatinate, and by the Prussian King, to northern Italy to boost Prince Eugene's efforts there.

Although Marlborough achieved a good deal in 1705, the campaign as a whole was a distinct disappointment. It was true that the French arrangements had been seriously disrupted; their carefully constructed lines of defence had been demolished, their baggage trains harried, and their troops out-marched and out-manoeuvred. Marlborough had demonstrated his own dominance over his opponents in this theatre of war. Despite all this, due largely to the lack of will on the part of his allies, his schemes and designs had fallen very far short of his hopes. He looked forward to the campaign in 1706, where he had plans for operations on a far wider stage.

NOTES
1. Marlborough letter to Robert Harley, dated 19 August 1705. See Murray, G (ed.), *Letters and Dispatches of the Duke of Marlborough*, Vol II, 1845, p. 225.
2. Although most of the prisoners taken at Blenheim fell into the hands of Marlborough's Wing of the army, they were divided in more or less equal proportions with Eugene's Wing. This was both in recognition of the valour of the Prince's attacks that day and in the interests of Allied harmony.
3. Due to the poor state of the roads, and the cost of maintaining large numbers of troops in the field, not least forage for the horses, the armies would only actively campaign throughout the months from early summer to late autumn. The cold months would be spent in training, recruiting and rest – in theory at least. In practice, the soldiers and junior officers, if not on recruiting duties, largely kicked their heels in dingy billets, while the senior officers (Marlborough was no exception) went back to their respective capitals to lobby persons of influence, curry favour for themselves and their families, and play at 'politicks'. However, the Duke never left for home before his last necessary task, whether at his headquarters tent or in some princely capital, was completed.
4. House of Lords address, in Churchill, W S, *Marlborough: His Life and Times*, Vol II, 1947, p.914.
5. The Margrave of Baden was obstinate and pompous, but he was also a veteran and courageous commander, and it seems unlikely that his absence from the Moselle campaign in 1705 was for some trivial reason, or merely the result of petty jealousy. He was certainly not well, as his wounded foot refused to mend.
6. Chandler, D, *Marlborough as Military Commander*, 1973, p.159; also Lee, C, *History of the Tenth Foot*, 1910, p.130 for Blackadder comment.
7. *Letters and Dispatches*, p.249 (Camp Bulletin dated 18 July 1705).
8. The fight at the Lines of Brabant is the first recorded instance of the

employment of the platoon firing system in the French or Bavarian armies. This had been in use by the Allies for some time. The system was not widely adopted by France until 1707, although individual commanders, aware of the handicap under which their troops laboured in musketry contests on the battlefield, increasingly instructed their soldiers in its use before that date. The notable skill with which the Bavarian infantry extricated themselves from a very tight spot at Elixheim may be attributed, in part at least, to the employment of this flexible and effective system of firing. The French tended to use the method when in defence, relying on the bayonet rush when on the attack. Their army adopted platoon firing officially in 1755. See Nosworthy, B, *The Anatomy of Victory*, 1992, pp 58–60.

CHAPTER VII

The Glorious Success
The Battle of Ramillies,
Whit Sunday 23 May 1706

Up to our necks in deadliness and noise [1]

Marlborough had been unable to bring his opponents to decisive battle since Blenheim, and the unproductive campaign in 1705 was mainly due to the obstructive attitude of his allies. The skilful defensive performance of Marshal Villars in the Moselle valley, and the generally good fortune of Marshal Villeroi in Flanders and Brabant also had their effect. In practical terms it seemed that the year since the great victory on the Danube had been wasted by the Grand Alliance, and the bright promises of all that had been achieved on that Sunday had rather faded away.

Marlborough made it plain that he would not attempt another campaign under such absurd restraints. The Dutch States-General, to their credit, realised their error and the prospects for the new campaign in 1706 were much brighter. Still, it seemed unlikely that Villeroi would be bold enough to venture from his defensive position behind the Dyle, from where he could comfortably cover Brussels with little risk to his army. Accordingly, Marlborough devised ambitious alternative plans for an offensive in the Moselle valley (again), and in Alsace and the Upper Rhine-land. He even thought to march his army over the hills and far away to combine with Prince Eugene in northern Italy.

The Dutch looked upon such projects with caution, although they would not forbid the Duke to march. The German princes were also wary. As it turned out, a defeat inflicted on Eugene's army at Calcinato in April 1706 by Marshal Vendôme (the Prince was absent), and another in early May inflicted by Marshal Villars on the Margrave of Baden near Landau on the Middle Rhine, changed the whole picture. Once again the Dutch were in a state of alarm, and the Grand Alliance was off balance and rapidly losing the initiative to the French. Still, Marlborough hoped that Marshal Marsin on the Moselle would reinforce Villeroi so that the French might be encouraged to attempt something in Brabant. Although his intelligence gathering indicated that this might be so, he was not optimistic. On taking the field he wrote to his friend, Sidney Godolphin, the Lord Treasurer, in London in despondent and fretful tones, on 15 May 1706: 'As yet neither the artillery horses or the bread wagons are come . . . I go with a heavy heart, for I have no prospect of doing anything considerable in this country.'[2]

Marlborough was to be agreeably surprised, for King Louis XIV was concerned to demonstrate the vitality of the French war effort, despite an increasingly empty treasury, with decisive campaigning on all available fronts. The King wrote: 'I can think of nothing which can better induce them to come to an agreement which has become necessary now than to let them see that I have sufficient forces to attack them everywhere.'[3]

In addition to this overall strategy, the unsuccessful Allied campaign in 1705 encouraged the French War Minister, Michel de Chamillart, to believe that Marlborough was, after all, rather a mediocre general – and that his successes in Bavaria and at the Lines of Brabant were due to good fortune rather than to skill. This heartening sentiment was promptly communicated to Villeroi at his camp on the Dyle.

By the time Marlborough joined his troops in the field, Villeroi had his army concentrated near Louvain. The Marshal had recently received additional cavalry from Marsin, bringing his strength to about 60,000 troops. In addition, Marsin was moving quietly northwards to Namur. Louis XIV had encouraged Villeroi, in a letter dated 6 May 1706, to take the initiative and force battle on the Allies should the circumstances prove favourable. This was tantamount to a direct instruction to take the field and fight. Villeroi indeed expected further reinforcements, but he strongly suspected that Marlborough would move first against Namur, trying to turn the right flank of his strategic position in Brabant. So, the Marshal struck camp on 18 May and began his march southwards, firstly crossing the Dyle with a feint towards the Allied held fortress of Leau, a town lost by the French the previous year. He then swung southwards towards Tirlemont and Judoigne, heading for the convenient watershed between the Mehaigne and the Petite Gheete Stream near the village of Ramillies. This line of march offered easy passage as he moved eastwards, for the rivers in the area, while not very large, were marshy and difficult for an army to cross.

Marlborough's army, soon to be 62,000 strong, was concentrated a little to the south of Maastricht, with the Dutch corps at Tongres and the troops in English pay nearby at Bitsen. Still rather doubtful that Villeroi would risk a battle, the Duke was surprised to learn, on 19 May 1706, that the French were on the march and had already crossed the Dyle and moved towards Tirlemont. He immediately moved to challenge them, but the army was not entirely complete as many Dutch officers were still on leave, and the Prussian contingent had orders from their King not to cooperate in any campaign until a dispute over their terms of service was settled. The twenty-one squadrons of Danish cavalry, whose involvement in the events to come was so pivotal, only joined the march after the most forceful appeals by Marlborough to the Duke of Württemberg: 'I send you this express to request your Highness to bring forward by a double march your cavalry.' Perceptively, the order was worded in such a way that any half-sensible staff officer receiving it would put his troops on the march even though Württemberg might not be at hand to read the note.[4] The Duke pledged his own credit that the troops' arrears of pay would be forthcoming, and delayed his march for a full day near Corswaren, so that the Danish cavalry could come up in time.

That Marlborough now hoped to force battle before long, and that he foresaw the ground on which the actual engagement might take place, is shown in the following sentences, penned on 21 May 1706, less than forty-eight hours before decisive battle:

> The French having drained all their garrisons, had passed the Dyle and were come to the camp at Tirlemont . . . to-morrow we expect the Danes; then we design to advance in order to gain the head of the Gheete [the Ramillies watershed], to come to the enemy if they keep their ground. I think nothing could be more happy for the Allies than a battle, since I have reason to hope, with the blessing of God, we may have a complete victory.[5]

After some days of heavy rain, the weather turned fine on the morning of Whit Sunday, 23 May 1706 as the two armies, marching through the mist from opposite directions, drew near to the Plateau of Jandrenouille and the Plain of Mont St André. This was the convenient watershed between the Mehaigne and Petite Gheete referred to by the Duke in his letter of 21 May. The marching troops made fairly good time as the muddy roads dried, and the dramatic encounter of the armies probably took place twenty-four hours sooner than either commander expected. Villeroi plainly was not expecting to fight that day. His cavalry commander, Maximilian Wittelsbach, the fugitive Elector of Bavaria (and still Governor-General in the Spanish Netherlands), was absent that morning attending the Pentecost devotional celebrations in Brussels. Villeroi thought Marlborough was at Corswaren, while the Duke believed the French to be near Judoigne, and expected to get to the watershed before encountering the French. Plainly, both men were mistaken.

The opposing field commanders – the Englishman one of the greatest captains in history and the other a distinguished Marshal of France, were each served by good staff. That they were both taken so unawares is intriguing. The fog of war was very evident, and much depended upon their differing responses once the unexpected clash began in earnest.

However, Villeroi had scouted the watershed at Ramillies earlier that spring, before submitting his outline plan of campaign to Versailles for approval. He recognised the practical value of the dry ground, giving easy passage between the two rivers. Now, he was on the very spot, and was, in effect, deploying to give battle on ground of his own choosing.[6] At any rate, any 'fog' that existed was to be abruptly pierced by blinding light.

Shortly after daybreak that Sunday, Marlborough's Quartermaster-General, William Cadogan, rode forward from the Allied overnight encampment between Corswaren and Merdorp with an escort of 600 dragoons. He meant to scout the crossings of the Ramillies watershed and to decide the precise location of the Allied camping ground for that night. The morning was misty, and the ground still sodden from recent rain as they cantered forward. Suddenly, on the Plateau of Jandrenouille, not far to the west of Merdorp, his escort brushed with French foragers, looming out of the mist. There was a mutter of shots, more or less at random, but the foraging soldiers did not stay long, and the skirmish was not serious, so Cadogan and his group pressed onwards. As the pattering of hooves died away, he peered westwards through the gloom. The big Irishman could see the well ordered lines of the whole French army marching on the far side of the low Ramillies ridge.

Cadogan immediately recognised the valuable opportunity that this unexpected encounter presented, and sent a galloper back to find Marlborough, who had remained with the Allied advanced guard a few miles away. The Duke and his staff, including Count Overkirk, General Daniel Dopff, and a number of Walloon officers familiar with the area, detached themselves from the main army and came up in reponse to Cadogan's beckoning. The newly appointed Frisian Field Deputy, Sicco van Goslinga, attached himself to the group as they hurried forward to join Cadogan at about 10.00 am.

The ground itself was familiar to most of Marlborough's party; they had fought Caraman and d'Alègre near there the previous year at the breaking of the Lines of Brabant. Their soldiers that autumn had laboured to demolish the defensive works in the gently rolling fields all around them. The mist had conveniently now risen. To the west, across the plain and beyond the Petite Gheete valley, they could see the whole magnificent panoply of Villeroi's army as it deployed for battle along the forward slope of the low ridge-line that ran from Ramillies northwards to Offuz and south to the open fields that led to the boggy Mehaigne river. Colonel De La Colonie, whose infantry marched with Villeroi's right Wing that day, recalled that:

> So vast was the Plain at Ramillies that we were able to march our army on a broad front as we desired and the result was a magnificent spectacle.' He added that the French army was '. . . such a fine array

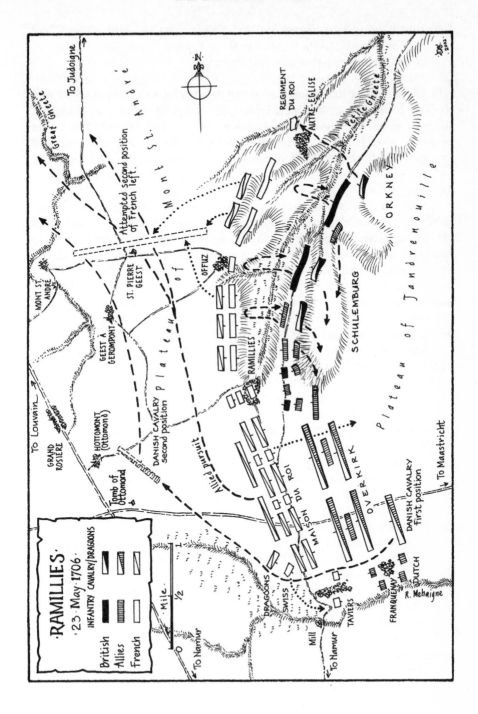

RAMILLIES·
·23· May·1706·
INFANTRY CAVALRY/DRAGONS

British
Allies
French

that it would be impossible to view a grander sight. France had surpassed itself in the quality of these troops . . . if defeated now, we could never hope to withstand them.[7]

The battlefield at Ramillies was about four miles in extent (remarkably similar in length to that of Blenheim), stretching from the village of Taviers on the Mehaigne, to the hamlets of Offuz and Autre-Eglise. In the southern part, between Taviers and Ramillies, the ground was open and the gently rolling farmland, although still rather muddy after the rains, offered excellent fields of view. This was good country for the employ-ment of massed cavalry. To the north of the small village of Ramillies, in the valley of the Petite Gheete, the terrain was much more broken and the whole stream valley itself was a wet and marshy obstacle nearly 200 yards across in places. The Walloon officers, who accompanied Marlborough's party as he viewed the French deployment, were sure that an attack across such a bog was bound to fail. They pointed out that the vicinity of Offuz and Autre-Eglise farther north was extensively farmed with small fields, gardens and orchards, all providing excellent cover for the deployment of infantry. The terrain was well suited for defence, and virtually impassable for cavalry. Nothing should be attempted there.

As the Duke peered through his spyglass, it was soon apparent to him that the position being occupied by Villeroi on the opposite ridge was rather concave in shape. The Marshal did so in order to cover his wide frontage fully, and to take advantage of the potential strong-points offered by the villages on the far flanks – Taviers to the south, and Autre-Eglise to the north. As a result, Marlborough had the immediate advantage of a shorter frontage to cover with his numerically stronger army (62,000 soldiers opposed to 60,000). His punch, when it came, would accordingly be more concentrated and have more power. He had the added oppor-tunity to operate on internal lines when shifting troops from one flank to the other, for the French soldiers would have farther to march in deploy-ing from one sector to another.

First Marlborough had to force his opponent to commit to a fight. At a word of command from the Duke, Allied cavalry squadrons went pouring forward, just in case the French commander should attempt, even now, to draw off and avoid battle. With the Allied cavalry darting towards him, any attempt to do so would result in a damaging running battle with the Marshal's rearguard in peril of being overwhelmed.

Villeroi's military career had prospered and been sustained by his long friendship with Louis XIV. He was not brilliant but was certainly capable enough, and he acted swiftly to establish his troops in position, immediately inclining to the defence. His horizons plainly did not stretch very far, and he let an opportunity to threaten Marlborough's flanks pass by. The watershed forming the oval and open plateau between the

Mehaigne and Gheete rivers offered a good position for a solid defensive battle, but Villeroi could, if he saw the opportunity, move forward onto the Plateau of Jandrenouille to envelop the flanks of the Allied army as it deployed for battle. Such a venture depended upon speed – once the Allied troops were in position and ready to strike, the French commander would have no opportunity to seize the initiative until he had first withstood the shock of Marlborough's attack.

At this stage, if Villeroi felt that his army was outmatched, he could fall back towards the Dyle river. Once behind it, Marlborough would be hard put to get at him, and the feared stalemate would become reality. Once again, such a course called for bold decisions, and this was not in Villeroi's style; he would comfortably arrange his army in the good position it occupied, dig in his heels and await Marlborough. The villages along the ridge above the Petite Gheete stream were quickly garrisoned and barricaded in strength, and French and Walloon infantry deployed into the intervening fields and orchards. Villeroi concentrated eighty-two squadrons of cavalry – including the elite Maison du Roi, in the mile and a half of open fields on his right to the south of Ramillies. General Guiscard commanded the cavalry in this part of the field. On Villeroi's left, on the Plateau of Mont St André behind Offuz and Autre-Eglise, he placed fifty squadron of Bavarian and Walloon cavalry. They would be commanded by the Elector of Bavaria, whose return to the army from Brussels was hourly expected.

Although the French had some rather peculiar three-barrelled cannon (apparently much was expected of them, but they must have been very strange to work in action), Villeroi was able to field only sixty artillery pieces, whereas Marlborough had ninety guns and a number of mortars. The French skilfully placed their batteries to cover the approaches to the barricaded villages, particularly at Ramillies where twenty heavy guns were put in place. However, north of there, the slopes of the Petite Gheete valley must have made it difficult for the gunners to obtain a good field of fire.

Now deployed for battle, Villeroi, although first on the field and quite ready to fight, was already curiously off-balance at an alarmingly early point, although it is very unlikely that he realised this important fact. Of the three options open to any commander before the onset of battle – whether to retire, to attack, or stand and fight – he had given up the first immediately, as his baggage train cluttered the ground immediately to the very rear of the line of battle being formed by his troops. To withdraw in good order and good time, with the aim of drawing Marlborough on to fight at a more advantageous position, perhaps on the Dyle, was an option he had thrown away. There is no sign that Villeroi gave any consideration to advancing to threaten the Duke's advance guard on the Plateau of Jandrenouille. Even had he done so, Marlborough, having neatly fixed his opponent and forced a commitment to fight, could fall back eastwards to Merdorp where his main army was massing and would have plenty of time and space to deploy. Instead, Villeroi chose the simplest option (which, in fairness, was respectable enough given the natural strength of the Ramillies position); he stood and fought from where he first observed the Allied approach.

On the other side of the tactical hill, the more agile Marlborough retained the ability to adopt any of these three options. He was able to retire and decline battle, although to do so was against the whole thrust of his campaign aims. If his army stood and deployed on the Plateau of Jandrenouille, the Duke had a good chance of defeating any French attack. Best of all, as he promptly deployed his advance guard, he committed Villeroi to fight a major battle on the Ramillies ridge-line, and this chance was something Marlborough had longed for ever since Blenheim. Partly through good fortune (the French disdain for Marlborough's abilities making them bold), and partly through good management (the Duke driving forward as soon as he encountered Villeroi's army), a decisive encounter was about to take place.

Cadogan was urging the troops to come forward from Merdorp as fast as possible. At about 11.00 am the Allied army crossed over the ruined Lines of Brabant, levelled by the same soldiers the previous autumn. The veterans amongst them might have remembered the carnage of the Battle of Landen under the Dutch King William in these fields just to the north. The army deployed from three marching columns into eight columns of advance, preparatory to forming line of battle on the ridge-line facing Ramillies and the Petite Gheete stream. Now, moving like a dark but welcome cloud over the sunny fields, Württemberg's Danish cavalry at last joined the line of march – their squadrons closing up to the left of the Duke's army, as Ramillies came into sight.

The Allied army now comprised 123 squadrons of cavalry and seventy-four infantry battalions. Amongst Marlborough's first moves was to bring forward a great battery of thirty 24-pounder guns, laboriously dragged forward by oxen teams to a slight rise just to the east of the Petite Gheete valley near Ramillies. The Duke guided these heavy guns into position personally. Nineteen English and Scots infantry battalions were marched towards the right flank, opposite the hamlets of Offuz and Autre-Eglise, under the command of George, 1st Earl Orkney. In the centre Count Schulemburg and Charles Churchill commanded the infantry. Twelve Dutch and sixteen Saxon and Swiss battalions in the Dutch service led by Schultz and Spaar were moving into position opposite Ramillies itself. The four-battalion Scots brigade in Dutch service added weight to this part of the attack.

The bulk of the Allied cavalry, Overkirk's forty-eight Dutch squadrons and Württemberg's twenty-one Danish squadrons, were drawn up to face the glittering array of French cavalry on the open plain between Ramillies and Taviers. Nineteen battalions of Dutch infantry stood in their support. Colonel Wertmüller, with an excellent brigade of four battalions of Dutch Guards and a section of guns, was detailed to hold the extreme left flank of the Allied line, near the marshes of the Mehaigne river. Fifty-four squadrons of cavalry, including the English and Scots cavalry and dragoons under Henry Lumley, were kept on the Allied right Wing to support Orkney and his infantry. On both sides, the artillery was readying for action, and Marlborough's infantry were prudently drawn up slightly in rear of the shallow ridge-line from which they must mount their attack, to gain some cover from enemy fire while their preparations were completed.

At this early stage Marlborough apparently fully appreciated that the ground was favourable for moving troops from one flank to another. He regarded the cavalry of his right Wing, where the terrain was much less suitable for their proper employment, both as an asset with which to threaten his opponent and hamper his tactical arrangements, and also as a reserve held ready for use along the entire line of battle, wherever the opportunity arose.

In a set of instructions issued from Versailles on 6 May 1706, Louis XIV warned Villeroi to be on his guard against the dangerous red-coated English soldiers. Attentively, the Marshal watched with particular care the orderly and impressive movement of Orkney's infantry and Lumley's cavalry towards the left of his position. Both the Marshal and the Elector (when he at last arrived) chose to take up position near to Offuz, from where they could best control the fighting in the area. They plainly anticipated that the crisis would come in that sector as the British infantry drove forward, and even at this early stage, Villeroi began to shift towards the left those infantry battalions intended for the support of the cavalry on the right Wing. This seriously weakened Guiscard's cavalry, and Colonel De La Colonie wrote afterwards of the concern he felt when he arrived on the scene with his brigade in the late morning. He saw the inferiority of the available infantry support, and the ominous gaps between the squadrons of cavalry, which themselves were only three ranks deep rather than the more customary four:

> I noticed, when passing the Maison du Roi, that there were large intervals between the squadrons, and that their formations were disproportionately extended. This made me think that the principal attack was not to be made here; that there was some other and more dangerous part that had to be provided for.[8]

Although the Colonel was writing with the benefit of hindsight, this is a very perceptive comment, as his commander really was shifting still more infantry to his left. Just as at Blenheim, the French cavalry were getting off to a bad start, through tactical mismanagement, and an advantage was being handed to Marlborough.

In addition, Villeroi was lax in still not ordering the baggage of his army to be sent to the rear of the Plateau of Mont St André, well out of the way of the battle-line. Neglect of this simple administrative preliminary to combat would have serious repercussions. However, his position overall was naturally strong, with the protective marshes of the Petite Gheete valley covering much of his front. His tactical arrangements in many respects were perfectly sound – the powerful Régiment du Roi in Autre-Eglise secured his flanks in the north, while the Mehaigne and its marshy tributaries sheltered his right flank. Here, the hamlet of Taviers was being put in a state of defence by two battalions of veterans from the Greder Suisse Régiment.

However, one flaw in Villeroi's arrangements was that the small hamlet of Franquenay, a few hundred yards in advance of Taviers, was not properly secured for defence. When, belatedly, this omission was rectified, some companies of the Greder Suisse were sent forward to line the walls and roofs of the few cottages and barns. They were dangerously exposed, and were well beyond the immediate support of their comrades in Taviers, yet they were not in Franquenay in sufficient numbers to hold the place against a determined attack. There was a distinct danger that the Swiss detachment would be isolated and overwhelmed in detail.[9]

At about 1.00 pm the opposing batteries opened fire and a brisk artillery exchange began along the centre and northern part of the ridges. The fire was particularly severe between the heavy guns around Ramillies, but the artillery tactics of the day were not sufficiently developed for the gunners to seriously impede the continuing deployment of the opposing armies. The billowing smoke from the bombardment rapidly degraded the ability of the commanders to see adequately the unfolding events of the afternoon. The general with the surer touch and the better and more developed methods for rapidly gathering information, such as the Duke's running footmen, was at a distinct advantage.

Marlborough seized the initiative at 2.00 pm. He directed Overkirk to send Colonel Wertmüller to storm Franquenay and Taviers, and eliminate the threat that the Swiss troops placed there posed to the left flank of the Allied cavalry as it deployed south of Ramillies. Making good use of dead ground in their approach, and supported by the fire of the two field guns boldly manhandled forward by their crews on their right flank (an imaginative tactical innovation at any time), the Dutch Guards soon overwhelmed the defenders in Franquenay. The Swiss soldiers fled in disarray back across the pastures to Taviers, but the Dutch were close behind, and a brawling and bloody battle at bayonet point followed through the gardens and alleys of the village.

The Greder Suisse fought with their customary courage but they were completely routed. Outnumbered, outgunned and unsupported, they were unable to stand the devastating close-range cannon fire and the ferocity of the Dutch attack. The drills for such an assault were well practised; selected infantry companies would advance, covered by the fire of their comrades, and only after sufficient progress was made would additional troops be fed into the battle. The soldiers would cover each other by fire as they advanced, and each cottage would be carefully cleared of defenders before pressing on. In the cramped village of Taviers there was little occasion for mercy and the Swiss soldiers were ruthlessly driven along the smoky alleys. By about 3.00 pm the Dutch Guards were left in firm possession of this key position at the extreme end of the French line of battle. Despite the speed of their advance, this had been no easy victory for Wertmüller's troops – as De La Colonie recalled: 'The fighting there was almost as murderous as the rest of the battle put together.'[10] The Dutch infantry suffered heavily, and their mood was ugly as they took up fresh positions at the edge of the village.

General Guiscard, the French cavalry commander on the right Wing, watched the fiasco along the Mehaigne river with mounting exasperation. He took rapid, if rather ill-judged, action to remedy the loss of Taviers and ordered a swift counter-attack on the Dutch Guards. Orders went to fourteen squadrons from the King's, Notat, La Reine and d'Aubigni Régiments of dragoons to leave their horses near the ancient hilly feature known as the Tomb of Ottomond, and move forward across the fields to retake the village. Their advance was to be supported by two more battalions of the Greder Suisse Régiment, under the command of Brigadier-General de Nonan, who were sent forward by the French infantry commander south of Ramillies, General de la Motte. Additional infantry reserves would presumably follow up the move. Overall, this was probably the correct response to the Allied opening attack – the sooner they hit back the more likelihood of success. However, little effort seems to have been made to co-ordinate the different components of the French counter-attack across the open plain, and it failed disastrously.

The dragoons were ill-supported in their advance by the Greder Suisse, who were some hundreds of yards behind them and laboriously threading their way between the massed squadrons of cavalry. They were raked with canister from the brace of Dutch guns on the edge of Taviers village and the Dutch Guards poured in a merciless musketry from the shelter of the cottages. The attacking dragoons wilted under the storm of shot. Furthermore, as they grimly struggled forward into this hail of fire, six squadrons of Danish cavalry came sweeping effortlessly across the cornfield, charging in at their left flank and that of the approaching Swiss. This was the leading echelon of Württemberg's cavalry corps, just moving forward into position to face Guiscard's cavalry. The shock of the onrushing horsemen was too great to withstand, and de Nonan tried to bring his disordered troops back beyond the shelter of the small Visoule Stream. There they became hopelessly entangled in the marshy ground (the dragoons in their long boots were particularly clumsy). Colonel d'Aubigni tried to rally his men into something like a line of battle, but was mortally wounded by a Dutch musket ball.

As a result of the complete failure of this inept counter-attack on Wertmüller's brigade, the French cavalry on the right Wing were reduced from eighty-two to sixty-eight squadrons, without the slightest benefit being obtained. The sparse infantry support for Guiscard's cavalry was correspondingly lessened by the scattering of the Swiss battalions. This had a detrimental effect on the balance of the French army quite out of proportion to the potential benefit that the retrieval of Taviers might have offered. In any case, both that place and Franquenay remained firmly in Dutch hands, and Villeroi's whole right flank was now in the air and dangerously exposed.

Worse was to happen. Colonel De La Colonie received orders to move his own regiment forward, from a position in the fields just to the south-west of Ramillies, to bolster the support of the scrambled counter-attack on Taviers. This was just reinforcing failure, although the extent of the Swiss defeat was not entirely apparent yet, but the soldiers of the Grenadiers Rouge and the Cologne Regiment, with which they were brigaded, stepped out readily enough. The gentlemen troopers of the Maison du Roi cheered their advance, the Grenadiers à Cheval waving their fur caps with grateful applause, as the Colonel put it. They recalled the fine performance of his regiment and their renowned stand at the Schellenberg fight, nearly two years previously, as the grenadiers marched through the intervening gaps in the squadrons. Soon, however, everything started to go wrong. Even before they got properly into action, De La Colonie's brigade commander cantered on rather too far in his enthusiasm and his horse became stuck in the marshes of the Visoule Stream, where the dragoons still floundered. Despite his calls for help they could not approach him and De La Colonie remembered: 'He would never have got out of it had it not been for the enemy's assistance, who promptly carried him off as prisoner.'[11]

As De La Colonie approached the scene of the defeat at the stream's edge, the ranks of his grenadiers were disrupted by the flight of the French dragoons and the Swiss, who had at last broken and were bolting for safety. The Colonel's soldiers promptly also lost their nerve and took to their heels, although he manfully sought to hearten the men, seizing the regimental colour of his grenadiers and calling on those around him to rally: 'I cried out in German and in French like one possessed. I shouted every epithet I could think of . . . I gradually rallied my French grenadiers and several companies of the Cologne Regiment.'[12]

106

After extraordinary effort, De La Colonie succeeded in gathering a much-weakened force of his grenadiers, Germans, and fugitive Swiss. He was also able to rescue some of the stranded French from floundering in the marshes, and at whom the Dutch were gleefully taking shots. In this way he gathered in a handful of rather sheepish looking dragoons to add to his force. The Colonel took up a fresh position to the west of Taviers but the Dutch Guards did not attack him there, thinking that his force was stronger than it was – perhaps there were more tempting prizes on offer than a grubby and expensive fight across the marshes. However, this valuable if minor service of holding Wertmüller in Taviers diminished as the afternoon wore on, for most of the Dutch Guards were drawn away into the fighting farther north. By then nothing that De La Colonie attempted around Taviers would matter very much to Villeroi, as he struggled desperately to withstand Marlborough's crushing attack.

While the Dutch attack in the south was gathering pace, George Orkney got word from Marlborough, at about 2.30 pm, to move into the attack against the villages of Offuz and Autre-Eglise in the northern part of the battlefield. For this purpose Orkney deployed twelve battalions of English and Scots infantry, in an attacking wave of two lines about 200 yards apart from each other. The soldiers, who had been lying down in the warm sun, rose to their feet, shouldered bundles of fascines (gathered while they were waiting) and move forward with drums tapping and regimental colours flying bravely. They descended the shallow eastern slopes of the Petite Gheete valley, their grenadiers leading the way to clear French and Walloon skirmishers out of the thickets as they advanced. Flinging their fascines onto the boggy ground, the advancing infantry then had to struggle calf-deep through the valley bottom. There they were met with a hedge of bayonets and heavy musketry fire – a four-battalion brigade of tough Walloon infantry had been sent forward from the far ridge-line to make a fight of the passage of the stream.

Thomas Kitcher, a Hampshire farm labourer who fought as a private in Meredith's Regiment that day, spoke afterwards to the curate of his home village of the heavy cost of the advance across the Petite Gheete marshes. The attackers were staggered by the well-directed Walloon musketry and many in the leading ranks fell. Kitcher, who was apparently in the second rank, got his feet entangled in the entrails of one of his fallen comrades. The curate wrote:

> They were then commanded to cross the marsh by means of fascines and many were shot and maimed, or killed, by the French outposts, which they carried and layd down their foundations [fascines]. He told me that limbs and bodies, of which it was impossible always to ascertain whether or not they were dead, were used to pass the quagmire at some points, and that one redcoat that he knew of raised

himself from the supposed dead at the indignity of the treatment and turned upon the pioneers who had thought him one of their bundles of faggots and flayed them with his tongue.[13]

Despite their losses, Orkney's soldiers reformed quickly on the drier ground and returned volley for volley with the Walloons. The growing numbers of the British quickly told and the defending infantry slowly fell back up the slopes. The French commander in Offuz village, Major-General De Guiche, did not attempt to hold the line of the stream for long, but withdrew his battalions in good order to their original positions. He completed the difficult manoeuvre up the gentle incline, under fire from Orkney's forward battalions, with great skill. Kitcher, with a casual disdain for his foes, was not impressed however, and he recalled in salty language that as they pushed boldly towards the barricaded villages: 'The Frenchies seemed surprised and showed no mind to fight much. Some of them I saw turned tail and I spiked one of their officers through the gullet, and another through the arse.'[14]

Around the villages on the low ridge a bitter struggle began as the attacking troops pressed towards the hastily erected barricades in the teeth of a heavy and well directed fire. The cottages were loopholed for sharpshooters, and the defenders had the advantage of good cover and clear fields of fire. They were there in numbers at least equal (if not actually superior) to the British attackers. Orkney wrote later of the assault, that 'I think I never had more shot about my ears.'[15] In Autre-Eglise on the far right, the Cameronians, under Lieutenant-Colonel Cranstoun, fought their way into the houses and lanes despite the best efforts of the defending companies of the Régiment du Roi. Lacking support, apart from a few of Lumley's dragoons who were able to get over the marshy valley, the Scottish soldiers were unable to hold onto their slim gains. They fell back into the shelter of the Gheete valley to recover their order and prepare for a fresh effort.

Meanwhile, in the centre of the field, the twelve battalions of Dutch infantry pressed forward against the stronghold of Ramillies, while the German infantry shook out to their right, attempting to work around the northern edge of the village. The garrison in Ramillies alone comprised twenty first-class French battalions, a strong brigade of German infantry, and the Jacobite Irish Clare Regiment of dragoons. As the attackers closed upon the village, a roar of musketry from the breastworks and cottages engulfed them. The leading ranks reeled in the hail of fire and the smoke, but their officers urged them forward and they gallantly closed up the gaps and came on again, supported by the Scots-Dutch brigade under John Campbell, 2nd Duke of Argyll. Seeing the ferocious resistance they faced, Marlborough directed Murray's small protestant Swiss brigade to close up to the village also, ready to go in on his command. He then sent for three of Orkney's reserve battalions, the Buff's (Churchill's), Scots Fuziliers, and Macartney's Regiment, to be detached from the right Wing and move southwards to add weight to the attack on Ramillies. This was the start of a significant shift in the balance of the Allied army during the course of the conflict, from right to left.

Villeroi is unlikely to have appreciated the peril in which he now stood and may well have felt that he had fought a good battle up to this point. Although closely engaged along the length of the field from Ramillies to Autre-Eglise, he still had reserves in hand, and the Plateau of Mont St André was plentifully lined with infantry and cavalry, held ready for the anticipated breakthrough from the Gheete valley by Orkney's infantry. It is not at all clear to what extent the Marshal appreciated the effects of the Dutch success in unhinging his line on the right. The nonsense of the failed defence of Franquenay and Taviers would have seemed to be capable of remedy, given time, for he had plenty of infantry that could be sent southwards.

Perhaps neither commander, Marlborough or Villeroi, was yet fully aware of the profound extent of Wertmüller's achievement. Significantly for the French Marshal's decision-making process, the sheer intensity of the attacks against Offuz and Autre-Eglise, and the massing of the Dutch and German brigades against Ramillies, impressed the vital need to move more of his reserves of infantry away from the cavalry on the right. He used them to bolster still further the forces behind the villages on his left and the result was that the Danish cavalry faced no opposition as they began to slide menacingly around the right flank of the French army.

This was in accord with Marlborough's rapidly unfolding plan. Villeroi was not granted sufficient time to recover his balance once the Duke took the initiative; the pace that he was dictating on the battlefield allowed the Marshal no time for calm reflection and analysis of what threat he really faced. Ironically enough, both commanders were now looking in opposite directions; Villeroi felt impelled by the ferocity of the infantry attacks aimed at him to reinforce the villages in the north. Marlborough, meanwhile, put additional weight into his own cavalry attack, across the open cornfields to the south. With deadly pace, having subtly decoyed his opponent on the right, the Duke was now shifting the full weight of his attack to his left Wing.

On the marvellously wide and open plain to the south of Ramillies, Count Overkirk had completed the deployment of his own forty-eight squadrons of Dutch cavalry and the twenty-one squadrons of Danes under Württemberg. At about 3.30 pm their advance, at a steady trot, began in earnest. To Colonel De La Colonie the Allied cavalry seemed to come on:

Like solid walls, while we had but three lines, the third of which was

composed of several squadrons of dragoons with plenty of gaps
between them . . . It seemed that the enemy's cavalry advanced upon
our people at first at a rather slow pace and then, when they thought
they had gained a proper distance, they broke into a trot to gain
impetus for the charge.[16]

A fierce cavalry battle erupted across the length and breadth of the plain
in the south, and for over two hours something like 25,000 horsemen
engaged in a vast surging struggle. Due to Villeroi's faulty dispositions,
the French had inadequate infantry support from the very beginning and
their thinned ranks were soon hard pressed. The gaps between the
squadrons, noticed by De La Colonie, allowed the Dutch to thread
through, and the French troopers found that they were attacked not only
from the front but also from the flank and sometimes even the rear. Before
long the first line of Guiscard's squadrons were thrown back on their
supports, but despite this the French rallied and the fighting was fierce
with charge and counter-charge coming fast upon each other. Officers of
high station were prominent for their valour, and in the mêlée a French
trooper hacked down the young Prince Lewis of Hesse-Cassel, for war is
no great respecter of rank.

These cavalry were the best the French had, elite squadrons finely
mounted and well trained – the Gardes du Corps, Grenadiers à Cheval,
the Mousquetières Noir and Gris, the Royal Carabiniers and the Gens
d'Armes. The pride of France was on the field and Guiscard was riding
valiantly amongst the ranks and shouting words of encouragement,
calling out to the Gentlemen troopers by name. The second-line French
squadrons coolly closed up the gaps, the scanty battalions of French
infantry stepped boldly forward and delivered their volleys, and the
Dutch horsemen were forthrightly and unexpectedly repulsed with
shaken ranks.

As the battle swirled around and around on the trampled wheat, a
spirited counter-charge by thirteen squadrons of the Maison du Roi
suddenly broke through the ten Dutch squadrons immediately opposing
them. These scattered in considerable disorder, and threatened to uncover
the left flank of the Dutch infantry just then forming for a fresh assault on
Ramillies. Marlborough was nearby, anxiously watching the ebb and flow
of battle for the outcome of the day was by no means certain. He had
already ordered the bringing up of eighteen more squadrons of Dutch
cavalry from his right Wing towards the cavalry battle in the south. Now,
sending orders to call forward all the remaining cavalry on the right
except Lumley's English and Scots squadrons, the Duke rode ahead to
hearten the shaken Dutch troopers. He was attended only by his
trumpeter and a couple of aides, and became dangerously exposed near
the milling French horsemen. Conspicuous in his red coat and Garter sash

amongst the grey and blue uniforms of the Dutch, Marlborough soon attracted the attention of the French. 'They fired their long pistols at him', and the Duke's horse stumbled and threw him heavily to the ground. 'Milord Marlborough was rid over' George Orkney wrote after the battle, and the exultant French troopers surged forward to finish his career one way or the other.[17]

Helped to his feet by his trumpeter (who in all likelihood saved the Duke's life), Marlborough moved with commendable speed for a 56-year-old man suffering the effects of a bad fall. His preference for wearing linen gaiters rather than leather-riding boots was fortunate and he darted nimbly up a short grassy slope to the nearby protection of two battalions of Murray's Swiss infantry. The Duke had only just seen to their placing in the line of battle, and they served him well. He was just able to reach shelter within their ranks when the onrushing French cavalrymen attempting to ride him down were themselves resolutely thrown back by the bayonets of the Swiss soldiers.

There was a flurry of anxious activity around the Duke – Overkirk sent to enquire after his safety, and Murray offered him his own horse. An aide, Captain Molesworth, hastened to bring up a fresh mount, and Marlborough was once again in the saddle, a little shaken and bruised, but his adventures that afternoon were far from over. As he changed horses a little later, a French roundshot from a battery in Ramillies skimmed the saddle, and neatly decapitated his aide, Colonel James Bringfield, who held the stirrup. The lifeless body, fountaining blood, fell at Marlborough's feet, and the grisly episode was subsequently recorded with some relish on a lurid set of playing cards that enjoyed great popularity in England.

It was now about 4.30 pm and the battle, for both foot and horse, had raged for over two hours in the fine May sunshine. Little progress was made by the Allies along much of the line but everywhere the two armies were in close and deadly conflict. Now the renewed infantry assault on Ramillies went in – Dutch, Swiss, German and British troops took part, and 'Red John' Campbell, 2nd Duke of Argyll, sword in hand, was amongst the first to reach the French barricades at the head of his Scots brigade. Borthwick's Regiment led the assault, and they encountered hedge-lines thronging with French infantry who had every intention of staying put. Suddenly, the opposing infantry were stabbing at each other through the foliage, as the Scottish attackers struggled to clear the way forward with the bayonet.

Almost at once Ramillies was a seething cauldron, with hand-to-hand fighting in the clamouring streets and alleys of the village. The struggle was hard, and ferocious volleys of musketry were exchanged at close range. Attacks followed one another in quick succession, and at one point Borthwick's Regiment lost their colours to a driving French counter-charge. The ensign, James Gardiner, was shot in the mouth and left for dead alongside the churchyard wall, while the French and Scottish soldiers viciously clubbed and grappled together in a sloping field of rye next to the church. At last the colours were saved by the regiment's grenadier company under Captain Jemmy Campbell.[18]

Meanwhile, along the roaring ridge above the Petite Gheete valley, the infantry attacks were pressed home by Orkney's battalions with the astonishing violence that comes so easily to young soldiers when under pressure. The grim determination of the defending French, Walloon, German and Swiss infantry not to yield even so much as an inch was remarkable, while around them the opposing batteries duelled without pause, the begrimed gunners on both sides moving in a daze from the repeated concussions of the pieces.

Marlborough's unfolding plan to fix Villeroi firmly in position, rapidly conceived as he viewed the enemy army on reaching the Plateau of Jandrenouille that morning, was reaching fruition. The whole French and Bavarian line from Ramillies to Autre-Eglise was held in a deathly grip by the ferocity of the Allied infantry assault. Now, the Duke sent word to Orkney not to press home his infantry attacks on Offuz and Autre-Eglise, but instead to retire and reform on the ridge from which he had set off. Orkney, standing with his English grenadiers amongst the burning cottages of Offuz, was indignant at such orders, for he had seen the beginnings of success as his tough soldiers battled their way into the barricaded villages. What was needed, he argued, was reinforcement of his success, not an unnecessary and inexplicable recall. However, a succession of aides came with the same instruction to retire, the very last being William Cadogan, to be sure that there was no misunderstanding about what the Duke intended.

Heated words were now exchanged between the two generals. Orkney could see no good reason to suspend his attacks, and suspected that Marlborough was unaware of the extent of his hard won gains. Cadogan loudly insisted however, and at last the order was grimly given to withdraw – the troops disengaged from their hectic assault and fell back into the valley. This rearward move was greatly resented by both officers and men, who felt that victory only waited to be grasped, and was being idly snatched away from them. Thwarted, they had no way to know that Villeroi's massed reserves of both cavalry and infantry awaited, admirably placed on the Plateau of Mont St André to strike the tired British troops once they passed the barrier line of the villages. If they had not been brought back they must very likely have been cut to pieces in the Franco-Bavarian counter-attack. Unknown to all but a few, the British infantry were part of a wider and more ambitious plan, and retire they must.

The English and Scots soldiers gradually walked back down the slopes, strewn with the wreckage of their advance, re-crossed the Petite Gheete marshy stream and resumed their starting position on the far ridge. De Guiche, like the good soldier he was, promptly sent forward his infantry to press the withdrawing soldiers. His attempts to turn the retirement into a rout were foiled by the cool discipline of the Allied soldiers, and by the steady volleys of musketry of the 1st English Foot Guards and the 1st battalion of Orkney's own regiment, who formed a rearguard under the Earl's personal direction, and were the last Allied troops to re-cross the stream. Thomas Kitcher recalled:

> We had the order to give ground and make way back to the river. 'Pray, what's this?' said my Lord Orkney, so his servant told me after. He had no mind to give ground when we were giving no quarter, nor we hadn't neither, being up to our necks in deadliness and noise. But so it was ordered and we went back and back across the river, and there we stayed awhile, with the cannon peppering us but not getting no success, our cover being good.[19]

On the ridge to the east of the Gheete valley, near to the hamlet of Foulz, Orkney's infantry re-formed and Marlborough's intentions became clear.[20] Under Cadogan's direction, the first line of infantry stood fast and turned to face their enemy across the valley once again. The second line, however, were ordered to re-form their ranks and turn southwards and march off, comfortably shielded by a shallow fold in the ground that hid them from the view of the French on the ridge opposite. Their regimental colours were left in place (indicating in some respects that they were not yet the treasured symbols that they would one day become). This gave the vivid impression that these second-line battalions were still there on the Allied right Wing, ready for a fresh effort at any moment. In reality, Marlborough's reserves of infantry and cavalry were being moved stealthily southwards towards Ramillies, as if by some sleight of hand. The Allies could not be strong everywhere, they enjoyed no overwhelming advantage in numbers, but, having fixed his opponent's infantry firmly to the ridge-line, the Duke was about to deliver the devastating punch elsewhere. Unknown, unsuspected and unseen, he was dramatically shifting the balance on the battlefield, and the destruction of Villeroi's fine army was about to commence.

By imaginative and careful management, Marlborough had been able to oppose the French cavalry to the south of Ramillies, firstly with sixty-nine Allied squadrons (Overkirk and Württemberg), then eighty-seven squadrons (with the first reinforcement from the right Wing), and finally a total of 108 squadrons (with the second reinforcement). Opposed to this solid mass Villeroi could only field the sixty-eight squadrons left to Guiscard after the French dragoons were wastefully routed around

Taviers. Unless the French commander took decisive action in good time to employ the fifty reserve squadrons held back behind Offuz, disaster threatened the right Wing of his army.

The time was approaching 6.00 pm and a fine evening was coming on. To the south of the main cavalry battle, the right flank of the French army remained glaringly in the air after the loss of Taviers and Franquenay. Villeroi should have addressed this danger, but with his attention so firmly concentrated on the desperate infantry fighting on his left, the opportunity never came. As the cavalry action wore on, the outnumbered French squadrons became increasingly tired, and the volleys of their few supporting infantry were ragged. Their weary battle lines contracted and this unavoidably opened wider the fatal gap to their south. This was fearfully dangerous and into the void was thrust, firstly, Opdham's regiment of Dutch Dragoons and then Wertmüller's brigade of Dutch Guards advancing from Taviers. With their support Württemberg was able to pass his entire twenty-one squadrons of Danish cavalry virtually unmolested through the gap, right past the open flank of Villeroi's army. Captain Robert Parker wrote:

> They [the Dutch] pressed home upon the enemy, and made them shrink and give back. At this very instant the Duke of Württemberg came up with the Danish Horse and pressing an open between the village of Franquenay and their main body, fell in on the right flank of their horse, with such courage and determination.[21]

Württemberg's troopers were relatively fresh, for the brunt of the cavalry battle so far had been borne by the Dutch squadrons. The Danes were able to form up quite unopposed near to the Tomb of Ottomond, and drove off a faint attempt to prevent their deployment by a remnant of the same dismounted French dragoons who had earlier failed to re-take Taviers. The fleeing dragoons, whose mounts had taken themselves off across the fields (some finding their way to their own stables twenty miles away), were chased, harried and cut down, but Württemberg was careful to keep his troopers in hand, and this pursuit was not pushed too far.

The Danish squadrons were now moved into place, facing northwards to Ramillies and Offuz. The opportunity for a marvellous cavalry stroke presented itself, but it had to be delivered promptly – for Württemberg's massed squadrons could hardly conceal their presence on the open fields for very long. In fact, many of the French had already noticed the move around their right, and urgent messages were flying to Villeroi, who was still near Offuz with the Elector of Bavaria. The thin squadrons of the French right Wing, so steadfast and brave, were worn out and had no reserves left to meet the impending catastrophe.

At about 6.30 pm Marlborough and Overkirk cantered over the

trampled wheat to join Württemberg in front of his squadrons. There was a pause while the Danish officers tidied their troopers' dressing, and the alignment for the advance was checked. The self control of the Allied commanders, high and low, was impressive – nothing was rushed, no chance of mishap was allowed, nothing was to be thrown away. The Danish cavalry were staring at the raw open flank of the enemy's army, and at the word of command they rode steadily forward with their ranks well closed up – *en muraille* as the technique was known.[22] The advance was plainly seen by Villeroi, for he was now hurriedly re-deploying his numerous reserves, held in needless idleness in rear of Offuz, to meet the threat. Nearly all the fifty squadrons of French, Bavarian and Walloon cavalry on the Plateau of Mont St André to the north scrambled to change front to their right and to form a new line. Utterly unprepared, they had to face the storm.

In addition, the re-deployment of Villeroi's reserves was fatally hampered by the mass of baggage which, so inexcusably, had not been sent to the rear when the battle commenced. All at once the French, who had fought well up to now, were desperately off balance, and reduced to plugging a gaping hole in their line of battle so ruthlessly created by Marlborough's subtle and imaginative techniques.

Villeroi's new line – a gaggle of cavalry squadrons and infantry battalions rapidly drawn up without properly thought out order – could do nothing against the disciplined rush of Danish horsemen. Simultaneously, the final reinforcement of cavalry, brought forward from the reserves on the Allied right Wing at Marlborough's request, rode forward to bolster the tired Dutch squadrons in a fresh effort in the centre. Under the weight and dash of the combined cavalry attack, the elite squadrons of the Maison du Roi were driven in disorder. The Elector's cavalry on the Plateau of Mont St André, brought round to face the Danes, took their cue from their comrades and broke in their turn, riding madly through the ranks of the Walloon and Bavarian infantry who were still trying to deploy and give their support. An Irish officer in French service, Captain Peter Drake, wrote afterwards that the cry 'Sauve qui peut' rang through the army at this moment. 'Then might be seen whole brigades running in disorder.'[23] Cohesion and self-control snapped and the right Wing of Villeroi's army simply disintegrated in utter rout, with cavalry and infantry fleeing to the north and west. The implacable Danes, burning to avenge the recent massacre of their countrymen at Calcinato in Italy, chased them, cutting and slashing amongst the fugitives.[24]

Meanwhile, in the shambles of Ramillies village, two tough battalions of German infantry – the Cologne Guards and the Bavarian Guards – fought on from the shelter of a sunken lane that leads gently upwards from the cottages to the Plateau of Mont St André. Their commander, Count Maffei, was an accomplished soldier, a veteran of the fights at the Schellenberg,

Blenheim and Elixheim, and his position was well chosen and his flanks secure. He tried desperately with his small brigade to form a stout hinge on which the shaken right Wing of Villeroi's army could swing back and find time to recover. Unfortunately, he incautiously rode over to some nearby horsemen to give them instructions, not having noticed, in the smoke and confusion, the tell-tale green foliage field symbols in the rider's hats. He found himself promptly taken prisoner by Dutch troopers: 'I went towards the nearest of these squadrons to instruct their officers, but instead of being listened to I was instantly surrounded and called upon to ask for quarter.'[25] It was fortunate for the Count that his captors were not the marauding Danes, who were in no mood for prisoners. Deprived of their commander, the German troops in the lane lost heart and quickly joined the general flight towards the north.

At this time, Argyll's Scots-Dutch brigade, supported by the British troops feeding down the re-entrant from the north, forced their way into Ramillies for the final time that day, and the village was at last firmly in Allied hands. The exiled Irish Catholic, Charles O'Brien, Viscount Clare, was killed while fighting with his regiment of dismounted dragoons, and the soldiers of the Picardie Régiment were driven from their breastworks after a particularly bitter struggle with the Buffs and Scots Fuziliers. Bayonet and musket but were freely used, and the French dead and wounded lay in thick heaps along the alleys and hedges, full evidence of their devotion. The fleeing soldiers fell into the path of Borthwick's Scots Regiment as it pushed forward from the churchyard where they had rallied after their earlier repulse. Colonel Borthwick was killed in the fighting, but his men completed the rout of the French, many of whom were taken prisoner.

Standing on the ridge-line opposite Offuz and Autre-Eglise, it was clear to Orkney that the French right Wing had disintegrated, and that the rear of their army was in chaos. Needing no further instructions, he promptly ordered his battalions back across the valley of the Petite Gheete into a fresh attack. Unsurprisingly, the defence of the villages on the opposite ridge was shakier than before, but seven fine squadrons of Bavarian Electoral Guards and Walloon Horse Grenadiers, who had stood inactive all afternoon behind Offuz, came hastening forward to throw the Allied infantry back. Orkney's men met the attempt with their customary deadly volleys, and the cavalry front rank was thrown into confusion. The disordered troopers were then put to flight by the Queen's Regiment of Horse and Wood's Horse. To their right Ross's Irish Dragoons and Stair's Scots Dragoons moved rapidly forward into Autre-Eglise as the Régiment du Roi pulled back from their positions. Taking the rare opportunity for a charge at full tilt, the British dragoons just overwhelmed the famous French regiment as the soldiers attempted to recover the knapsacks they had dropped as they went into position earlier in the day.

1. John Churchill, 1st Duke of Marlborough.
Artist: Godfrey Kneller
(By kind permission of His Grace The Duke of Marlborough)

2. Queen Anne.
Artist: Edmund Willey
(By kind permission of His Grace
The Duke of Marlborough)

3. Prince Eugene of Savoy.
Artist: Godfrey Kneller
(By kind permission of His Grace
The Duke of Marlborough)

**4. William,
1st Earl Cadogan.**

**5. The Duke of Marlborough
and his Chief Engineer,
Colonel John Armstrong.**
Artist: Enoch Seaman
(By kind permission of
His Grace The Duke of
Marlborough)

6. Marshal Villeroi.

7. Marshal, the Duke of Vendôme.

8. Marshal Villars.

9. Henry of Nassau, Count Overkirk.

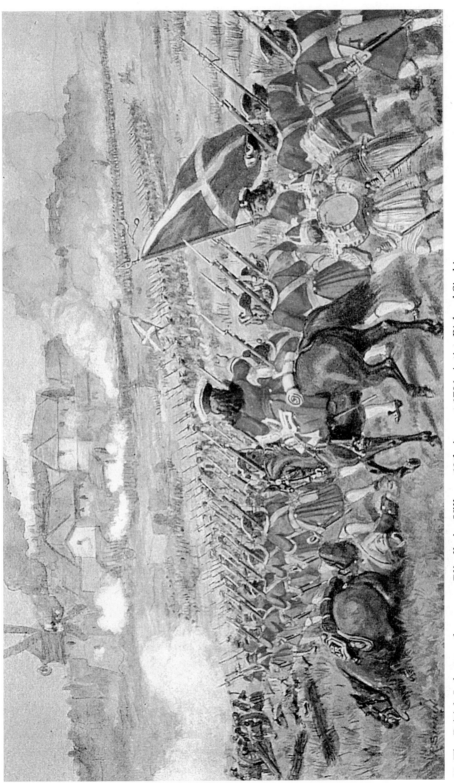

10. The British Infantry advance on Blindheim Village, 13th August 1704. Artist: Richard Simkin

11. The Plain of Höchstadt – scene of the great cavalry battle at Blenheim.

12. The Ramillies – Offuz Ridge, where the British infantry attacked on 23rd May 1706.

13. Malplaquet, 11th September 1709. Marlborough's squadrons move through the Allied gun-line, 1.00 p m. Artist: N Dupray (Courtesy of Ian Fletcher)

14. Malplaquet. Bois de Thiery seen from Bois de Lanieres. The Dutch infantry surged around this copse in their doomed attacks on the French right Wing.

15. The Plain of Malplaquet, viewed from the French monument, scene of the great cavalry battle in the afternoon.

Marshal Villeroi and the Elector of Bavaria were caught up in the appalling confusion and nearly taken prisoner, but they managed to escape from the field. One of Marlborough's cavalry commanders, Lieutenant-General Wood, was nearby on his great bay horse, Corialanus, and he saw the two enemy commanders, but did not recognise them in the smoky twilight. Instead he directed his men to seize some other senior enemy officers close at hand. The troopers of the Queen's Regiment of Horse managed, in addition, to triumphantly capture the silver kettle drums of the Electoral Guards, together with their celebrated negro drummer. The redoubtable female dragoon, Mrs Christian Davies, was wounded in the head at this time (apparently by a shot fired from the tower of Ramillies church). Carried to the regimental surgeon, she was too stunned to conceal her sex as he tended her wound, and so the secret was discovered.

Although isolated groups of French, Walloon and Bavarian infantry fought bravely on, pouring their volleys into the opposing cavalry from hedges and ditches, nothing could now hold the hectic Allied onrush. Villeroi's army was in a state of collapse; parts of the left Wing preserved a semblance of order in the retreat, but that was all. Along the country lanes leading north and west the fugitive soldiers and their camp attendants were jammed together in a desperate search for safety. The deeply rutted lanes, themselves sunken well below the level of the surrounding fields, proved all but impassable, particularly for the passage of wagons and guns. Accordingly, almost all were lost to the Allies. Thomas Kitcher's salty commentary ran: '. . . and the last we saw of 'em was with their breeches seats to face us.'[26] At the close of a tiring day, unlike the cavalry and dragoons, he could perhaps look forward to leaning on his musket and lighting his pipe.

The Allied cavalry, in no need of orders, were off the leash like a hunting pack, and the pursuit towards Louvain continued well into the darkness. Through the night subordinate commanders, requiring no instructions, pressed onwards towards the Dyle river. By midnight a bruised and weary Marlborough was still in the saddle with only a small cavalry escort over twelve miles beyond the battlefield, somewhere near Meldert. At about 2.00 am on Monday 24 May, the tired pursuers were called to a halt. They were able, at last, to reflect in quite some wonder on the victory they had won the previous day – for they had destroyed the only French field army in the Spanish Netherlands.

Even as victors, the Allied troops were in a state of great disorder, so complete and sudden was their success and headlong pursuit. George Orkney said in a letter that he dictated at the roadside at Beauvedon on 24 May 1706, at 7.00 pm:

You will be extremely glad to hear we have fought a great battle yesterday and beat the French, and I am in good health, but am hardly able to hold up my head, I am so weary and faint, for it is 48 hours I have not eaten or drunk . . . Mr Lumley and I had resolved to march straight to the Dyle to their lines. But we are endeavouring to make camp and form in some order, for we look like a beaten army.[27]

However, that army still had the vigour to press on with their chase (in strict contrast to their exhaustion on the evening of the Battle of Blenheim). Everywhere columns of tired Allied troops marched on through the darkness, heading for the Dyle crossings. No coordination was possible that night; individual commanders just did what they thought best as they pressed on. Marlborough slept for a few hours under a cloak thrown on the ground and he shared his rough shelter with the newly appointed and extremely argumentative field deputy, Sicco van Goslinga, who had relished his first battle, galloping enthusiastically about the place, offering ill-judged advice and generally getting in the way.

By this skilful operation Marlborough met, and in only a brief afternoon, broke apart Villeroi's fine army. Suddenly, to be a soldier of Louis XIV in the Spanish Netherlands was to be a fugitive running through the darkness, and fully a half of Villeroi's army ceased to exist as a fighting force that astonishing day in May. One hundred and twenty French, Walloon and Bavarian regimental colours and standards were captured, together with all cannon, ordnance, tentage, wagons and baggage. Over 13,000 French soldiers and their allies lay on the battlefield, or were taken as unwounded prisoners, and many more deserted or defected in the coming weeks. Upon the proclamation by the Brabant States-General of the Austrian Archduke Charles as King Charles III of Spain, which soon followed the battle, many Walloon soldiers changed their allegiance. As a result, seven excellent battalions of these veteran troops joined Marlborough's army.

In this astonishingly complete victory, Marlborough's losses amounted to a fairly modest 1,066 killed and 2,567 wounded. Despite the severity of the infantry fighting along the Ramillies–Offuz ridge, and the tempestuous cavalry battle in which the Dutch were tested so severely, this toll was significantly less than that at Blenheim. This added considerably to the general wonderment of the world on hearing of the Duke's triumph. In stark comparison to his gloomy expectation of a fruitless campaign on the end of the leading strings of the Dutch, Marlborough was able to conduct a virtual triumph over his prostrate opponent in the Spanish Netherlands. These vital territories, over which a great and costly campaign of many years might have been expected, were now laid open for his armies to occupy, almost at will. So rapid and headlong was the Allied pursuit, that the enterprising French Governor of Namur was able to send out working parties onto the battlefield to rescue some of the guns abandoned by Villeroi's army. In the same ironic way, many Allied soldiers, who had dropped their packs when moving rapidly forward across the fields from Meldert into battle, had no chance ever to reclaim them. Their marches did not again take them back to Ramillies, in all the years of war that followed.

Marlborough's letter to Sarah announcing the great victory at Ramillies was dated 11.00 am, Monday 24 May 1706:

> God almighty has been pleased to give us a victory. I must leave the particulars to this bearer, Colonel Richards, for having been on horseback all Sunday, and after the battle marching all night, my head aches to that degree it is very uneasy to me to write. Poor Bringfield, holding my stirrup for me, helping me on horseback, was killed.[28]

The Duke wrote with an air of calm triumph to his Queen:

> I humbly crave to congratulate your Majesty with all humility and respect on the glorious success wherewith it pleased God yesterday to bless Y.M.'s arms and those of your allies over the enemy, who were equally desirous to come to a battle with us, having got together all their strength in these parts. I have been on horseback the whole day and last night, in order to press the enemy in their retreat, and am just come to my quarters to send Colonel Richards to Y.M. with an account of this action, wherein all the troops, both officers and soldiers, have behaved themselves with the greatest bravery and courage . . . I hope the troops will be able to march again tonight, in order to see if the intrenchments behind the Dyle may be attacked.[29]

The news of the victory was greeted in England on 27 May 1706 to tremendous acclaim. On 29 June Queen Anne attended another great Service of Thanksgiving in St Paul's Cathedral with Duchess Sarah at her side. The rejoicing was all the greater because so little had really been expected from the campaign: 'The whole nation rang with the highest acclamation of his extraordinary merit.'[30] Meanwhile, it took two days for rumours of the grim events at Ramillies to reach Versailles. Many there waited anxiously for news of husbands, brothers and sons. Louis XIV had to ask courtiers and servants what they had heard – it was a dreadful time. St Simon wrote: 'Never was seen such consternation. What was worse was that for six days there was no mail. The King was reduced to ask news here and there.'[31] At last the awful tidings came, and War Minister Chamillart (who had been so keen that Villeroi should seek battle) was sent to the front to verify the truth of the incredible news of disaster.

For the French, the immediate consequences of the battle, quite apart from the heavy casualties and loss of materiel and munitions, were far-reaching. Amongst Villeroi's first actions, once across the Dyle, was to order the destruction of the great depots and magazines in Louvain. Huge quantities of stores were dumped in the river, or set on fire. With no heart for another fight, the beaten French soldiers hurriedly fell back from the line of the Dyle towards Brussels and beyond as the Allied columns approached. Charles Churchill seized that great city itself in a dazzling and virtually uncontested advance on 28 May 1706. He welcomed his brother into the city the following day and Marlborough was received with all pomp and ceremony by the magistrates and dignitaries, as was his perfect due as their conqueror.

Messengers now came in from the east, where Prussian and Hanoverian troops were pressing forward from the Rhine crossings, eager to join the campaign. Marlborough's generals were sent ranging far and wide to ensure that no respite was allowed to the French. However, despite the magnitude of his victory at Ramillies, and the bonus that many stout towns would give up without much of a struggle, Marlborough's conquest of the Spanish Netherlands was to be no simple triumphal procession. Although utterly defeated on the field of battle, Villeroi was no fool. He prudently gathered together what troops he could muster, stripping some good garrisons to the bone in the process, and fell back behind the shelter of the Scheldt river. In this way he hoped to retain control of the strategically important towns of Ghent and Bruges, and the valuable waterways in that region. With the generally poor state of the roads in northern Europe at this time, particularly in bad weather, the ability to use the highly developed river and canal system to transport guns and supplies was a significant asset to any commander. Simultaneously, to deny their use to the Allies would be an important tactical advantage.

Marlborough was too swift for the Marshal once again, and he struck directly across the Senne and Dender rivers towards the crossings over the Scheldt at Oudenarde and Gavre. In this way he threatened Villeroi's communications with France. The French commander had no alternative but to fall back to cover Courtrai on the Lys, and to abandon the greater part of the Spanish Netherlands to the Duke. Chamillart met Villeroi at Courtrai on 31 May, and the War Minister approved his decision to abandon the line of the Scheldt. Villeroi was an honest and brave soldier whose great misfortune was to meet an opponent so immeasurably his superior. He always believed afterwards that his prompt retreat, and the wholesale abandoning of the Spanish Netherlands, saved the bulk of the French army from Marlborough's clutches. It perhaps enabled others to pursue a fresh and largely successful campaign the following year. On the battlefield, the Marshal's soldiers had fought with commendable tenacity in the hot May sunshine, but the pace of events dictated by Marlborough was altogether too dynamic, too indomitable, to be resisted. Despite the excuses Villeroi sought to offer, there was no disguising the scale of the disaster that had engulfed them.

The valour of the French, Walloon, Swiss and Bavarian soldiers was, quite naturally, obscured by the magnitude of their defeat at Ramillies, and some officers spoke of how poorly the troops had performed compared with Tallard's army at Blenheim, who had stood the storm longer. Certainly, a number of French regiments were not up to scratch, partly because of the habit of raising new, untried regiments rather than bringing seasoned veteran regiments up to full strength with recruits. This unwise practice, the evils of which were remarked on by De La Colonie and others, enabled Louis XIV to satisfy the numerous requests for regimental colonelcies from within his Court, but did absolutely nothing for the quality of his armies. St Simon wrote of the state of the French army at this time:

> Permission was given to raise a number of new regiments, and a vast crowd of new colonels and their staffs had to be paid for, which was a very great error. Instead of new battalions and squadrons being added to existing regiments, so that they became imbued with the regimental traditions, there was the disadvantage of having raw troops formed into small regiments, which were promptly destroyed.[32]

The severity of the combat at both Ramillies and Offuz says a great deal for the fighting quality of Villeroi's troops, but, while strict comparisons can be misleading, his army did collapse at Ramillies considerably more quickly than Tallard's had done at Blenheim. Perhaps Marlborough was on better form.

Villeroi wrote a remarkably frank letter to Louis XIV setting out the errors his own generals felt he had committed at Ramillies. The defeated Marshal rebutted the charges one by one but admitted, with perceptive clarity, that good reasons were no explanation for catastrophe. He added, rather sadly, that he could look forward to only one happy day – that of his death.[33] However, when the Marshal was at last persuaded to relinquish his command (he was perversely reluctant to do so), and returned to face his sovereign in Versailles, the King showed him the same unwavering kindness that was offered to his faithful but unsuccessful generals. He, greeted him with the soft words. 'At our age, Marshal, we must no longer expect good fortune.'[34] Villeroi would campaign no more, he was never again offered a field command.

In the Spanish Netherlands during the weeks that followed the battle, towns which in the past had defied their enemies for long months (sometimes years) – Louvain, Oudenarde, Ghent, Bruges, now surrendered in mere days before Marlborough's generals. The bulletin to the Allied army, dated 3 June 1706, described the surrender of Bruges. It ran:

> My Lord Duke went about noon to the city, and was met at the gate by the magistrates, who presented him the three keys in a gold basin, which his Grace returned . . . In the evening the magistrates attended his Grace again at his quarters and made their formal submission to King Charles [the Austrian claimant].[35]

Ostend (which withstood a Spanish siege of three years and three months between 1601 and 1604) surrendered in less than three weeks in 1706. On 4 July a Dutch battalion, led by a forlorn hope of fifty English grenadiers, stormed a breach in the town walls and, despite a valiant French resistance, the town had to fall. This gave the Duke an excellent port with convenient links to southern England. The great citadel at Antwerp capitulated to George Orkney, and the first-rate fortress of Menin, well supplied and commanded by Count Caraman, fell on 4 August when exposed to assault. Dendermonde surrendered on 6 September, and Ath on 2 October 1706. Foul weather then brought the campaign to a close and the soldiers trudged off to their dreary winter quarters, still shaking their heads in amazement at what they had achieved.

Marshal Marsin had already moved to garrison Mons, Mauberge, Ath and Charleroi, soon after the battle, but Louis XIV felt obliged to plunder his other armies to replace the soldiers lost at Ramillies, and to protect northern France. Amongst the most significant of the after-effects of the battle was the inability of the Duke de Vendôme to exploit his victory at Calcinato in northern Italy, as battalions were stripped away from him to be sent to the north. He bitterly commented that the French defeat on the Ramillies ridge that Sunday was the most disgraceful thing he had ever heard. Certainly, the effect on the French war effort was considerable, although the King's reaction to the defeat was probably over-done. Shocking though the battle was for French military ambitions, Marlborough's brilliantly successful army was still faced with a formidable belt of first class fortresses along France's border. Dealing with these strongholds, while powerful new French armies gathered against him, would be another matter entirely. [36]

The Ramillies Battlefield Today

The wide landscapes and rolling fields that Marlborough and Villeroi saw in 1706 are still easily recognisable today. There has been little modern development along the Ramillies–Offuz ridge and the surrounding farmland is lightly wooded, open and attractive. The villages themselves, all still separate and distinct from one another, have been rebuilt and partly enlarged in the intervening years. Standing on the ridge on the eastern side of the Petite Gheete valley (now only a channelled watercourse, hidden by willow trees and no longer a marshy obstacle), Ramillies and Offuz are just across the way. It is easy to visualise what Orkney's British infantry saw as they filed down the gentle slope to cross the marsh and come to grips with De Guiche's French and Walloon soldiers. Tom Kitcher would know the place today.

In Ramillies itself, there are one or two farm buildings that are contemporary to the battle, but most of the village has been rebuilt, and the car park of the church had some First World War relics scattered about. In the wonderfully wide cornfields to the south of the village, however, the visitor has the chance to view the scene of one of Europe's great cavalry battles, virtually unchanged over three centuries. The level ground, with really no obstacles at all to rapid movement, is absolutely ideal horse country. The commanders each chose this spot well – Villeroi quite rightly drew up his best cavalry on this ground, and it was here that Marlborough struck them so devastatingly with his Dutch and Danish squadrons.

The small hamlets of Franquenay and Taviers are not greatly larger than in the 18th century. Walking from one to the other the marshy nature of the fields on either side of the country road, particularly to the southwards, indicate very well how it was that the French dragoons could get embroiled as they attempted their doomed counter-attack. The Visoule Stream has all but disappeared. On the horizon to the west stands the Tomb of Ottomond (an ancient tumuli). Gazing north from here, in virtually unbroken line of sight, the church towers of Ramillies, Offuz and Autre-Eglise can be clearly seen across the flat plain. It is immediately obvious what an extraordinary opportunity was presented to the Danish cavalry on their deadly mission when they slipped past the French right Wing so dramatically that Sunday afternoon.

NOTES

1. Wykes, A, *The Royal Hampshire Regiment*, 1968, p.29.Comment by Tom Kitcher, a soldier in Meredith's Regiment.
2. Churchill, W S, *Marlborough: His Life and Times*, Vol III, 1947, p.82.
3. Chandler, D, *Marlborough as Military Commander*, 1973, p. 170.
4. Murray, G (ed.), *Letters and Dispatches of the Duke of Marlborough*, Vol II, 1845, p. 517.
5. Letter to M Hop, dated 21 May 1706 – *Letters and Dispatches*, p. 518.
6, Chandler, p. 172.
7. De La Colonie, J, *Chronicles of an Old Campaigner* (ed. W Horsley), 1904, p. 305.
8. Ibid., p.306
9. Some accounts of the battle have Taviers and Franquenay occupied by quite a substantial number of Swiss battalions. This is unlikely as, even today,

when some modern development has taken place, the two hamlets are small and straggling, and offer little scope for occupation by very many troops.

10. De La Colonie, p. 307.
11. Ibid., p. 308.
12. Ibid., p.309.
13. Wykes, p. 29. See also *Gleanings from the Cathcart Mss.* (ed. C T Atkinson), JSAHR, 1951 p. 64.
14. Wykes, p. 30.
15. Trevelyan, G M, *Ramillies and the Union with Scotland*, 1948, p.90.
16. De La Colonie, p. 312.
17. Churchill, p. 111.
18. Burn, W, *A Scots Fusilier and Dragoon under Marlborough,* JSAHR, 1936, p. 88. Attractive cottages now occupy this field. The colour ensign, James Gardiner, survived his dreadful wound. As a Colonel he was killed at the Battle of Prestonpans in Scotland in 1745, within sight of his own house.
19. Wykes, p. 29.
20. The hamlet of Foulz is now known as Foux les Caves. Many of the place names in modern Belgium are changed since 1706, so caution is required when reading maps.
21. Chandler, D (ed.), *Captain Robert Parker and Comte de Mérode-Westerloo,* 1968, p. 61.
22. Nosthworthy, B, *The Anatomy of Victory,* 1992, p.178.
23. Peter Drake was a real rogue, changing sides as his fancy pleased, and keeping just one step ahead of the hangman. He was convicted of piracy in 1708, but got off and ended his service under Marlborough's eventual replacement, James Butler, Duke of Ormond. See Burrell, S, *Amiable Renegade. The Memoirs of Captain Peter Drake, 1671–1753,* 1960, pp. 78–9.
24. Earlier that spring the Duke of Vendôme had defeated an Imperial army at Calcinato in northern Italy. The victorious troops ran amok, butchering many of the Danish contingent who had surrendered on terms. The Allied cavalry at Ramillies were eager for vengeance, and many of Villeroi's men who looked for mercy that afternoon did so in vain.
25. Churchill, p. 116.
26. Wykes, p. 29.
27. Churchill, p. 118. Also see Trevelyan page 117.
28. Churchill, p. 122.
29. *Letters and Dispatches*, p. 522.
30. Chandler, p.65.
31. Norton, L, *St Simon at Versailles*, 1958, p. 130.
32. Ibid., p.130. St Simon was not a dispassionate observer, having been deprived of his own regiment by Louis XIV in 1702.
33. Churchill, p. 130. The criticisms the French generals levelled at Villeroi for his handling of the army at Ramillies, were that he:
    (i) sought battle without ascertaining the enemy strength;
    (ii) fought without waiting to combine with Marshal Marsin;
    (iii) failed to reinforce his right Wing in good time;
    (iv) placed insufficient infantry to hold the marshes at Taviers;
    (v) erroneously deployed the right Wing on the field of battle.
34. Churchill, p. 131. See also Thompson, G M, *The First Churchill*, 1979, p. 186.
35. *Letters and Dispatches*, p. 556.
36. One of the consequences of Marlborough's triumphant year in 1706 was that the Ducal title was permitted to descend through the female line (his only

son, the Marquess of Blandford, had died young). This most unusual honour, proposed by a grateful Parliament and readily agreed to by Queen Anne, indicates the very high level of appreciation of the Duke's achievements in that campaign. See Coxe, W, *Memoirs of John, Duke of Marlborough*, Vol II, 1848, p. 29.

CHAPTER VIII
Endless Dusty Roads
The Lack of Success in 1707

The French do not seem inclined to attack us[1]

Marlborough's tremendous victories in 1706 rather perversely led to another year of frustrating disappointment. Allied unity was frittered away, for it was widely thought that France was beaten, and if that was so, the Allied powers were less inclined to agree with each other than before. Squabbles increased, narrow self-interest assumed greater importance than common purpose, and cooperation was not to be had at any price. In London meanwhile, on 17 March 1707, royal assent was given to the Act of Union between England and Scotland, henceforth known as Great Britain. [2]

At this time the Emperor in Vienna offered Marlborough the post of Governor-General of the Spanish Netherlands. Partly, it seems, this was to forestall a Dutch occupation and tax-gathering in areas which were viewed as Austrian possessions. In the warm after-glow of Ramillies, it seems unlikely that the Queen would have denied the Duke very much at all and had he pressed for this post he would in all likelihood have got it. However, Marlborough certainly knew the objections such an appointment would raise from the Dutch States-General, and he needed their continued support if the war was to be won. Additionally, there would be increased suspicion and envy in London over this (the annual stipend of the position alone was worth £60,000). So, the offer was politely refused on the rather spurious grounds that Queen Anne would not give her consent. Marlborough, so often accused of self-seeking and greed, had to let the tempting offer pass. The Dutch were highly suspicious of his motives all the same. Instead, a thoroughly unsatisfactory joint council of regency was established, in the name of the Austrian Archduke Charles, now grandly, and somewhat optimistically as it turned out, entitled King Charles III of Spain.

Still, despite these distractions within the Grand Alliance, all the hopes of the French King seemed to be brought to nothing. His armies were defeated in the Netherlands and in northern Italy (where Eugene brilliantly saved both Turin and Savoy for the Alliance). With a bankrupt treasury, Louis XIV wanted peace, and he now offered to abandon his grandson's claim to the Spanish throne. He would agree to trade concessions for England and Holland, the restoration of most of the Barrier fortresses to the Dutch, and to end his support for the Stuart claim to the English throne. Plainly, a good peace was to be had by some capable negotiation, even though the King never gave up trying to play off one enemy against the others. Only eighteen months previously so generous a French offer would have been beyond the wildest dreams of the Allied powers. Now, victory made them obstinate and greedy and they demanded more than Louis XIV would offer, and so his armies fought on while better terms were sought.

Marlborough had ambitious plans for a fresh offensive in the Moselle valley in 1707. In this way he could strike into the heart of France yet avoid the massive obstacle belt in Flanders. Almost inevitably, the Dutch were once again reluctant to see their armies march away southwards, and the Duke found that, while still steadfast and brave, they remained troublesome allies. Simultaneously, he had once again to keep King Charles XII of Sweden out of the war, as he had done in 1702. Any involvement by that volatile and dangerous monarch would prove very distracting for the Duke's German allies, particularly Prussia and Saxony, both of whom provided large numbers of excellent troops for the Allied armies. They were very susceptible to Swedish pressure, but in the end Charles XII went off to fight Russia, and was defeated at Poltava.

Elsewhere in the war, there were setbacks. In Spain, one of Louis XIV's best Marshals, Marlborough's nephew James Fitzjames, the Duke of Berwick, overwhelmed a smaller Allied army at Almanza. Meanwhile, Marshal Villars stormed the Lines of Stollhofen on the Upper Rhine, and the French took a campaign of fire and devastation into the princely states of middle Germany, from where so many of the mercenary soldiers of the Grand Alliance came. The Imperial commander in this region, the invalid Margrave of Baden, proved utterly incapable of coping with the French offensive. Soon French generals once again encamped their soldiers on the plain of Höchstädt beside the Danube. Perhaps they remembered their day of shame and defeat in those fields only three years earlier, and this was some compensation. A number of the officers enjoyed an excursion to the Schellenberg hill, to view the scene of the dreadful July battle and pick up scattered military mementos of the day.

One grand Allied project that did proceed that summer was a joint sea and land attack under the command of Prince Eugene on the great French naval base at Toulon. This operation was intended to cripple French power in the Mediterranean, and might in time lay southern France open to invasion. Despite the generalship of the Prince, who was not wholeheartedly convinced of the value of taking Toulon, the project miscarried badly. Eugene was obliged to raise the siege and hurry his army away empty handed, back to northern Italy, in late August 1707. Louis XIV's Mediterranean fleet was burned at its moorings and France was prevented from fully exploiting Berwick's recent successes in Spain. Some French troops were drawn away from Flanders and the Rhine, but this was fairly meagre stuff, and the failure of the Toulon operation was a distinct setback for the Alliance.

Meanwhile the Duke of Vendôme, a tough and brash campaigner, went to command Louis XIV's army in the Spanish Netherlands.[3] Impatient to regain strategic momentum in the region Marlborough manoeuvred hard to catch him at a disadvantage, but Vendôme had strict orders from Versailles to avoid a pitched battle, and he was too wily to be snared easily. A complex, wasteful and unproductive summer campaign followed. Despite a close shave near Soignes in early August, Vendôme managed to keep safe within fortified lines near Mons, while Marlborough's detractors commented acidly on his lack of success. Elsewhere, the Allied effort was progressively being dispersed, for the Austrians were diverting troops to the irrelevant (to all except Vienna) seizure of Naples and southern Italy. They also concluded a disgraceful local agreement to parole 20,000 French prisoners captured at the Battle of Turin, as long as they left Italy to fight the Allies elsewhere. All in all, the year 1707 passed in drift and confusion, and Marlborough was unable to point to a single major success on the field of battle. Instead, he had to hope for better fortune in the coming year.

At the end of the campaign that year, Captain Robert Parker of the Royal Irish Regiment wrote: 'As the country was very plentiful, our camp was sufficiently provided with forage till the middle of October, when we went into quarters.'[4] Despite such comforts, much of the Grand Alliance was stale and growing weary of heavy taxation and seemingly endless war. Marlborough returned to London to a sea of domestic troubles. His great friend and ally, the Lord Treasurer Sidney Godolphin, was under bitter attack in Parliament while the Duke's younger brother, Admiral George Churchill, stood accused (rather unfairly) of maladministration over the Toulon affair. Duchess Sarah was rapidly losing favour with Queen Anne, with whom she was developing a very unfortunate tendency to quarrel. The Duke was observed to be peevish, and perhaps he had good cause.[5]

NOTES

1. Marlborough letter to Mr James Stanhope, 30 June 1707. Murray, G (ed.), *Letters and Dispatches of the Duke of Marlborough*, Vol III, 1845, p. 449.
2. A valuable account of the negotiations that led to the Act of Union is G M Trevelyan's *Ramillies and the Union with Scotland* 1948.

3. Vendôme's lineage, as the descendant of a bastard son of Henry IV of France, and his vigour and flair on the battlefield, gained him acceptance, despite his sordid personal habits, into the inner circles at the Court of Louis XIV.

4. Chandler, D (ed.), *Captain Robert Parker and Comte de Mérode-Westerloo*, 1968, p. 68.

5. Chandler, D, *Marlborough as Military Commander*, 1973, p. 200.

CHAPTER IX
The Devil Must Have Carried Them
The Battle of Oudenarde,
Wednesday 11 July 1708.

We were obliged to pass a river and to engage them before the whole army was passed.[1]

In the spring of 1708 the Dutch States-General were, once again, at their most cooperative. They had the wit to realise that their difficult attitude the previous year had thoroughly exasperated the Duke of Marlborough and cost the Allied cause dearly. Assured of their renewed support, he looked forward to proceeding with an active and aggressive campaign in the Spanish Netherlands.

Elsewhere, the Allies stood on the defensive in Spain, but it was planned that the Duke of Savoy would make a demonstration of offensive intent in south-eastern France. The Elector of Hanover (one day to be George I of Great Britain) would maintain a strong front with his forces on the Upper Rhine, while Prince Eugene with his Imperial army made covert preparations to march from the Moselle valley to join Marlborough near Brussels. However, Eugene was at this time often away, attending to pressing state affairs in Vienna, and time was lost. The Duke devised alternative plans (which would come to nothing) for an amphibious 'descent' on the French coast, and even thought to abandon Brussels and fall back towards Antwerp, hoping to entice the French to battle away from their lines of defence.

King Louis XIV had his own plans for a campaign that summer, in order to force a good peace for France. His army commander in Flanders, the 54-year-old Duke of Vendôme, although an appalling man in many ways, was amongst the best soldiers France had. However, there was a significant fault-line in the French command arrangements. The Duke of Burgundy, Louis XIV's 26-year-old eldest grandson and heir to the throne (he would have been King one day had measles not intervened in 1712), was appointed to the nominal command of the army. His fond grandfather was keen that the refined and elegant young prince should have experience of the art of war, and become known to his armies. Accordingly, although Burgundy was a quiet and devout man, he was packed off on campaign with his grandfather's advice to heed what the hard-bitten veteran Marshal had to say. Unfortunately, with characters so unlike, the two men were on the very worst of terms.

Despite these difficulties, Vendôme had several promising options open to pursue, and he enjoyed a distinct numerical superiority over Marlborough. An advance against Oudenarde and Ghent would threaten the Duke's connection with the Channel ports and England and this was the thrust he most expected. Vendôme preferred to move to threaten the Allied fortress of Huy on the Meuse river, where he hoped to lure Marlborough out to fight in open country well suited to the employment of the powerful French cavalry. Burgundy, however, wanted to make a direct attack on Brussels, even though this would almost certainly bring on a pitched battle with Marlborough on ground, more or less, of the Duke's own choosing.

Vendôme concentrated his army of 100,000 troops (197 squadrons of cavalry and 124 infantry battalions) near Mons, and on 26 May 1708 he pushed his advance guard across the Haine river to Soignes, as if to threaten Brussels. Marlborough promptly moved to Hal, hoping to force an early decision point on the French commander. On 1 June Vendôme advanced towards Braine l'Alleud as if heading for the Dyle river and Louvain. Marlborough moved rapidly past Brussels to Terbanck, to the south of Louvain in order to meet the threat, but the French halted at Gembloux on 3 June, with the appearance of having been foiled by the Duke's prompt and confident response to their advance.

Marlborough's army at this point comprised about 90,000 men (180 cavalry squadrons and 112 battalions). He was dismayed to learn that Eugene would not fully assemble his army for the intended march to the Spanish Netherlands until 28 June, and as a result, the Duke had to employ patience and bide his time while reviewing his troops. At last Eugene began his march northwards from Coblenz on 29 June; there had been unexpected complications with the prickly Elector of Hanover, who could not bear the thought that he might be left out of things. Accordingly, the Prince was only able to take 15,000 troops rather than the 40,000 originally planned, and the highly capable Duke of Berwick was soon hot on his heels with a 27,000-strong force of French soldiers. However, Eugene had a three-day head start. Everything now depended on his energy – if the Prince made good time on the road to combine with Marlborough, the joint Allied army might fall on and defeat Vendôme before Berwick could come to his aid.

In the meantime, Vendôme was laying deep plans of his own, in the sure knowledge that much of the population of the Spanish Netherlands were now tired both of oppressive Dutch rule and taxation, and of the ravages of Allied foragers. Count Bergeyck, French Minister of War in the Spanish Netherlands, had put forward a scheme to seize certain key towns, and this was put into effect. The French commander sprang into action late on 4 July 1708. Leaving Braine l'Alleud (Brain la Leuze, as Mrs Christian Davies put it in her memoirs), his army marched rapidly westwards, crossed the Senne river and made for the Dender river at Grammont. Flying columns under Generals Chemerault and La Motte were sent ahead to Ghent and Bruges, the two most populous and important towns in northern Flanders. There the citizens welcomed the French columns and threw open their gates, and the few loyal Allied troops in each garrison could do little to prevent the occupation. Vendôme's army, led by an advanced guard under the Marquis Grimaldi, continued its march to cover these daring operations.

At a stroke, by this bold and skilful manoeuvre, the waterways of northern Flanders, so useful for the movement of cannon and supplies, were lost to Marlborough. His own line of supply to Antwerp and Holland, and his direct communications with England through Ostend were cut. The French army was soon in a good secure position behind the Dender, and was well placed to apply pressure on the Allied hold on Brussels. At the same time, the Allied garrisons at the fortified town of Oudenarde on the Scheldt, and Menin on the Lys river were threatened. However, a dispute now arose between Burgundy and Vendôme concerning the next course of action to be taken. Despite copious advice from Louis XIV that he should make use of the older man's considerable military experience, Burgundy preferred his own opinion and still held himself aloof from the rough soldier. For his part, Vendôme openly despised the elegant young man; the respective entourages followed their lead, and even while the campaign progressed, as few words were exchanged between the two parties as was practically possible.

In the opposing camp, the Count of Mérode-Westerloo (now in Allied service having switched his allegiance to the Habsburg claimant, Archduke Charles) claimed to have heard rumours of Vendôme's plans for a sudden offensive, but Marlborough supposedly paid little attention to the information:

> I had received news from a reliable source advising me to take good care of Ghent and Bruges, which were soon to be betrayed to the enemy . . . He treated my news as something of no account, telling me that it was impossible.[2]

The Count was prone to be wise after the event, and was not a particularly objective observer. In any case, the Duke suspected his newly acquired sincerity for the Allied cause against France.

Vendôme's offensive was both well planned and skilfully executed, but although Marlborough had been taken aback by the audacity and speed of the French moves, his reaction was prompt. A brigade of cavalry under Bothmar had been sent towards Alost on 5 July, while the main Allied army headed west to Anderlecht and Tourbeck. Misfortune dogged their steps – the roads were bad, the weather was foul, and the hard marching told heavily on the foot soldiers in particular. The fog of war once again cloaked the movements of the two armies, and Marlborough's keen instincts were temporarily foiled at this time. That evening the French rearguard at Goycke deployed between the Senne and Dender rivers under the Marquis d'Albergotti, and caused Marlborough to halt his columns and deploy for battle across the sodden and dusky fields. The hour was late and Marlborough appears to have taken a wrong road when on a reconnaissance. Having tramped about for an hour or two, the soldiers went off to their bivouacs. Such difficulties are to be expected on campaign, but precious time was lost, and there was more than a trace of confusion in the Allied camp. Gloom was spread by the dismal news that both Ghent and Bruges had, indeed, fallen to the French.

By the morning of Saturday 7 July 1708, the French were found to have successfully slipped away. In frustration Marlborough's cavalry pushed on in pursuit to Ninove, and there they ran into the French rearguard again, this time with the baggage column. A fight erupted along the Dender river, but apart from snapping up some French wagons and stragglers, the Allied troopers were unable to achieve very much. Vendôme's army fell back virtually unmolested to a good position at which to stand near Alost. Marlborough wrote home to London the following day:

> On Saturday morning we fell in with the enemy's rear-guard as they were crossing the Dender, but too late to do them much execution. We took about 300 prisoners, and some baggage that night, and yesterday we halted at Assche.[3]

The Duke did not forget to look farther afield and he put 700 fresh troops from Prendergast's Regiment and Waleff's Dragoons into the first-class fortress and town of Oudenarde on the evening of 7 July. This secured a toe-hold on the vital line of the Scheldt river, and the garrison were under the command of the Governor of Ath, the highly proficient Brigadier-General Chanclos. This robust officer promptly made it plain to the citizenry that he would not hesitate to burn their town around them, if there was any attempt to follow the example of Ghent and Bruges and open the gates to the French. The place remained quiet.

As the Allied army tried to close the gap, Vendôme's fertile mind next favoured an operation against the now well-equipped town of Oudenarde, while the main French army held the forward line of the

Dender against Marlborough's counter-moves. Burgundy, however, wanted to re-establish direct contact with northern France, and to move closer to supply depots and magazines at Tournai and Lille. The successful marches which gave them possession of Ghent and Bruges had the corresponding counter-effect of laying the French lines of communication and supply open to Allied attack. With this in mind, Burgundy suggested that a siege of Menin should be the next step, and there was sense in this, but Vendôme appears to have thought it too timid. He was not inclined to give up so much territory to Marlborough unless under real pressure. As they could not agree on the best course to take, the matter had to be referred to Versailles for a decision, and Vendôme in the meantime prepared to invest Oudenarde. He made his army ready to close up to the Dender crossings around Lessines for the covering operation.

From here Vendôme could cover his conquests in northern Flanders, and simultaneously threaten both Antwerp and Brussels. All the while his army would have the protection of the Dender, which could not be forded and needed bridging. If his army were pressed by Marlborough he could still slip away, using the cover of the equally difficult Scheldt, to northern France and the protecting fortress belt there. Time would allow him to then combine with the Duke of Berwick, while strong French garrisons would remain in many of the key towns of northern Flanders, and Marlborough's scope for further operations placed under severe strain. All told, the French general was playing his cards rather well, while Marlborough appeared to be fumbling.

Despite his lack of accord with Burgundy, Vendôme had achieved a considerable coup in the virtually bloodless re-capture of much of north and western Flanders, under the very nose of Marlborough. The trick now was for him to hold on to the gains, while Berwick, obliged to move on the outer curve of the marching arc, hurried up from the Moselle to join forces with him. The French commanders had no pressing need to seek battle, beyond an obvious necessity to cover both the river lines behind which they lay and their lines of communication and supply with northern France. With careful planning Vendôme could avoid any serious engagement with Marlborough before Berwick's arrival.

At the same time, Vendôme could not safely ignore Allied moves to sever his communications with France. The holding of the line of the Dender was a necessary preliminary to whatever should be decided in Versailles regarding the respective merits of Oudenarde or Menin as his intended victims. The river gave protection against Allied thrusts, but this protection required close attention, and had to be held at the point of actual threat to be effective. Therefore, Vendôme had to manoeuvre to place his army to dispute any river crossings that Marlborough attempted. Hampered by the need to refer vital decisions to Versailles, there was the likelihood that an alert Marlborough could take the initiative in the next phase of the campaign. However, complications on the line of march from the Moselle valley were taking their toll, and Eugene made slower progress than expected, while Berwick was pushing his troops hard to overtake him. While waiting for the Prince to arrive, Marlborough had put his army into camp near Assche to the west of Brussels. Frustrated and unwell with migraine headaches, he faced an apparently dismal prospect, and on Sunday 8 July he did not venture from his tent; the orders for the day were issued by Count Overkirk.

Later that same day Eugene rode into the Allied camp to confer with his friend. He had outstripped the marching pace of his own army, still toiling along the roads to Flanders, and intended to pay a brief visit to his aged mother in Brussels. The Prince was alone but for a mounted escort of Hanoverian dragoons and some wild looking Imperial Hussars. His timely arrival cheered Marlborough, who shook off his migraine as the two comrades considered how best to counter the French offensive. Eugene placed little importance on the loss of the towns, arguing that a victory in open battle would set all to rights, even though time was pressing as Berwick drew nearer. The Duke's spirits lifted immediately, and his lively mind began to devise daring plans. The Allied campaign sprang into life.

Marlborough's original scheme to combine his army with that of Eugene and attack Vendôme was plainly not possible in the time available. The decision the Duke now took was to force battle on the French with his army alone, and this action was fully endorsed by Eugene. They plotted to bring on a battle without delay, and this required the subtle placing of Marlborough's numerically inferior army so close to Vendôme that he could not refuse to fight. Such an ambitious course called for skill and judgement, and the hectic marching campaign that now began would be a race for control of the river lines of Flanders.

Action was almost immediate, indicating that Marlborough had not been wasting his time in idleness, even while in his tent sick with migraine. On the evening of 8 July 1708 the Allied advance guard under William Cadogan broke camp and marched south from Assche through Herfelingen and Ghislengien to Lessines on the Dender river. The main body of the army followed at 2.00 the following morning, 9 July. George Orkney was left with a brigade of infantry to ensure that no sudden dash by Vendôme across the rear of the Allied army would threaten Brussels. Arnold Joost von Keppel, the astute Earl of Albemarle, had thirty squadrons of Dutch cavalry to protect the baggage trains, and to maintain a link with Orkney.

The pace that Cadogan set was fast, and one young dragoon, whose troop had to be recalled from a foraging expedition, recalled that the whole army seemed to be hurrying along. Charles Cathcart wrote of being present with two squadrons of British dragoons who had been detailed to drive off some French marauders, but were recalled and had to force the pace to catch up with the speeding Allied army.[4]

By noon on Monday 9 July, after a march of nearly fifteen miles, Cadogan's soldiers reached Herfelingen. Prince Eugene, who had completed his fleeting visit to his mother in Brussels, rejoined the army at this point, still with only his small escort. Marlborough urged his army onwards, heading for the river crossings. The Duke had delayed a letter to the Secretary of State in London, begun the previous day, in order to bring him up to date with the news of the march. Making his intentions for an offensive brilliantly clear, he added:

> We began our march again at 2.00 o'clock in the morning (9 July), and about noon came to this camp [Herfelingen], where we shall only halt till about 7.00 o'clock in the evening, and then pursue our march towards Lessines, to endeavor to pass the Dender, in order to attack the enemy.[5]

Meanwhile, Vendôme also intended to secure Lessines to cover the operations against Oudenarde. His army was on the march past Ninove and Voorde, on a generally converging course with Cadogan's column, but the French troops moved at a rather gentler pace than those of their alert opponents.

Cadogan wasted no time; Ghislengien was passed and daybreak on 10 July saw his soldiers resting in the streets of Lessines, while their pioneers laboured to add pontoon bridges to those already across the Dender. By noon that day, his detachment was across the river while the main body of Marlborough's army was hurrying along to Lessines, marching in four great columns with the cavalry on either flank. This was a remarkable feat of marching, for the Allied troops had covered thirty miles in less than thirty-six hours to secure the river crossings. The French army was not operating under the same urgency and was not there to oppose them. Vendôme had now lost the initiative in this campaign.

During the morning of 10 July, French cavalry were seen to be approaching Lessines along the road from Voorde. These scouts soon withdrew as Cadogan's presence was detected. They took back to Vendôme the unwelcome news that he had lost the line of the Dender, unless he was prepared to commit to a battle then and there. The aggressive French commander's inclination was to do just that, to advance and attack the Allies as they crossed the river. This was probably the correct response, but Burgundy would not agree to such a hazardous course, and he urged that the army would be better placed to offer battle from the security of the far bank of the Scheldt. Fuming with frustration, Vendôme drew his army off towards the river crossings at Gavre, six miles downstream from Oudenarde. Once snugly across that wide river obstacle, he could deploy to oppose any Allied crossing, or fall back at leisure to a suitably strong position of defence. In this way Ghent and Bruges would be covered, and operations could proceed against Menin; it was probably not possible now to take on Oudenarde as Marlborough approached. Despite some recent hesitancy, Vendôme's situation was not too awkward at this point, if he remained alert.

This whole series of marches and manoeuvres is a demonstration of the professional supremacy of Marlborough, when compared with the fractious command neglectfully exercised by Vendôme and Burgundy. Each hour that passed brought the Allied army decisively closer to their opponents, while the French commanders, flushed with their recent successes but without a clear idea of how to deal with Marlborough's counter-offensive, reacted inexpertly to his moves. Intent on the defence of firstly, the Dender, and then the Scheldt, it seems that they had no inkling of the determination of the Duke to close with and destroy their army. For this lack of awareness the performance of the veteran Duke of Vendôme looks feeble for an army commander, while the Duke of Burgundy is exposed as a reluctant amateur.

At 1.00 on the morning of Wednesday 11 July 1708, Cadogan began a forced march with his advance guard along the rough by-road leading from Lessines to Oudenarde. He took with him six British battalions under Sabine, four Dutch and two Scots-Dutch battalions under Plattenberg, and four Prussian battalions under Evans. He also had eight squadrons of Hanoverian dragoons, from the Liebregiment, and the regiments of von Bulow and Schulemberg, under the command of Jorgen Rantzau. Thirty-two light field guns (attached to the infantry as 'battalion' guns) accompanied the column, and marching along were parties of engineers and pioneers with the train of 'tin boats' to construct the essential pontoon bridges. The column totalled about 10,000 men – little enough really to take on the might of the French army. With an uneven road the going was not easy, but Cadogan's march of sixteen miles to the hamlet of Eename, on the hills overlooking Oudenarde and the Scheldt river, was successfully completed in little more than eight hours. It seems that the sweating soldiers encountered not a single French scout or picket on the road. This admirably urgent pace was at complete variance with the leisurely march of Vendôme's army, as it moved majestically, and in sublime ignorance of the Allied approach, to the crossings over the river.

As William Cadogan looked down from the hills of Eename on the Scheldt, at about 9.30 that morning, the day was fine and the sun shone brightly on the stretches of water and marshy meadow below. Beyond the river was a great amphitheatre of low-lying and heavily cultivated ground, cut through with the Norken, Diepenbeek and Marollebeek Streams, all bounded by the low hills of the Boser Couter to the left and

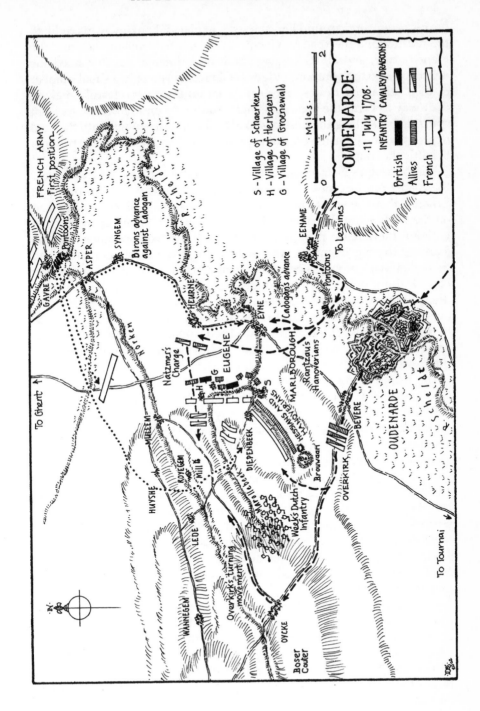

the higher ground around Huyshe straight ahead. Looking to his right, to the north along the road to Ghent, Cadogan could plainly see that the French army, and all its baggage and impedimenta, still thronged the approaches to the pontoon bridges at Gavre. As yet, only a small number of their advanced troops were safely across the river, steadily making their way towards the protective high ground. At once, messengers went spurring back along the Lessines road to find Marlborough with the vital news – that the French were not yet across the river, and could be brought to battle that day.

Marlborough's instructions to Cadogan had been plain – he was to clear the road from Lessines to the Scheldt and seize the crossing places at Eename; there he was to lay pontoon bridges and establish a bridgehead on the far bank of the river sufficient to allow the Allied army to cross without interference from the French. Such a major operation held no fears for the big Irishman, who was amongst the most competent and trusted of Marlborough's generals. Getting his troops down onto the river bank without delay, Cadogan directed his pioneers to lay their bridges, dragged up by oxen-teams at about 10.30 am after their laborious journey over the hills. Prudently, he also sent men to help Chanclos improve the two stone bridges in Oudenarde town itself, and to lay additional pontoon bridges there, foreseeing that these would be in demand as the day progressed.[6]

The march of the main body of the Allied army, which began from Lessines at 8.00 am, was at a good pace. Marlborough and his staff galloped ahead with an escort of twenty squadrons of Prussian cavalry under Dubislaw Natzmer. As in the earlier march through Herfelingen to Lessines, the troops responded enthusiastically; the men (and the few women amongst their ranks) could be seen doubling along the road, shrouded in great clouds of choking dust, eager to get to the field of battle. Those soldiers detailed to the rather humble task of guarding the wagons left their posts, tipping officers' equipages gleefully into the ditch whenever they encumbered the road, before heading over the hills towards the beckoning clamour of battle, as morning gave way to afternoon. Deputy Goslinga, although always a sharp critic of Marlborough and his methods, wrote excitedly afterwards: 'It was no longer a march, but a run.'[7]

As his pioneers worked to put the bridges across the Scheldt, Cadogan could see that their presence was not really detected by the French who appeared to have mistaken his activities for those of foragers or working parties from the garrison in Oudenarde. With one singular exception, the French attention seems to have been entirely on their own steady progress across the river and up onto the 'heights' at Huyshe above the Norken Stream.

By mid-day Cadogan was able to push his infantry battalions across the completed pontoon bridges onto the meadows on the far bank. The soldiers moved out of the constricting bridgehead at the water's edge, trudging towards the tree-lined Ghent road and on to the first real natural obstacle that would offer a place to make a stand against any French attack. This was the sluggish Diepenbeek Stream, which ran to its marshy confluence with the Scheldt near the hamlet of Eyne, about one mile downstream from the crossing points. The four Prussian battalions, under Cadogan's immediate command, stayed as guard at the water's edge. Joseph Sabine's British infantry brigade (marching into battle under the bravely flying Union flags for the first time) took the left, more exposed flank near the road, while Plattenberg's Dutch and Scots-Dutch battalions took the flank nearer to the river. Rantzau's Hanoverian dragoons formed up to the left of Sabine's brigade; here they covered the left flank of the infantry, and were free to probe ahead, across the water-meadows into the orchards and gardens of the low-lying and highly cultivated countryside around them. Without any interference, Cadogan's advanced guard was able to shake out into good order, and this major hurdle for Marlborough's successful deployment was safely crossed.

However, the seemingly not too onerous task of watching this leftwards flank of the French army, as it moved across the Scheldt, was entrusted to the Marquis de Biron. He had command of two brigades comprising seven good battalions of Swiss infantry in the French service, from the Villars, Gueder and Pfeiffer regiments, and these were moving steadily upstream towards the village of Heurne. Unaware of the Allied approach, the troops marched at ease, and were not in battle order. In support of Biron were twelve squadrons of French cavalry, the nearest at hand being those of the Royal la Bretache Régiment. These troopers, recently deployed from the line of march, had been foraging, but now stood beside their grazing horses in the fields between Heurne and the Ghent road. In all, Biron had about 5,000 men immediately at hand.

At around 1.00 pm shots crackled briskly across the water meadows as Rantzau's dragoons brushed with Swiss pickets near the hamlet of Eyne. Biron's second in command, Major-General Pfeiffer, was on the spot with the advanced brigade, and he pushed his leading companies forward into Eyne to find out what really was there. He only had four battalions, and so called for the second Swiss brigade to come forward. Biron hurried ahead, and as soon as he reached the vantage point of the windmill at Eyne, he could plainly see the scale of Cadogan's bridging operations along the banks of the Scheldt and the growing infantry deployment. Worse still, beyond the blue-coated Prussian infantry standing at the pontoons less than a mile upstream, the road that led over the hill from Lessines was filled with marching soldiers – cavalry, foot and guns. This was a great army on the march. Biron was now thoroughly alarmed and he hurried back to bring forward his infantry supports, and to give instructions to the nearby cavalry. Meanwhile, messengers were sent to find Vendôme with word of this alarming and unexpected development – help was urgently needed for the threatened Swiss detachment.

At last, at about 2.00 pm, word reached the French commander of Cadogan's bold crossing of the Scheldt; the enemy army thought to be fifteen miles or more away was now bearing down on him. Ironically, at this time both Vendôme and Burgundy were each enjoying al-fresco lunches, in their separate parties, beside the Ghent road, while the main army threaded its stately way along the track from Gavre towards Huyshe. When the incredible news was broken to Vendôme he exclaimed sceptically: 'If they are there, then the Devil must have carried them. Such marching is impossible.'[8]

The whole notion of such a daring enterprise – flinging a forward detachment of an army across a wide river in such close proximity to an opponent's main force – seemed reckless and preposterous. Still, scanning the horizon, as the Marquis de Biron had done before, Vendôme could now see the dust clouds boiling above the hills, a sure sign of great numbers on the march. They told a plain enough tale. Grimly, he sent a reply to Biron that he should attack the Allied bridgehead at once while he brought the cavalry of the left Wing of the army round into position to support the advance. Meanwhile, a message was sent to Burgundy that the whole weight of the infantry of that Wing should follow the cavalry. A rapid assault in force should set things right, and this was quite obviously the correct course of action. The key to French success was to deploy their superiority in numbers as soon as possible and to smash the Allied bridgehead.

However, as Biron moved forward his reserve brigade of Swiss from Heurne, he was stopped by the Marquis de Puysegur, Vendôme's chief of staff. Earnestly helpful, but mistaken, Puysegur insisted that the ground to their front was marshy and difficult for cavalry to cross; the infantry advance would be unsupported and vulnerable. Then Marshal Matignon rode up, apparently oblivious to the approaching crisis but looking for a place to mark out an encampment. He readily agreed with Puysegur and forbade Biron to continue the operation, taking upon himself the responsibility of countermanding Vendôme's order. Shortly afterwards, Vendôme himself came along the Ghent road leading the cavalry of the left Wing that had been gathered to support Biron's thrust. He furiously demanded to know why the Swiss soldiers were standing idle. Puysegur and Matignon explained their doubts about the state of the ground. Baffled, but in no position to question his chief of staff's apparently superior knowledge of the terrain, Vendôme bitterly countermanded his orders for the cavalry to advance farther to the support of the Swiss. He then flounced off to find Burgundy, perhaps to try and co-ordinate an attack from a different quarter.

During this fraught period of increasing confusion in the French command, Burgundy, seeing that Vendôme was not pushing forward, had begun to draw up the main body of the army north of the Norken Stream, along the heights of Huyshe. This was a perfectly satisfactory defensive position, but it contributed nothing towards the elimination of the dangerous Allied bridgehead. The time was now nearly 2.45 pm and the afternoon was being frittered away. Biron was left to his own lonely fight on this flank without real support, unable to influence the wider battle as it spread quickly out along the Diepenbeek and Marollebeek Streams.

Marlborough and Eugene had now arrived at the Allied bridgehead, and fresh British and German battalions, under John Campbell, the 2nd Duke of Argyll were preparing to cross the pontoon bridges. Marlborough quickly approved Cadogan's dispositions and ordered him forward to clear the line of the Diepenbeek. He also ordered a battery to be placed to cover the inn at Schaerken (it was actually a brothel) on Cadogan's left.[9] Sabine's and Plattenberg's infantry were already deployed into line of battle along the stream from the Scheldt to Schaerken, exchanging shots with the Swiss skirmishers. The Allied troops had very prudently been provided with bundles of fascines with which to bridge the boggy watercourse, and at about 3.00 pm they advanced boldly to drive in the leading enemy troops. As soon as they were pressed the forward Swiss companies fell back on their supports, but they became increasingly disordered in the rearward movement. Rantzau's dragoons came promptly forward, the leading squadrons dismounting to ford the stream with little difficulty, although the Electoral Prince, one day to be King George II of Great Britain, fell off his horse into the mud. Lapping around the right flank of the withdrawing Swiss infantry, the Hanoverians rode amongst the increasingly disordered soldiers, driving them in confusion. Marlborough wrote afterwards: 'Major-General Rantzau, who commanded a detachment of eight squadrons, was first to charge, and contributed greatly to our happy success.'[10]

The pace of the Allied attack, a forthright and confident infantry advance coupled with a sharp flanking movement by the cavalry, plainly caught the normally reliable Swiss soldiers off balance. Three of their battalions were routed and dispersed, many of the soldiers being taken prisoner in Eyne itself, Pfeiffer amongst them. The fourth battalion broke and ran for Heurne where the remaining Swiss brigade still stood. The fugitives were ruthlessly ridden down by Rantzau's dragoons, and fully a half of Biron's detachment had been destroyed in short order. Some of the Swiss infantry left in Heurne eventually managed to rejoin the left Wing of the main French army, but, later that day, the Marquis de Biron himself became the reluctant guest of the Duke of Marlborough when he fell into the hands of Allied soldiers. Cadogan had secured the right flank of his developing line with this swift and capable attack, and the first and most dangerous phase of this extraordinary battle had passed off successfully. Marlborough had his foot planted firmly on the far bank of the Scheldt river.

Flushed with this easy success over the Swiss, Rantzau's dragoons now surged along the line of the Ghent road, apparently without receiving any order to do so from Cadogan. They soon encountered the squadrons of the Royal la Bretache Régiment and, charging at full tilt, they drove them in flight towards the Norken Stream; the French regimental commander was amongst those taken prisoner. This hectic and scarcely controlled pursuit soon involved Rantzau's squadrons in a furious mêlée with the cavalry of the French left Wing (those same squadrons that Vendôme had originally intended to support Biron). These were making for the heights of Huyshe, but now they deployed to meet the approaching threat. Badly out-numbered, and harried by a French battery emplaced near Mullem, Rantzau ordered a withdrawal, but in the confusion the Electoral Prince was once again thrown, as his horse was shot. His squadron commander, Colonel Loseke, sprang to the ground and helped the young prince into his own saddle so that he escaped the encircling French horsemen. The gallant colonel, sword in hand, was cut down almost immediately afterwards.

Proudly carrying off dozens of prisoners, two kettle-drums and ten captured French standards, Rantzau's breathless dragoons rejoined Cadogan's infantrymen near Heurne. John Dalrymple, 2nd Earl of Stair, had not been able to restrain his enthusiasm, and gathered together a band of quartermasters with whom he had ridden ahead to scout the ground. He charged in with this motley group to assist Rantzau in his withdrawal. Charles Cathcart, who was in Stair's party, described the Hanoverian dragoons as being broken, but it seems most likely that he mistook their state from the rapid and breathless withdrawal they made under French pressure. John Deane of the 1st English Foot Guards remembered:

> A noble action it was, and the behaviour of all from the highest to the lowest the same. The royal Prince of Hanover in this action behaved himself with undaunted courage, exposing himself in the thickest of the fire at the head of his troops until his horse was shotte from under him.[11]

At about 4.00 pm the lead element of the main Allied army, twenty battalions of British, Hanoverian and Hessian infantry under Argyll, were filing across the pontoon bridges and through the bridges in the town, and moving out towards the Diepenbeek Stream.[12] Natzmer's Prussian cavalry, who had provided Marlborough with his escort that morning, also began to move across the pontoon bridges. Several of these squadrons were detailed to remain to the east of the river for the time being, and to watch for any signs of French interference from the direction of Gavre against the vital Lessines road. The remainder moved to join Rantzau on the right flank, while Sabine and Pallandt edged their infantry leftwards towards Herlegem, Schaerken and Groenewald to link up with Argyll's newly deploying troops. Meanwhile, Marlborough sent gallopers back along the road from Lessines, urging the toiling columns on. He was heartened by the inexplicable lack of a proper French response to his audacious coup, but was still heavily outnumbered on this side of the river, and the lack of direction and harmony amongst the French commanders could not be counted on to last.

Vendôme still had several perfectly good options open to him as the Allied troops poured across the Scheldt bridges. He could form line of battle on the heights of Huyshe and dare Marlborough to attack him there – it is unlikely that the Duke could have gathered his full force in time to do so before darkness fell on 11 July, so the French had ample time to prepare a good defence for the following day. Alternatively, the French army could continue its march towards Ghent and deploy a stout rearguard to cover its trains. In this way they could draw out of contact and stand to fight elsewhere on another day, while simultaneously protecting their precious conquests. However, best of all was still to attack the Allied bridgehead with all the considerable force they had at hand, and to drive Cadogan and Argyll and their few brigades of infantry to destruction in the Scheldt river.

A vigorous thrust by Vendôme at this point had every chance of succeeding. He had considerable superiority in numbers on the actual battlefield, and his soldiers were comparatively rested, unlike the panting Allied infantry stepping manfully out along the rough roads leading to the Scheldt. However, the antagonism between Vendôme and Burgundy, and the general astonishment felt at Marlborough's advance, fatally hampered the chances of an adequate response. Little effort was made to properly assess the threat the Allied thrust posed. The French leadership remained sadly divided and no attempt was made to form a concerted plan of action which, although time was pressing, was essential to any effective response.

As a result of this lamentable state of affairs, without any real effort to confer with each other, or to co-ordinate the actions of the Wings of their army, the French commanders allowed themselves to drift into a pitched infantry battle in the densely hedged close country around the Diepenbeek and Marollebeek Streams. This was the very kind of action which, with their superiority of cavalry, they should have avoided and which Louis XIV had explicitly warned against in one of his frequent instructions to his generals in the field. Conversely, despite his lack of numbers at the initial point of contact, Marlborough had by speed and daring firmly fixed Vendôme, forcing him to commit to battle in unfavourable circumstances. Lacking proper direction, the French army, although at this stage vastly more numerous and first on the ground, was obliged to stand and fight at Marlborough's bidding.

Shortly after the news reached Burgundy of Rantzau's impudent success in driving in the French cavalry on the left, the indignant young Duke ordered six battalions of infantry from the right Wing of the army forward to the hamlet of Groenewald. From that point they would threaten Cadogan's left flank, which was still exposed as he re-formed and extended his battle-line to cover the Marollebeek Stream. Argyll's infantry were still moving forward across the meadows from the Scheldt bridges, and could be brushed aside with a vigorous effort.

The French infantry attack took time to arrange, but shortly after 4.00 pm, as their leading infantry advanced through the orchards and gardens near Groenewald, they ran into two battalions of Prussians, just released by Argyll's arrival from guard duty at the pontoon bridges. The French were coming on in dense battalion columns – due to the close country it was difficult to find a place to form. The Prussians, although outnumbered, were already in line and had a distinct advantage in the initial exchanges of fire. A vicious close-range musketry battle blew up with astonishing speed. Both sides were using versions of the highly effective platoon firing method to deliver continuous fire, but the Prussians were rather more proficient at this technique. The crumbling effect of their fire forced the French to fall back northwards towards Mullem to re-form their battered ranks. Here Vendôme, who had yet to confer with Burgundy, came upon them. Outraged at their repulse, he ordered up another six battalions to join them in a renewed attack, and soon afterwards personally led twelve more battalions on foot into the escalating French assault towards Groenewald.

The Prussian infantry were a tough lot, and their remaining two battalions soon came up from the bridges to join in the fight for the hamlet. They were well posted behind hedges and fences, and their volleys tumbled the onrushing French soldiers down in large numbers, but by 5.00 pm Vendôme's heavy attack succeeded in driving them away from Groenewald. These were the last uncommitted troops Cadogan had in hand to deploy, and all now depended upon the Duke of Argyll. As the hamlet fell to the French, he at last got his battle-line in place, extending the Allied left along the Marollebeek Stream with sixteen Hanoverian and Hessian and four British battalions. As they were coming into action opposite Vendôme's right flank, the French were now, in their turn, in danger of being enveloped from that direction. Frustrated and furious, all the French commander's soldierly ardour was now thoroughly aroused. Half-pike in hand, he thrust more and more battalions from the right Wing of the French army – the French and Swiss Guards, the renowned

Régiment du Roi, the Picardie, Royal Roussillon, Alsace, Saintonge and Guyenne Régiments – into the battle along the boggy streams.

The fighting was blunt and bloody, the veteran troops standing in ragged lines and exchanging volleys and bayonet thrusts at close range. It was a pure infantry battle, there was little for the artillery to do in the close country, and for the same reason the cavalry were onlookers for the most part. Junior commanders on both sides exerted themselves selflessly in the ordering and arranging of their companies in the confusing and tangled lanes and gardens. Each French regiment, as it hurried into line, found an opposing Allied battalion, hot and dusty from the line of march, forming up to meet it. The smoke hung heavily between the hedges, a dusky pall shot through with the flash of musketry volleys and the glint of bayonets. The pace was dramatic and hectic, but every time Argyll's British and German troops lapped around the French right flank, they found their opponents breaking through hedges and leaping ditches to get into place to hold them.

Spontaneously, the battle lines opened out like a great fan from Herlegem and Groenewald towards Schaerken and the gardens and orchards beyond. By calling on every unit at hand, at 5.30 pm Vendôme had achieved a local tactical superiority with fifty battalions in line, opposed by only the thirty-six Allied battalions of Cadogan and Argyll. Now was a vital opportunity for the French commander to strike with all his available force and sweep Marlborough's exposed vanguard into the wide waters of the Scheldt.

Such a mighty stroke required proper co-ordination, and Vendôme was embroiled in the infantry battle. Still, as this teeming and confused struggle raged on, he sent an aide, Captain Jenet, to find Burgundy. Vendôme demanded that he order the left Wing of the army, still standing inactive on the high ground behind the Norken Stream, to strike southwards along the Ghent road and rout the Allied troops holding the right flank. This spot was increasingly vulnerable as the fighting spread away to the west, for the Allied centre of gravity shifted with it – Cadogan's infantry had increasingly and necessarily been pulled away from the right by Vendôme's attacks on Groenewald. Allied infantry were pouring down the hill from Eename to the pontoon bridges, but they needed time to get into place. At this moment Vendôme's gallant soldiers were holding the battle-line of Cadogan and Argyll firmly in position, so Marlborough was fighting at full stretch with not a soldier to spare.

Only Rantzau's Hanoverian dragoons (rather battered and blown) and Natzmer's twenty Prussian squadrons guarded the right flank of the Allied army on the Ghent road. Henry Lumley's British cavalry was on the road at Bevere, watching the left flank and the exit points from Oudenarde. Fleetingly, and for a second time that afternoon, the French had a chance to use the uncommitted left Wing of their army and sweep along the bank of the Scheldt and roll up the Allied army. Now was the moment for Burgundy to strike.

The Duke of Burgundy at this time seems to have been unaware of the escalating extent of Vendôme's attack. Taking position with his entourage (which included his younger brother, the Duc de Berri, and the Pretender to the English throne, the Chevalier de St George) on high ground near the windmill at Royegem behind the Norken, he watched in apparent puzzlement as if he were just an observer of the dramatic events unfolding in the close country ahead. The field of view from Royegem, or from the heights of Huyshe nearby, was not particularly good, as the undulations and folds in the terrain put much of it in dead ground to any onlooker. But any competent commander must get to where he can see what is going on. The smoke and noise from the savage infantry battle stretching westwards from Groenewald added greatly to the general confusion, and the sheer rapidity with which events were taking place defied the inexperienced young man's ability to make firm and calm decisions. The deferential staff officers clustering at his elbow, many of them veterans of long campaigns, appeared pathetically reluctant to offer advice.

In fairness, Burgundy was by no means entirely idle, and he made some attempts to re-establish control within the French army. Shortly after 5.00 pm he requested the Marquis de Grimaldi, with sixteen squadrons of cavalry under command, to move forward to Vendôme's support. Puysegur again made his baleful influence felt by assuring Burgundy that the ground in front along the Norken Stream was quite impassable (on what authority he had this information is very unclear). The leading squadron, under Colonel Sisterne, soon trod marshy water and, rather tamely, the advance was called off. The difficult country between Groenewald and Schaerken certainly offered little scope for effective mounted action, but thereafter the thousands of soldiers of the French left Wing watched, as if fascinated, while Vendôme's troops fought a pitched battle against the increasingly powerful Allied army. Nothing was done to help them. Captain Jenet was sent back with the grim news, but this unfortunate officer was killed on the way, and Vendôme was never told that he had to fight on alone. The old Marshal held his valiant infantrymen to their terrible task all that late afternoon and evening, while the shadows lengthened and Marlborough's army outreached and overwhelmed them.

In spite of the folly of these misunderstandings, the ferocity of the French assault showed no signs of slowing, for the cream of their infantry were engaged here. The conduct of Vendôme's men deserves high praise, but again and again the disciplined volleys of the massing Allied infantry broke up their attacks. Argyll's line was now extended towards the ruined château of Brouwaan by Count Lottum's twenty Prussian and Hanoverian battalions as they came doubling breathlessly over the pontoon bridges. Despite this the French troops closed up the gaps in their ranks and came on afresh, once more and once more, and the success of the day hung dangerously in the balance as Marlborough's infantry tired, and threatened to give way. Still, the Duke was always at hand, exposed and conspicuous with a small escort in the smoke and din – calmly giving instructions to his commanders, showing the newly arrived battalions where to form, and the best position to be taken in the line of battle.

The Allied right was now under the command of Prince Eugene, while Marlborough controlled the line of battle stretching towards Brouwaan on the left. At about 6.00 pm some relief for the battered Allied infantry was received, as eighteen fresh Hessian, Saxon and Hanoverian battalions streamed along the road from Lessines. Marlborough promptly put them into place to bolster Lottum's soldiers on the left. Then, with great confidence in the abilities of his junior commanders, he deftly extracted Lottum's battalions from the firing line. His soldiers left their regimental colours in place to deceive the French (rather as the British infantry had done at Ramillies), and quickly re-ordered their ranks. Grabbing handfuls of ammunition from quartermasters standing at the roadside, they strode off to the right flank to bolster Cadogan's infantry in the increasingly desperate battle for Groenewald and Herlegem. This was just as well, for by 6.30 pm those hamlets were entirely in French hands, and the right flank of the Allied line was threatening to collapse. Lottum's arrival steadied the situation and Groenewald at least was recovered after a fierce hand-to-hand struggle. So neatly was this crucial movement carried out, that Vendôme was unaware of any switch in the Allied effort from left to right.

During the afternoon, Marlborough learned from his scouts (almost certainly drawn from Lumley's British cavalry, at that time still on the Allied left flank)[13] that the Boser Couter hill, overlooking the battlefield from the west, was unoccupied. He discussed this with Count Overkirk, the commander of the Dutch and Danish troops of the left Wing of the army. These men were still on the march from Lessines, but the Duke gave Overkirk instructions to take his powerful corps, comprising twenty-four battalions of infantry and twelve squadrons of cavalry, past the hamlet of Oycke and onto the hill, to turn the right flank of the French army. Marlborough expected this to take place by about 6.00pm, but to his great frustration nothing seemed to happen.

All that dangerous summer afternoon, Marlborough was looking over his shoulder towards the road from Lessines, awaiting the arrival of Overkirk's columns. At last, disappointingly late, these soldiers in their blue and grey coats came teeming over the brow of the hill and down to Oudenarde town. Directed to the two stone bridges and the two pontoon bridges erected earlier in the day, the soldiers were then caught up in an awful bottleneck in the narrow streets which maddeningly delayed their progress. Perhaps the pontoon bridges so hastily thrown up earlier in the day were unequal to the task, for at least one collapsed. It was not until about 7.00 pm that Overkirk's troops began to move out of the town past Bevere and onto the Boser Couter. Even then the twelve squadrons of Danish cavalry under Count Tilly had trouble getting into place, apparently finding it difficult to negotiate a belt of trees, and it took British officers to lead them into position.[14]

While this was done, Marlborough's line of battle remained under intense French pressure. He urgently sent to Overkirk for some support in the battle which raged on with astonishing and unabated fury around the château at Brouwaan. Badly outnumbered here, the weary Allied soldiers were beginning to give way in face of a fresh French attack. Overkirk promptly responded to Marlborough's request for support – 'Avec la docilite d'un subalterne'[15] – and he detached Major-General Week with eight Dutch battalions (the Nassau-Woudenburg Regiment and a brigade of the Dutch Guards) from the line of march onto the hill, to move down from Oycke towards Brouwaan. These troops wheeled into line and moved swiftly across the slopes to the seething battle. The right-hand-most battalion of Dutch Guards had the château immediately to their front, and the French were suddenly taken in flank and driven back. Their line was now refused and bent at a sharp angle back upon itself, as they struggled to avoid envelopment by Overkirk's accelerating attack.

In the smoke and dust, and the fading daylight, it is not at all certain what the French officers can have made of the Dutch and Danish troop movements across the Boser Couter. Much of the hill is so gently sloping that soldiers crossing the feature would not be in dead ground to an alert observer in the fields along the streams below. In the event, no one seems to have taken much notice of them and the sudden arrival of Week's column both shook the French and steadied the hard pressed Hessian and Saxon soldiers. Vendôme's commanders found that, once again, they were threatened with envelopment and were thrown back away from the Diepenbeek Stream.

Meanwhile, time had to be bought for Marlborough's infantry as the Dutch and the Danes moved steadily into position on the Boser Couter. At 7.00 pm he instructed Lumley to take the seventeen squadrons of British cavalry from Bevere, where Overkirk's arrival had made their watch on the road from Oudenarde superfluous, across the rear of the army to join Eugene on the right flank. As this fresh support came up, the Prince immediately ordered forward Natztmer's twenty squadrons (the same Prussian troopers who had escorted Marlborough along the road from Lessines) in a daring attack on the French left flank around Herlegem.

The grimy line of Allied infantry opened briefly to allow the Prussian cuirassiers and gendarmes to advance to their left front. Their charge across the Ghent road met with swift initial success (the rapid progress of these horsemen demonstrating Puysegur's complete error in warning against an advance by the French cavalry over pretty well the same ground earlier in the day). Natzmer's squadrons pierced the line of opposing cavalry and, edging to their right, charged and broke two French battalions and went on to over-run a battery of guns in quick order. The scattered French battalions lost their colours and the guns were abandoned as the crews fled towards Royegem.

In the excitement Natzmer was unable to hold his squadrons together and, almost inevitably, they went too far. Raked with canister from a concealed French battery, they were then struck by a violent counter-charge by superior numbers of the scarlet-clad Maison du Roi, who came teeming forward from their position near Royegem. The Prussians were overwhelmed and scattered, while Natzmer was surrounded in the mêlée and, despite his own swordsmanship, was repeatedly cut about the head. He narrowly escaped with his life, leaping his mount over a water-filled ditch in which at least one dead horse lay. Many of Natzmer's troopers were ridden down in the pursuit by the elite French cavalrymen, and his squadrons were sadly depleted as they sought sanctuary behind Cadogan's battle-line between Herlegem and Groenewald. The blown French squadrons, wisely, did not press their counter-attack, as Lumley's British cavalry and Rantzau's Hanoverian squadrons patiently awaited them. This dashing Prussian exploit, although very expensive in men, gained a respite for the Allied army as Overkirk readied himself for his attack. Once again the attention of the French commanders was directed away from the really important spot by the dynamic actions of their opponents.

Schaerken was now ablaze as the Allied infantry drove forward in dogged determination. Many of the French wounded, who had hoped to find shelter in the outbuildings, were burned to death. John Deane, who took part in the ferocious action, remembered that:

> Our forces pressing vehemently on them at once gave then such a vigorous attacque and furiously rushing into the village, drove them cleanly out of the village, setting some of the houses on fire in wch, the enemy put abundance of their wounded.[16]

Meanwhile, at the other end of the battlefield Tilly and the Swedish soldier, Count Oxenstiern, arranged their squadrons and regiments on the Boser Couter, comfortably aware that they faced the raw, open right flank of the French army. There was no formed body of troops to oppose them.

The extraordinary climax of the day, perceived with clarity by Marlborough early in the afternoon, and held in his mind throughout the anxious hours of battle, was now at hand. In his skilful and determined hands, the entire Allied battle-line pressed forward, holding the tough French infantry in an iron grip. At 8.00 pm Overkirk gave the word and Tilly and his Danish cavalry swept down from the high ground behind the right flank of the French army. Simultaneously, Oxenstiern struck against the right flank of Vendôme's infantry line, between Brouwaan and Schaerken, with sixteen Dutch battalions. Simultaneously, and in complete accord with Marlborough's unfolding plan, Eugene urged Cadogan's infantry forward in a fresh effort, past the smoking ruins of Groenewald and Herlegem on the right flank, heading inwards towards the windmill at Royegem.

The cavalry of the Maison du Roi, a little ragged and blown after their hectic pursuit of Natzmer, now attempted to change front along the line of the Norken Stream to counter Tilly's rushing squadrons. They were badly out of position and unable to offer any particularly effective reply to the new attack. All of a sudden, Vendôme's flanks were turned both right and left, and he was entirely off balance and in peril. It began to rain.

From his vantage point at the windmill, the Duke of Burgundy and his noble entourage could not decide how to respond to these awful events. The Allies apparently called on an endless stream of troops to join the fast paced infantry battle raging in the low ground before them; long lines of British and Hanoverian cavalry, dimly visible and impressively motionless behind the smoking shambles of Groenewald, plainly indicated the weight of reserves available to their opponents. The red-coated British infantry had turned the left flank of his army, now the thunderbolt of Overkirk's great attack came boring in on the right. The drizzle and growing twilight added to the confusion as Burgundy stood irresolute, for this thrust came from such an unexpected direction, and threatened to encircle the whole right Wing of the French army. To the dazed watchers at the windmill, it seemed in the failing light that Vendôme's battalions were being gradually encircled by glowing snakes of spitting fire.

The Duke of Burgundy had troops in plenty at hand, for the left Wing of the army was hardly engaged all day, but he had not the experience or presence of mind to use them to any effect. He certainly shifted some grenadiers and dragoons to meet the new Allied attack, but it was a wholly inadequate response. Had the veteran soldier Vendôme been at his side to assess the threat and offer firm directions, things might have been so much better for the French that day. Instead they were separately responding to Marlborough's dictation of the battle. Standing so far outside the Duke's devastatingly effective decision-making cycle, Burgundy and his hapless staff were frozen in the face of unbelievable catastrophe. This magnificent French army, numerous and well equipped and under the command of a veteran general, was simply being shaken to pieces by Marlborough in the smoky evening twilight. Mrs Christian Davies remembered:

> The French were driven from hedge to hedge and everywhere trodden underfoot; however, they behaved very gallantly and defended every inch of ground, till, being taken in the rear by 18

152

battalions and some horse, they began to lose courage, quitted the field, where they left a great number of dead.

Sergeant Milner of the Royal Regiment of Ireland, wrote:

> ... we drove the enemy from ditch to ditch and from hedge to hedge, and from one scrub to another.[17]

At 8.30 pm, as the Dutch and the Danes pressed ever closer to Royegem, Burgundy decided that his party at the windmill was in too exposed a spot. What command and control the army had enjoyed that day was now gone anyway, with battalions and squadrons fighting as best they could manage in the teeming confusion that was now the French right Wing. Burgundy and his party called their aides, mounted their horses and rode off for a safer spot along the Ghent road. Gradually, the left Wing of their army trickled off past them, looking to find sanctuary in Ghent and Bruges – those very same towns that had welcomed them so warmly as liberators only a few days before.

The delays on the line of march that Overkirk encountered, and the exasperating struggle to get his men into position on the Boser Couter, meant that Marlborough narrowly missed the complete destruction of Vendôme's army. The Duke could not hold back the onset of night, and soldiers on both sides were now volleying into their comrades in the wet and smoky twilight of evening, as the Wings of the Allied army closed towards each other below the heights of Huyshe. At one point Cadogan's British soldiers exchanged shots with Oxenstiern's Dutch infantry near Huyshe itself. As darkness fell, Marlborough called his troops to halt, and the process of scooping up French prisoners in the tangled gardens began.

Vendôme, grimy with exertion, blackened with powder and smeared with blood, joined Burgundy and his lordly party on the Ghent road at about 10.00 pm. The two French commanders had not spoken to one another since before 2.00 pm that day and they now exchanged hot and bitter words of recrimination. Vendôme charged the young Duke with cravenly watching a battle being fought before his very eyes without moving to his general's aid. He protested that he found it amazing that 30,000 Frenchmen had thought fit to stand by while an army fought for its life all afternoon in front of them.

Burgundy let the cutting insults pass, to the dismay of his own aides, while the older man raved on in his anger and frustration. At last, controlling himself with difficulty, Vendôme demanded that the intact left Wing of the army be gathered together on the heights of Huyshe and readied to renew the struggle with the dawn. Burgundy replied that the army was disordered, which was true, and the troops were short of ammunition. This lack seems unlikely, but Burgundy insisted that nothing but a retreat would do. Puysegur and Matignon galloped up at that point, and they supported Burgundy's view. Perhaps they understood rather better than the hot-headed Marshal did, what terrible moral and physical blows their army had suffered. Vendôme shouted at those around him, urging that the battle be resumed and calling on them to support him, but they heard him without making reply. The general fell silent for a moment; then he bitterly gave his consent to the withdrawal, spitting out the insulting and venomous words at Burgundy: 'And you, Monsieur, have long had that wish.'[18]

Vendôme took himself off through the drizzle to Ghent in a rage of frustration, apparently oblivious of the ordering of his army during its withdrawal. Dismounting outside his quarters in the town, he grossly and insultingly relieved the needs of nature in the road, in full view of his staff, and went off to bed and slept for a full thirty hours, giving no orders and calling for no reports in his neglect. Marshal Matignon was left to arrange the withdrawal of the battered army, and in the dismal darkness this was a nightmarish task, which he accomplished with competent skill.

Below the Boser Couter hill, throughout the wet night, the rounding up of dazed French prisoners proceeded. Deluded by bogus drum beats, and calls of encouragement in French from Huguenot officers in Allied service, large numbers of prisoners strayed into Marlborough's hands. As it was, many more French soldiers escaped encirclement and capture than might have been expected. Colonel De La Colonie, whose brigade served with the left Wing of Vendôme's army that day, wrote: 'Our army did not quit the field until two o'clock [12 July] and then directed its march upon Ghent.'[19] So, it is apparent that there was no clean break between the opposing forces. Much activity, coming and going, brushes between pickets and skirmishes, went on across and around the dark and wet battlefield well into the night. Soldiers in both armies stumbled and fumbled to find their regiment or squadron and, given the extreme nature of the conflict, this was unavoidable.

The merciful and baffling cloak of night hid a good deal, and General St Hilaire, the French artillery commander, whose crews had little opportunity for action that day, brought off almost all his guns safely to Ghent. The next morning, the Marquis de Nangis (who had conducted an amusing, and not very innocent, intrigue with the young and sprightly Duchess of Burgundy in the recent past) found the squadrons of cavalry from the left Wing standing at their posts along the track from Gavre to Huyshe. They were apparently forgotten in the general flight of their commanders. After various adventures, the Marquis brought this immensely valuable body of cavalry, which must have numbered at least 5,000 troopers, to the safety of the French encampment at Leeuwarden, a small town on the Ghent–Bruges Canal.[20]

In the damp light of dawn on 12 July, the Allied soldiers were roused from their sodden brief bivouacs on the battlefield. Looking around them they found only the wreckage of the French army – the dead, maimed and bemused. Once again, Marlborough's soldiers stood as victors on a field of battle. The dangers, frustrations and delays of the previous day were forgotten as the process of gathering the prisoners and booty continued, but John Deane wrote: 'The dead lye in every hole and corner and to hear the cryes of the wounded was saddening.'[21]

Vendôme and Burgundy lost about 5,500 men killed and wounded at Oudenarde, with another 9,000 unwounded prisoners being captured. Amongst these captives were nearly 800 officers, and over 100 regimental colours and standards, 4,500 horses and mules and ten pairs of kettle-drums were taken by Marlborough's army. In addition large numbers of Vendôme's soldiers were fleeing as fugitives towards the safety of the nearest French garrison. They were now at the mercy of the peasantry upon whom they had so often imposed themselves. Once again, as after Elixheim and Ramillies, to be a French soldier in the Spanish Netherlands was, for many, to be a fugitive.

Marlborough's losses that day amounted to 2,972 killed and wounded (of whom only some 230 were Britons) – an extraordinarily modest figure considering the severity and scale of the infantry battle. These losses were soon made good by defections and desertions from France's allies, and many experienced Swiss, Walloon and German soldiers enlisted for the Allied cause in the wake of Vendôme's defeat.[22]

At 9.00 on the morning after the battle, 12 July 1708, Marlborough, who had spent the night in the rain on the battlefield, rode into the town square of Oudenarde to be received by Brigadier Chanclos. The place was teeming with French prisoners, and these men pressed curiously forward to glimpse this extraordinary general who had brought about their downfall. There was nothing threatening in their interest and the Duke graciously acknowledged them, doffing his hat to the salutes he received.

Those who had refused to back Vendôme the previous night may have appreciated that a large part of Marlborough's army was not yet on the battlefield. As many as a third of the Allied troops were still on the march, and long columns of men and guns continued to pour along the road from Lessines down to the bridges on the Scheldt. Marlborough probably got only about 60,000 troops into action on 11 July, while across the field the French left Wing had stood idle. The overall effect was that the troops actually engaged were probably about equal in numbers, but the mode of their employment was startlingly different. The Allied bridgehead could have been crushed several times over if the French commanders had only stirred themselves sufficiently before it was strengthened. Instead, Marlborough had seized the initiative and never let it slip.

A prompt pursuit of the beaten army was ordered, and forty squadrons of cavalry under Lumley and von Bulow, backed by thirty-four battalions of infantry commanded by Meredith, trooped along the road towards

Ghent. Here, a stout French rearguard was in place, backed by artillery and Pentz's Hanoverian dragoons, leading the Allied advance, were roughly handled and driven back.

Although the delay in Overkirk's turning movement, and the onset of darkness (unseasonably premature because of the drizzle) robbed Marlborough of the destruction of Vendôme's army that was planned, the French summer campaign was now in ruins. At 4.00 pm on 12 July 1708 Marlborough, after a few hours' snatched sleep, held a council of war with his commanders in the Governor's palace in Oudenarde. It was evident that the previous day's success had stripped away Vendôme's ability to take the initiative or to deploy effectively in the near future. His battered force was now widely separated from Berwick's approaching army, while the victorious Allies (soon to be reinforced by Eugene's troops as they approached Brussels) firmly held the ring in between. It remained to be seen what moves the astute Marshal Berwick would attempt to remedy the terrible situation that the French now faced. In the meantime, it was for Marlborough to dictate the pace of events in the coming campaign and glittering opportunities presented themselves. The northern border of France was starkly laid open to invasion, and a powerful Allied thrust might bring the war to an end.

Lord Stair, who had joined Rantzau in his tumultuous charge the previous day, was entrusted by Marlborough with the dispatch announcing the victory to Queen Anne in London. The Duke wrote: 'I hope I have given them such a blow to their foot that they will not be able to fight any more in this year.'[23] Stair was able to perfect his own account of the action that day while becalmed on board ship in the Channel. He subsequently received a purse of £1,000 from the Queen for bringing the glad news to London but the victory was greeted more with weary resignation and relief than joy. The world was becoming tired of the war, the costs and risks seemed to be never-ending, and taxation was heavy.

In France, on 11 July 1708, a sumptuous picnic had been arranged at Versailles to celebrate the capture of Ghent and Bruges by the Duke of Burgundy. News soon arrived that all was not well and that a great battle had been fought on the Scheldt river; no one yet knew the outcome with certainty. In Versailles Louis XIV prowled the state-rooms and waited anxiously for news from the field, opening every letter himself and scanning the pages swiftly. It was whispered that the great English Duke, whom the King remembered as the youthful 'Le Bel Anglais', had once again brought his army down – all that remained were for the doleful details to arrive. He finally received the news on 14 July, just after midday. Vendôme's battle-report, when it belatedly came, very dishonestly commented on the defeat his army had endured:

The enemy would not have been successful, had we not freely given them the victory by our retreat. We had gained some ground. I cannot comprehend how 50 battalions and 130 squadrons could be satisfied with observing us engaged for six hours and merely look on as though watching the opera. [24]

In this, at least, the French commander spoke with justice. Before long, many of Vendôme's generals also sent partial and somewhat untruthful accounts, each attempting to avoid the blame for the shameful mishandling of the army that day.

The French army was still in the field, more or less, but their losses and the damage to morale inevitably meant that it was crippled in offensive potential for the summer. With luck, the French could hold on to Ghent and Bruges, but they could hardly interrupt Marlborough's progress towards the French border. The Duke's telling comment to Sidney Godolphin in London was: 'Our greatest advantage consists in the fear that is amongst their troops.'[25]

The Duke of Berwick learned of the defeat of Vendôme and Burgundy from the French governor of Mons on 12 July 1708, when at Sart la Bussiere on the Sambre river. He pushed twenty squadrons of cavalry towards Mons itself, and sent his infantry marching to Valenciennes. His small army was now virtually the only immediate defence that France had against Marlborough. Berwick wrote afterwards of his immediate concerns:

> I went post haste to Tournai, to have a nearer view of the situation of things. There I found a great number of straggling parties of the army. Upon a review of them, the whole number at Tournai, Lille and Ypres, amounted to upwards of nine thousand men; the enemy had made as many prisoners. As it would be some days before my infantry could come up, and the frontier was entirely destitute of troops, I divided these parties amongst the three places. [He went on] It had always been found, that the loss of one battle was followed by that of all Flanders, for want of garrisons.[26]

In Oudenarde itself, Marlborough firstly gave instructions to Count Lottum to march with a strong force of cavalry and infantry to take the unoccupied French defensive lines between the Lys river and the fortress of Ypres. These works were to be levelled and made useless without delay, and the Count got on the march at midnight on 13 July. Berwick foresaw this likelihood and sent a mixed corps of foot and cavalry to interrupt Lottum's operation, but the Count got into place on 15 July and the work of destruction commenced. In this practical way the road to the French border was cleared for the Allied armies soon after the battle, and Marlborough could move forward to an advanced position beyond the

Lys. In contrast, Vendôme in sullen mood entrenched a defensive position for his battered army between Ghent and Bruges. A major tactical effort would be required for Marlborough to engage the French commander in these lines, with the shelter of the Ghent–Bruges Canal, and it seemed far more profitable for the Duke to let him languish in his failure. Elsewhere, on 16 July Eugene's Imperial infantry marched into Brussels, and the combined Allied army was now in the field. Marlborough wrote to the Secretary of State in London that evening:

> On Friday at midnight, we detached M. Lottum with forty squadrons and thirty battalions towards Menin, with orders to pursue his march directly towards the enemy's lines between Warneton and Ypres, and to endeavour to force them, and the army followed at break of day on Saturday morning. We are now levelling them. The enemy's army continues encamped behind the canal between Ghent and Bruges, whither they retired after the battle, but it is expected they will soon march this way to defend their frontiers. Our next care must be to re-possess Ghent, the lack of which obstructs the bringing up of our great artillery by water. The last of the foot of Prince Eugene's army arrived yesterday, near Brussels, where they joined the rest of his troops, and are to remain while the French continue near Ghent.[27]

The concentration of Eugene's army to the west of Brussels was a considerable relief to Marlborough. If Eugene were not there, at his back, the armies of Vendôme and Berwick could harry his lines of communication and supply without hindrance. The Prince was given the immediate task, not only of covering Marlborough's rear, but also of bringing forward supplies and heavy ordnance from Maastricht. Marlborough wrote to Secretary of State Boyle on 23 July 1708 that:

> We are at present at a stand for want of our heavy artillery, which we are using all possible diligence to bring up . . . in the meantime we are doing all we can to annoy the enemy . . . [they] continue to fortify themselves between Ghent and Bruges notwithstanding they have the canal before them, and we hear their troops are still under great consternation. [28]

By doggedly clinging to the line of the Ghent–Bruges canal, Vendôme managed to inconvenience Marlborough's arrangements. The Duke's concerns regarding transportation are clearly seen from his letters. The French commander, by making a virtue of the necessity of reconstituting his crippled army from a strong position of defence, in a quite subtle way managed to exert a drag on his opponent's freedom to exploit the recent success. In the meantime, by 30 July Lottum completed his work at levelling and spoiling the defensive lines along the Lys, and the main baggage of the Allied army came up from Brussels. With his forces now concentrated and re-equipped (but for his heavy guns) Marlborough could press his campaign onwards to the French frontier.

The Battle of Oudenarde was a pell-mell encounter battle with battalions rushing into the line instead of forming up neatly. It has few parallels in any period, let alone the eighteenth century, when set-piece engagements, with each commander consenting to the ordered onset of the fighting, were the norm. The forced marches, the ad hoc grouping of regiments and squadrons, the spontaneous and, on the French side, entirely unexpected explosion of violence along the streams, lanes, gardens and orchards at Oudenarde, were of a kind entirely novel in that age of formal battles. In the handling of this complex and adventurous operation, the contrast between the cool and harmonious conduct of Marlborough and Eugene and the fractious bickering between Vendôme and Burgundy could not be starker.

Despite the customary Thanksgiving Service for victory in St Paul's Cathedral in London, Queen Anne's tired response to the news of the battle – 'Oh, when will this dreadful bloodshed cease?' – provoked a particularly severe quarrel with the Duchess of Marlborough, who took exception to this lack of appreciation of her husband's efforts. The Duke's letter to his wife with the news of the victory was unfortunately worded, suggesting that the Queen was inclined to be unappreciative and Sarah did not hesitate to show her this letter. Indignant at the implied rebuke, Anne wrote to her Captain-General with crushing civility on 24 July 1708:

> You say after being thankful for being the instrument of so much good to the nation and to me, *if I would please to make use of it*. I am sure I will never make an ill use of so great a blessing . . . I should be glad to know what is the use you would have me make of it.

Not for nothing had Marlborough been a courtier and he wrote with urbane charm in reply on 2 August:

> Your Majesty might see, by the shortness of the letter that was shown you, that I was in great haste when I writ it, and my fullness of heart for your service made me use that expression.[29]

Such a fulsome and apologetic letter to the Queen would have smoothed things over nicely but, at one point on the way to the Thanksgiving Service, Sarah picked an argument with Anne over the choice of jewels to be worn that day. On stepping out of the coach at the steps of St Paul's, the Duchess then commanded the flustered Queen to be quiet, in the shocked hearing of others standing nearby. This was all very unfortunate for the security of Marlborough's position, both at Court and on campaign. Clouds of envy and intrigue were growing in London, where the Duke's Tory enemies worked cleverly to bring him down. Meanwhile, the valuable friendship between Duchess Sarah and the Queen became cold.

All the same, at that very moment in Flanders the Duke's armies were sweeping across the French border. He could now point to four significant victories on a large scale, in addition to smaller successes such as Elixheim. He had acquired a reputation for success – nothing less than victory was expected of the Captain-General.

Marlborough, who never ceased to look at the far horizon, had developed a great plan for a thrust by the combined Allied armies upon Paris itself. Supported by naval landings on the coast of the Pas de Calais and Normandy, the seizure of the French capital and, perhaps, Versailles itself, would be sure to bring the war to an end. However, imaginative as it was, this was undoubtedly also a risky enterprise. The Duke of Berwick was now at Menin, and could be counted upon to either harry the Allied advance from the flank, or to invade Brabant. In conjunction with Vendôme he might attempt to seize Brussels and Antwerp; perhaps even southern Holland would be invaded once more. Prince Eugene, often the most daring of commanders, was firmly against Marlborough's plan, as were many of his general officers. The Duke wrote to Godolphin: 'I have acquainted Prince Eugene with the earnest desire we have for our marching into France. He thinks it unpracticable till we have Lille.'[30] Disappointed, Marlborough gave way with his customary good grace, and turned his attention instead to the capture of that great and significant city of Lille, Vauban's defensive masterpiece.

The Oudenarde Battlefield Today

Modern development of Oudenarde has spread along the bank of the Scheldt river, so that the small hamlets of Eyne and Heurne are suburbs of the town. There is little sign of the marshy water-meadows across which Cadogan's infantry boldly advanced to drive in the Swiss in 1708, although groves of willow trees betray the natural wetness of the ground. Light industrial and commercial development along the main Ghent road has covered some of the battlefield along the line on which the armies of Marlborough and Vendôme fought it out toe-to-toe in 1708. However, most of the cultivated low-lying country below the heights of Huyshe and the Boser Couter hill, remain as smallholdings, farms and the gardens of small, attractive residential villas. The desperate and confused afternoon battle, fought along these lanes and hedges, may still be freely imagined.

The higher ground around the battlefield is largely undeveloped, and good vantage points can be found beside the (modern) windmill at Huyshe, and on the road past Oycke on the Boser Couter hill. It is easy to see how difficult Burgundy would find making any sense of the confused infantry battle below him – the folds in the ground hide much of the terrain, and on a moderately misty day (let alone in the drizzle, rain and failing light of evening) even an experienced field commander might be forgiven for hesitation and confusion. The view obtained from the Boser Couter, in particular, sets the whole battlefield nicely into perspective. Although the modern town intrudes on the scene to the south, it is plain what an enormous advantage Marlborough gained by firstly occupying this high ground, and then throwing Overkirk's corps of infantry and cavalry out around the exposed right flank of the French army.

NOTES

1. Marlborough letter to Queen Anne, dated 23 July 1708. Coxe, W, *Memoirs of the Duke of Marlborough*, Vol II, 1848, p. 280.
2. Chandler, D (ed.), *Captain Robert Parker and Comte de Mérode-Westerloo*, 1968, p. 201.
3. Murray, G, (ed.), *Letters and Dispatches of the Duke of Marlborough*, Vol IV, 1845, p. 100.
4. Atkinson, C T (ed.), *Gleanings from the Cathcart Mss*, JSAHR, 1951, p. 65.
5. *Letters and Dispatches*, p. 110. Written in camp at Herfelingen. The Duke delayed posting the letter by a day, so that he could update those in London with the news of the march to battle.
6. The use of pontoon bridges, copper plated 'tin boats', mounted on wagons and dragged along the muddy or dusty roads with great effort, was highly developed in both armies. Despite their clumsiness they could be rapidly laid over quite wide obstacles and greatly aided tactical mobility in this area of dense rivers and canals.
7. Belfield, E, *Oudenarde 1708*, 1972, p. 49.
8. Churchill, W S, *Marlborough, His Life and Times*, Vol III, 1947, p. 358.
9. Schaerken is variously described as a village, cabaret, hamlet and inn. Coxe refers to it as a public house, but the place was actually a brothel. Modern residents of Oudenarde confirm that Schaerken was indeed once a house of ill repute.
10. Atkinson, p.67; *Letters and Dispatches*, p. 110.
11. Chandler, D (ed.), *Journal of John Deane*, JSAHR, 1984, p. 61.
12. Ibid., p.59. Deane makes it plain that his own regiment, the 1st English Foot Guards, were marched through Oudenarde town and not across the pontoon bridges downstream. Despite this time consuming detour, the soldiers got into place in time enough to make their mark in the line of battle.
13. Atkinson, p.66.
14. Ibid. Lumley's British cavalry watched over the exits from Oudenarde, and guarded the Allied left flank, for much of the afternoon. As Vendôme had little, if any, cavalry on this flank they were not heavily engaged, but Marlborough usefully employed them to scout the routes over the Boser Couter hill.
15. Edwards, H, *A Life of Marlborough*, 1926, p. 220.
16. *Journal of John Deane*, p. 61.
17. Churchill, p. 382; Defoe, D (ed. J Fortescue), *Life and Adventures of Mrs Christian Davies*, 1929, p. 99.

18. Belfield, p. 65; Churchill, p.379.
19. De La Colonie, J (ed. W Horsley), *Chronicles of an Old Campaigner*, 1904, p. 329.
20. Norton, L, *First Lady of Versailles*, 1978, p. 267; Churchill, p.380.
21. *Journal of John Deane*, pp. 62 and 86. Deane also gives an interesting account of the fate of soldiers falling into the hands of the 'Boors' or peasantry who had for so long suffered the attentions of the campaigning armies: 'A corporal of the Hanovers they hanged up dead in a tree'.
22. The pressing need for veteran soldiers was so great at this time that a bounty of two pistoles was offered to any French soldier who came across to change his coat. A bounty of two crowns was awarded to any Allied soldier who brought a deserter in to the colours. Amongst those captured at Oudenarde were numbers of Allied soldiers (including Britons) who had been taken prisoner at Almanza in Spain the previous year, and subsequently pressed into French service. It seems that they were allowed to return to their true allegiance without too close a questioning – an interesting indulgence granted to common soldiers at that time, in certain matters – but then, veteran soldiers are hard to come by, and should not be wasted. See Atkinson C T, *Queen Anne's Army*, JSAHR, 1958, p. 58.
23. Coxe, pp. 271–4; Churchill, p.382.
24. Chandler, D, *Marlborough as Military Commander*, 1973, p. 222; Churchill, p. 390.
25. Churchill, pp. 390–1.
26. Petrie, C. *The Marshal, Duke of Berwick*, 1953, p. 229.
27. *Letters and Dispatches*, p. 112.
28. *Letters and Dispatches*, p. 126.
29. Churchill, pp. 413–5.
30. Churchill, p. 399; Trevelyan, G M, *Ramillies and the Union with Scotland*, 1948, p. 368. Marlborough readily amended his plans to accommodate his comrade's concerns about by-passing a major fortress like Lille. See *Letters and Dispatches*, p. 147.

CHAPTER X
Terrible Dark Winter
The Great Frost and the Missed Peace

Two of our sentinels were found frozen to death.[1]

In the high summer of 1708 Marlborough began a vast and complex campaign to capture Lille, the most important city in northern France. The city itself and the great citadel, each a masterpiece of military engineering, were held by the 64-year-old Marshal Boufflers and a strong French garrison. From the east Marlborough's nephew, the Duke of Berwick, manoeuvred to obstruct and disrupt the Allied campaign, and a determined attempt was made by him to seize Brussels. To the north the Duke of Vendôme tried to hinder the flow of supplies and reinforcements which sustained the Allied operations. Marlborough skilfully countered all these threats, but the siege operations were time-consuming and expensive in manpower, and the casualties were heavy amongst the attackers. Prince Eugene was one of those shot and wounded in the Allied trenches, and the elderly Count Overkirk died from strain.

Lille surrendered after an epic defence on 25 October 1708. The citadel held out under Boufflers until 9.00 pm on 9 December, when he signed the capitulation, and the garrison marched out on honourable terms, two days later. The Allies went on to recapture both Ghent and Bruges in late December and early January 1709, when the French commanders rather tamely capitulated, and control was re-established over northern Flanders. This was a particular disappointment to Louis XIV for, even after the fall of Lille, he had hoped to retain control of this important area, exerting pressure on Marlborough's communications. At last the weary troops could trudge off to their winter quarters, unusually late in the season.

The soldiers of all armies found shelter not a moment too soon, for the winter of 1708/9 was one of the most severe on record. There was widespread famine and distress in Europe, pack-ice blocked the English Channel and ice sheets formed on the Rhone river in southern France. The vines died of frost in Avignon, and soldiers expired of the bitter cold while on the march. In Versailles wine froze in the glass even though fires were blazing in the hearth. Mrs Christian Davies wrote: 'A very great frost immediately followed the taking of Ghent and two of our sentinels were found frozen to death.'[2] The French, so worn down by war and taxes, were in a terrible state in those appallingly cold months; their harvest had failed in 1708 and vital imports of grain purchased from North Africa were captured or sent to the bottom of the Mediterranean by the ships of the Royal Navy, prowling out of newly captured harbours at Gibraltar in southern Spain and Port Mahon, Minorca. Marllborough's armies had ravaged Artois and Picardy and there was famine in much of France.

Back in London, in the spring of 1709 Marlborough asked Queen Anne to appoint him as Captain-General for Life. In this way his position would be made secure against spiteful attacks at home, and his standing in the courts and council chambers abroad would be enhanced. Whatever the merits of the request, he chose a bad time. The Queen was thoroughly exasperated with the ill temper of her old friend, Duchess Sarah, and she had tired of the war. Those same enemies against whom the Duke wished to secure himself increasingly enjoyed her confidence, and they muttered that what he intended was enthronement of 'King John' when the crown became available. The Queen had little hesitation in turning down Marlborough's request, perhaps remembering that the last man to hold the post had been a Cromwellian soldier, George Monck. Of course, the refusal soon became common knowledge and Marlborough's standing was diminished accordingly.

By this time, the Grand Alliance had effectively won the war with France. In the most important theatre of the war, the Spanish Netherlands, the French armies were baffled and beaten, morale was low and the ranks were thin. Louis XIV's treasury was empty and his Marshals were in despair. Negotiations were in progress at the Hague to conclude an agreement for peace. The great King would accept whatever terms were asked of him – he would cede territory and fortresses (Alsace and Picardy were to be sacrificed), French-held territory in Italy would be abandoned, as would the lucrative trade with the Americas. His troops would be removed from Spain. Most importantly, he would accept the Habsburg Archduke Charles's claim to the throne in Madrid, at the expense of that of his own grandson, Philip. The Allies were confident of success. Marlborough wrote to Sir Philip Meadows on 31 May 1709:

> I am now glad to acquaint you that after many tedious conferences we have at last, I hope, brought our affairs to a happy issue, and that the Allies will soon reap the fruits of this bloody and expensive war. We have agreed upon the [peace] preliminaries but the French Ministers pretending there are some articles to which they are not authorized to give their consent, M de Torcy went from here on Tuesday for Paris to lay the whole before his master.[3]

The Grand Alliance badly misjudged matters, failing to see that they had to deal not with one king, but with two. Philip V of Spain (every bit a grandson of Louis XIV) was proving to be rather popular with his adopted people, and he really had no intention of abandoning them. Still, this was what the Allies insisted upon – the cry 'No Peace without Spain', first coined in England, found a ready audience in their victorious capitals. A clumsy and ultimately deadly provision, Clause 37, was included in the draft peace treaty sent for the French King to consider. This clause required him to use his own troops to go and depose his grandson if the young man refused to abdicate the throne in Madrid.

After the defeat at Oudenarde, the loss of Lille and the ravages of the terrible Great Frost, Louis XIV genuinely considered that he should agree to all the terms presented by his enemies. The alternative seemed almost certain ruin for France. However, in the Great Council in Versailles, his eldest son, the Grand Dauphin, bitterly condemned the fatal Clause 37, so injurious to the interest of his own son. He rounded on those advisers present who urged its acceptance, and pointedly reminded them that, one day, they would answer to him as their King, and that it was his own blood that they sought to deprive of the throne. Glaring at his father, the Dauphin declared that a King of France might make war on his enemies, but should not do so on his grandchildren. Those in the room were aghast at the unprecedented confrontation, but Louis XIV was profoundly moved by the Dauphin's passionate declaration. The treaty was returned to the Hague, rejected in its absolute entirety.

Meanwhile, the Allies, made careless and arrogant by success, were waiting for the French King's acceptance of their terms. They had pointlessly set a deadline of 1 June 1709 for an answer, and arrangements for the disbanding of their armies were underway. When news of the rejected treaty was brought, all were appalled at its implications. An astonished Marlborough commented: 'What! And is there then no counter-proposal?' No, there was none – desperate as she was, France would fight on, even if it meant destruction.[4]

The disgraced Duke of Vendôme had been posted elsewhere, and Marshal Villars was appointed to command the French army in Flanders.[5] Flamboyant, boastful, energetic and skilful, the Gascon soldier faced an immense task. Everything from trained men to horseshoes was in short supply, and the French soldiers, both high and low, had become wearily used to being beaten by Marlborough. Spirits were low and the officers had been selling their coats to get bread for the men. Ironically, gaunt recruits were pouring in to fill the depleted regiments for soldiers must be fed. Louis XIV remarked rather sadly that the young men only followed the bread carts, but this does them less than justice, as the coming campaign would demonstrate. Although his army was downhearted and badly equipped, Villars' enormous energy and popularity came into full play. His enthusiasm was infectious, and he openly commandeered bread to feed the army and bullied contractors into replacing arms and supplies. The morale of the French soldiers steadily revived.

NOTES

1. Defoe, D (ed. J Fortescue), *Life and Adventures of Mrs Christian Davies*, 1929, p. 122.
2. Ibid.
3. Murray, G (ed), *Letters and Dispatches of the Duke of Marlborough,* Vol IV, 1845, p 499.
4. Churchill, W S, *Marlborough: His Life and Times,* Vol IV, 1947, pp 548–50. The Duke had not forgotten his duty in eager anticipation of peace. The Allied army remained at twenty hours' notice to march throughout the entire period.
5. The Duke of Vendôme went to command an army in Spain, where he enjoyed considerable success before his death three years later.

CHAPTER XI

A Very Murdering Battle
The Battle of Malplaquet,
Wednesday 11 September 1709

In the heat of battle there was little quarter given on either side.[1]

At the end of June 1709 Marlborough's army deployed across the Plain of Lille. The start of the new campaign was later than usual; a product of the rigours of the recent winter campaign, and the delays caused by the abortive recent peace negotiations. Strong contingents of fresh troops joined the Duke's army as Allied princes clamoured to take part in his victorious progress, and he had over 110,000 men under command. The French army, under Marshal Villars, could field only about 90,000 troops. Villars was hampered not only by lack of numbers, but by the certain knowledge that he commanded virtually the only viable field army left to France. While Vendôme, Berwick and others had forces elsewhere, France's army along her northern border was the one on which all her war effort now depended. King Louis XIV wrote to Villars at this time: 'All I have left is my confidence in God and in you, my outspoken friend.'[2]

This imposed caution on the normally adventurous Marshal, and he stuck to the entrenched Lines of La Bassée stretching the forty miles or so from Aire to Douai. The strength of these works was enhanced by the winding course of the Lys and Scarpe rivers, and the poor weather that summer added greatly to the marshy obstacles behind which the French army could shelter.

Faced with such stout obstacles, Marlborough could see that an attempt to force open battle on Villars was unlikely to succeed. He turned instead against the important French fortress of Tournai on the Escaut (Scheldt) river. This modest opening to the new Allied campaign, just one more siege rather than a grand advance with his huge army, indicates very well the problem Marlborough faced after the hard winter. Taking the field so late in the year, he would have insufficient time to achieve anything very considerable before the onset of the next season of cold weather. Villars

167

recognised this difficulty for his opponent, and clung to his defences as long as he decently could.

The operations against Tournai proved particularly severe and expensive in men, although Marlborough skilfully decoyed the French army away from the area, and managed his approach march unimpeded as a result. The French commander, Seuville, deployed ingenious measures in the defence; the campaign was bitterly fought, and consisted of continuous trench raids, bombardments, assaults and mining. A soldier who fought in the trenches remembered: 'By the enemy's dayly springing of new Mynes our Ingeniers advance so very slowly.'[3] Whole companies of men were buried in the mining and counter-mining operations, and 5,000 Allied soldiers had become casualties when the town fell on 3 September 1709. With the place at last in his hands, Marlborough could turn his attention to St Ghislain and Mons, the possession of which would make complete the long-awaited return to the Dutch of their Barrier fortresses. More significantly, the capture of these towns would also open the road to Paris for a campaign in 1710, and this impending threat might tempt the French army out into the open to give battle.

Once the capture of Tournai was certain, Marlborough moved with his usual speed. Orkney and Pallandt arrived before St Ghislain on 3 September, with twenty squadrons of cavalry and composite storming companies drawn from the grenadiers of every battalion in the Allied army. Soon afterwards Prince Frederick of Hesse-Cassell marched right past St Ghislain with a corps of cavalry and infantry to isolate Mons. They waded across the Haine river on 5 September to accomplish the task, but not before a brigade of French dragoons and Walloon infantry were hurriedly sent in by Villars to reinforce the garrison. Sicco van Goslinga, who had insisted that such a rapid march so soon after a severe seige would fail, freely admitted that he was mistaken, and allowed Marlborough credit for the adventurous operation.

The Marshal was under strict instructions from Versailles to ensure that Mons did not suffer the same fate as Tournai, even though this fortress was of lesser importance. Louis XIV wrote: 'Should Mons follow Tournai, our case is undone; you are by every means in your power to relieve the garrison; the cost is not to be considered.'[4] Given Villars' passionate temperament, this instruction from Versailles was simply an open invitation to give battle at the earliest opportunity.

By 6 September, as the pace of operations quickened, both armies were edging towards each other along muddy roads. The next day the French army advanced from the vicinity of Valenciennes, and crossed the Hagenau river to openly challenge Marlborough's movement against Mons. The Scots Dragoons, part of Hesse-Cassell's cavalry screen, expected to be attacked at any time.[5] Soon the leading elements of the opposing armies lay only about five miles apart, separated by gently

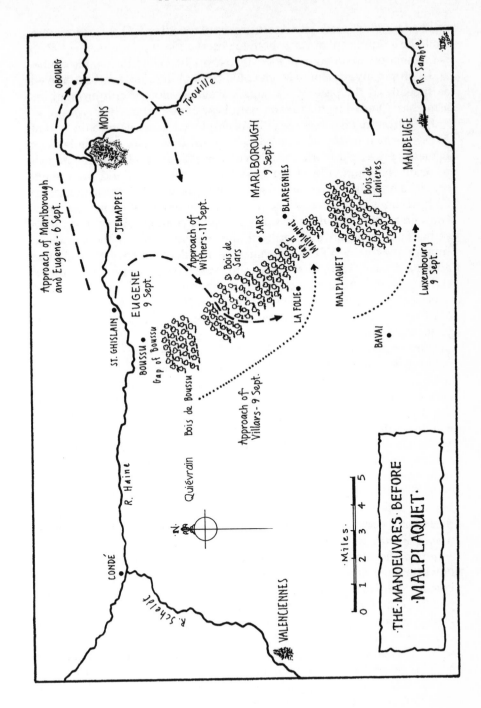

THE·MANOEUVRES·BEFORE·
MALPLAQUET·

Miles

0 1 2 3 4 5

rolling farmland laced with dense groves of woodland. This close country could be a significant obstacle both to observation and to movement. By 8 September the main body of the Allied army had closed up to the Haine, and a proper investment of Mons could begin. Villars, meanwhile, moved as speedily as the pace of his supply wagons allowed and brought his army past Quiévrain, his cavalry patrols probing cautiously forwards.

The adroit manoeuvres that Villars employed to close up to the belt of woods formed by the Bois de Sars, the Bois de Boussu, and the Bois de Lanieres, presented Marlborough with a significant problem. The French were on the blind side of the woodland to the Duke, and there were several demanding tasks he had to perform – he must cover the mopping-up operations at Tournai, while preparing the siege operations against St Ghislain and Mons. Simultaneously, he had to complete the concentration of his field army on the northern and eastern edges of the woods to counter moves by Villars to challenge his deployment. With all this activity, if the Duke was not careful, the French commander might suddenly slip through, achieve a temporary local superiority, and overwhelm one of the Allied detachments. If this occurred while Marlborough's army was scattered, a major setback to his whole campaign would result.

Marlborough seems to have delayed the approach from Tournai of the rear echelon of his army, a powerful mixed column of horse and foot under Lieutenant-General Henry Withers (nineteen infantry battalions and ten squadrons of cavalry), until the French intentions became clearer. The Duke's sensitivity on this score was understandable. A move by Villars northwards against St Ghislain would both turn the right flank of the Allied army as it formed up to the woodland belt, and threaten to detach him from his supply trains as they trundled along the rutted roads from Tournai.

On the level of grand tactics, Marlborough had taken the initiative by moving quickly to attack St Ghislain and Mons with hardly a pause after the fall of Tournai. Villars had now, in his turn, achieved a temporary local initiative with his well considered advance, using the belts of woodland south of the Haine to mask his approach. Neither commander was, however, tactically fixed by the other – the Duke could adopt a defensive posture at little risk to his army while besieging Mons, while Villars could pull back and manoeuvre for a better position if he was threatened. However, the urgent imperatives under which each operated dictated otherwise – Marlborough was driven by the need to seek open battle, and Villars was under firm instructions from Versailles to save Mons. It might be said that each commander, in his own way, was fixed by events.

On the afternoon of 8 September 1709 Prince Eugene's left Wing of the Allied army moved to observe the Gap of Boussu near St Ghislain and Jemappes, while Marlborough did the same at the Gap of Aulnois opposite to Bavai with the right Wing. It was thought that Villars would bring on a battle – Marlborough's intelligence gathering told him that much, and on that same day his cavalry patrols happened to capture the Marquis de Cheldon who was inclined to be talkative. He had no hesitation in confirming that the French commander intended to fight.[6]

At this point Villars' army was closest to the Gap of Boussu in the north. Therefore Marlborough was reluctant to devote too much force to the more southerly Gap of Aulnois, preferring to keep closed up to Eugene as long as prudently possible. He felt no pressing need to entrench his army. Such formal preparations, which would certainly serve to protect the operations against Mons, would also equally deter Villars from chancing battle against one or other of the Allied detachments in the open ground to the east of the woods. Marlborough decided to wait and see what he did next.

During 8 September Villars had sent his cavalry forward, under the Chevalier de Luxembourg, to reconnoitre the Gaps of Boussu and Aulnois. Finding that both were unoccupied by anything stronger than Allied scouts, Villars cautiously deferred a decision to immediately offer battle – perhaps he hoped that an Allied detachment would venture through the wood and offer a tempting prey. In the event he moved his army to the right on the following day and closed up to occupy, but not pass through, the Gap of Aulnois. At about 8.00 am on 9 September Marlborough and Eugene went forward with a detachment of Auvergne's cavalry. Finding French scouts forward of the eastern edge of the woods, Auvergne's troopers drove them off, but they soon ran into stiffer opposition as they probed farther into the slightly higher ground of the Gap itself. As the firing mounted in volume, the Allied commanders were able to glimpse Villars' army approaching the Plain of Malplaquet, coming forward across the gently rolling countryside to the north and west. The Marshal was committing his army to the Gap of Aulnois, and in doing so, effectively fixed Marlborough to making an attack on that ground.

The French advanced in four large columns of march, two of infantry, each led by the lumbering artillery, with a cavalry column on either flank. Their oddly measured pace caused considerable annoyance to the French soldiers and the curious formation, perhaps a result of the Marshal's certain knowledge of his inferior numbers, was at distinct variance with the skill and boldness he had employed over the preceding few days. It may have inhibited Villars in an attempt to catch Marlborough's advance guard unawares, but he might also have suspected that the Duke was in a position to surge through the woodland belt in force and confront him in the open.[7]

Things were very different on the other side of the tactical hill. To Marlborough it briefly seemed that it was Villars who would venture right through the Gap of Aulnois, where the Duke had only Daniel Dopff's division of Dutch infantry close enough at hand to support Auvergne's squadrons. The French might be trying to surprise the right Wing of the army as it came up to the Gap, as yet unsupported by Eugene. The danger was not acute as the Duke had no heavy equipment or guns in the area, and Dopff could fall back towards Eugene, only six miles away to the north, if he was pressed. In fact, properly handled, such a movement would serve to draw the French right through the Gap, where they would be a ready target for an Allied counter-stroke.

Villars was too experienced to fall into this trap, and shortly after noon on 9 September he began to entrench his army in the Gap of Aulnois and in the woods on either side. At about 2.00 pm the forward French batteries were able to engage Auvergne's cavalry, and these troopers prudently fell back out of range from their advanced positions at the small copse known as the Bois de Thiery. Dopff's infantry were now at the hamlet of Blaregnies, and Auvergne brought his squadrons back to support them. He thereby established the forward edge of the Allied position opposite the Gap. It was now plain that Villars had committed his army, so Eugene began shifting his Wing of the Allied army southwards, to combine with Marlborough. The first echelon of this movement, eighteen battalions of German infantry, began marching from the Gap of Boussu at about 3.30 that afternoon.

On the evening of 9 September Villars detached his reserve cavalry and sent Luxembourg to move off to the right flank to hold the Gap in the Bois de Longueville. This covered the approaches to Maubeuge, but the town was under no immediate threat, for Marlborough could not stretch out that far without exposing his own flank to the French, and further distancing himself from the tail of his army now nearing St Ghislain. What induced the Marshal to so materially weaken his cavalry is not now clear. It is possible that Villars contemplated another movement by his army around to the right, to cut in behind the Bois de Lanieres and turn the left flank of the Allied army as it lay in the Gap of Aulnois. This was unlikely to be successful, given the time available and the distance involved, and if it was considered at all nothing came of the idea.[8]

At a council of war late on 9 September 1709, Marlborough and his generals agreed that no attempt could be made to force the French position the following day. There were three main reasons for this hard decision, the most pressing of which was that the Allied artillery would not be fully in place until 11 September. Also, Withers' corps of almost 10,000 troops would not arrive from St Ghislain until then, and a major part of Marlborough's developing plan depended upon this reinforcement. Lastly the ground was marshy and difficult, and largely unknown to the Allied commanders. Of all these, the lack of artillery was vital, as any attempt to assault the strengthening French position depended heavily upon the preparatory bombardment and the support the gunners could give to the attacking troops. Time simply did not allow for the large number of cumbersome pieces to be brought into position sooner, and this seems to have been the decisive consideration for delay.

The difficulty in preparing a well co-ordinated attack across the uneven ground was well reported by Eugene in a letter he wrote to the Emperor on 9 September 1709:

> Since we do not know the lie of the land, we dare even less take any risks. The terrain is very uneven, and cut up by many small brooks and ponds swollen by the bad weather, and is full of water and gullies, paths and defiles, so that one cannot march directly forward.[9]

It was obvious that a good deal of time would have to be spent on careful consideration and preparation of the ground over which the Allied attacks were to be made. So, there seemed little alternative but to accept the delay in making the attack, even though the French, as a result, had a greater chance to entrench their position. Marlborough reportedly favoured making an attack the following day but this is far from certain, and ignores the benefit anticipated from the arrival of Withers' troops. He abided by the opinion of the council of war. The price of the delay had to be borne, and there was no evident dissent amongst the Allied commanders about the necessity. Accordingly, that night of 9 September their army closed up to its allotted positions opposite the Gap of Aulnois and lay on its arms.

This whole series of preliminary manoeuvres, which brought the two armies opposite each other with the intention to fight, saw the initiative pass from Marlborough (with his rapid advance on Mons) to Marshal Villars (with the movement of his army to the woodland obstacle belt). As the Marshal closed up to the Gap of Aulnois, he temporarily fixed Marlborough by forcing him to commit to an assault on a position chosen by his opponent for its very strength. Villars then let this advantage go by detaching Luxembourg's cavalry towards Maubeuge. The initiative was back with Marlborough – Villars had no reserve with which to harry a disordered or beaten opponent, while the Duke had a corps in reserve.

As the armies were now disposed, Villars had to fight for a draw at best; all his troops were committed to the defence of the position adopted; he could not pursue any advantage gained in battle. This is of particular importance, for his reserve echelon, that which he would use to strike, was employed elsewhere under Luxembourg. Meanwhile, Marlborough was holding Withers' column off to the northern end of the Bois de Sars (initially to cover the operations against St Ghislain). This had the obvious benefit of forcing Villars to commit all his available army to pitched battle, while this active and dangerous body of Allied troops was able to manoeuvre freely. Withers could be employed by the Duke at any point along the line of battle, although his troops' arrival at the scene would inevitably be delayed if they had to pass behind the rear of the Allied army to get into position. The original intention was apparently for Withers to reinforce the Dutch corps on the Allied left, but Marlborough decided to let him loose on the left flank of the French army instead. An added benefit, one which the Duke could only hope for, was that Villars might have no notion that Withers' corps was free to attack him, almost at will.

There were distinct dangers for the Duke in such a bold and innovative course. The concept of 'marching to the sound of the guns', although employed admirably at Oudenarde the previous year, was still rather unusual and staff procedures were not developed to cope with the complexities of such a course of action. Subordinate commanders, in the main, were mentally ill-prepared for such novelties. Additionally, Marlborough accepted a lessening of the force concentrated at the point of initial attack, while Withers faced the difficulties of marching in close country to join a confusing battle which was already in progress. Despite all this, there is no doubt that Marlborough had a great stroke in mind for Withers. Eugene referred in his letter to the Emperor, in which he bemoaned the state of the ground, to plans for '. . . the corps from Tournai [Withers] which is to make a special effort, and are to be let loose upon the enemy.'[10]

The French were busy making the most of the time allowed them to strengthen an already stout position. Their complex defences ran along a slight rise in the ground, gently sloping towards shallow muddy ravines leading to the north-east and the Allied army. Trenches, and log and earth breastworks, were constructed along the whole length of the line, reaching deep into the flanking woods. In these copses large numbers of trees were felled to provide material for the breastworks, and the underbrush was cleared to improve the fields of fire. The great tree trunks themselves were chained and roped together to add mass to the tangled lines of sharpened branches (abattis), facing towards the enemy, which ran in wide belts in front of the defences.

In the centre of the French position, on more open ground, a series of nine earthen redans were built and manned with infantry and artillery. The Bleiron Farm, slightly to the right of the French centre and partly masked to the front by the low ridge on which sat the copse known as the Bois de Thiery, was barricaded and made into a strongpoint under the command of General de Guiche (the veteran defender of Offuz at the Battle of Ramillies three years earlier). Nearby, a battery of twenty heavy guns, cunningly hidden in a shallow fold of the ground running north-east away from Bleiron Farm, added enormously to the firepower of the defenders in that sector. These guns were emplaced to fire obliquely across the front of the French breastworks on that side of the field, and would take in the right flank any troops approaching the Bois de Lanieres.

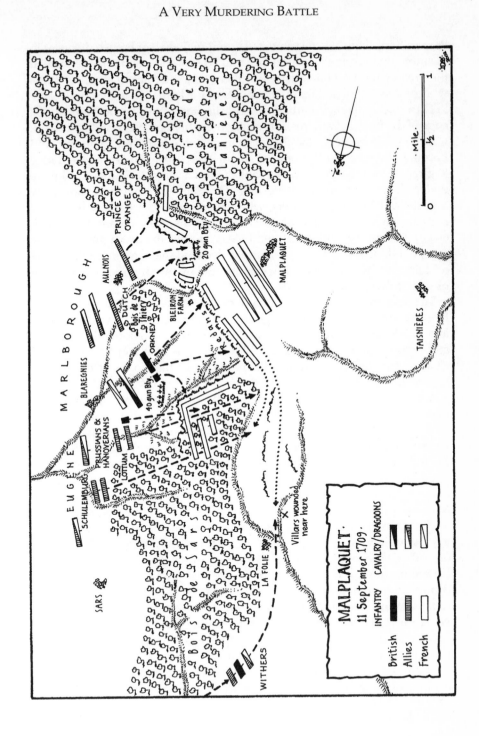

Preparations were also begun for a second main belt of French defences in the more open country to the south and west of the woods. These were in the area of the La Folie Farm, but there was insufficient time for these works to be completed before the onset of the battle.

Thirty-seven French battalions held the line from Bleiron Farm to the edge of the Bois de Lanieres, with eight more held in reserve. On this flank were the Grenadiers, the Royal Italians, the Montrou, Santerre and Lorraine Régiments. Supporting them were the Navarre and Alsace Régiments and the German veterans of the La Marck Régiment. All were under the command of the Comte D'Artagnan, alongside the vastly experienced Marshal Boufflers, who had ridden from Paris, with sword and breastplate, to offer his services to Villars as a volunteer. With elaborate courtesy Villars offered to serve under the distinguished older man, but Boufflers with equal courtesy declined the honour. Their shabby soldiers watched, and the army was cheered by this dignified exchange of niceties between the Marshals.

The French centre was occupied by seventeen battalions of Gardes Français and Gardes Suisses, together with the Picardie, Royal Roussillon and Greder Suisse Régiments. Another thirteen battalions, the Cologne and Bavière Guards, Clare and Dillon's émigré Irish and the Béarn and Champagne Régiments, linked the redans with the woods of the Bois de Sars on the left. In these copses forty French battalions under the Marquis d'Albergotti made up the left Wing of the army – the forward entrenchments held by the Royal La Marine, Charost, Saintonge and Provence Régiments. Deeper in the woods lay the depth battalions – the La Reine, La Roi and Bretagne Régiments. To the rear, on the open Plain of Malplaquet, no fewer than 260 squadrons of cavalry (many badly under-strength and indifferently mounted – even the elite Maison du Roi being in poor shape) were held in reserve behind the line of redans. In all, Marshal Villars had about 85,000 men on the position with eighty guns.

The French commander intended to meet Marlborough with an aggressive kind of defence, even though he was outnumbered. The woods on either side of the Gap of Aulnois thronged with his entrenched battalions, and all his preparations were intended to force the Allies to commit their infantry to an attack in the central killing zone in front of the redans. With the French artillery in the wood-line on either flank enfilading the attacking infantry and bringing them to a halt, his massed cavalry would sweep through the gaps between the redans and drive them back. The squadrons would then retire without getting tangled up with the numerous Allied cavalry. When the Allied infantry came on again, as they would be bound to do, the exercise would be repeated, and so it would go on – a battle of attrition with the French protected by their defensive works and by their firmly anchored flanks. The Allies would batter their fine battalions to flinders on the breastworks. Given the disparity in numbers, and the certainty with which Marlborough could be expected to attack, this was a perfectly sound approach for the Marshal to adopt.

However, Villars' arrangements for defence, while thorough and comprising several deep belts of breastworks and obstacles, meant that the left of his line in the Bois de Sars was 'short' and metaphorically in the air. He simply had insufficient troops to prolong the line on that flank far enough to prevent a determined turning movement. This would probably not matter if the Duke of Marlborough was fully committed to the forcing of the French centre and would, in his own turn, have no troops to spare. In fact the Marshal was relying too much on the shelter provided by the dense woodland off to his left, and he was unwittingly leaving his army open to precisely the kind of manoeuvre which Marlborough had in mind. The 'special effort' referred to by Eugene in his letter to the Emperor did not occur to the French.

At times during 10 September 1709 there were heavy exchanges of fire between the opposing batteries, but losses were modest. This activity seems to have had more to do with the gunners wanting to bed in the heavy guns on the soft ground and, possibly, a kind of reconnaissance by fire to see what response would be made to an artillery assault. That evening the small French garrison in St Ghislain were overwhelmed by an Allied assault under Colonel Haxhusion, who took 200 prisoners and five guns. This fully opened the way for Withers and his column to march straight onto the battlefield the following morning. Although the battle had of necessity been delayed, the hours had not been wasted by the Allies as, later that day, Marlborough ordered that a four-battalion German brigade be brought out of the force preparing to besiege Mons. They would give added weight to the infantry attack on the woods in the morning.

Marlborough's plan was simple and not unlike that employed at Blenheim and Ramillies, although on a far greater scale. His infantry would breach the French obstacle belts and exert intense pressure on the two Wings of Villars' army. When the Marshal had been forced to commit all his reserves and his centre was weakened, Marlborough would send forward his massed squadrons to engage and destroy the French cavalry on the Plain of Malplaquet. As always, he expected to take rapid advantage of any weaknesses in his opponent's arrangements. The Duke's numerical superiority gave him an obvious advantage, although this was partly offset by the sturdy defensive works Villars had been allowed time to construct. The important added factor in Marlborough's calculations was Withers and his corps marching against the French left flank once Villars was committed to battle; the Marshal would have no corresponding reserve to deploy while Marlborough's main army held him fast.

The hours before the battle were alive with the pop-popping of musketry as opposing patrols felt their way forward in the woods. There was no moon that night and the rigid and formal procedures for battle commonly employed at this time had no place in the dark and dangerous thickets as the two armies stealthily stretched out to grapple with one another. Colonel De La Colonie wrote: 'There we awaited them, lying that night in battle formation, whilst our patrols and those of the enemy kept up a constant fire whenever they came across each other.'[11]

Despite this dangerous activity, a number of Allied officers took advantage of an unofficial kind of truce, proposed by d'Albergotti, to go forward and converse with acquaintances and friends in the French army. With the polyglot nature of the army, a few Allied soldiers could even count relatives serving with the army across the way from them. Matthew Bishop, who fought the following day, wrote that: 'a sergeant that belonged to my Lord Hartford's Regiment, had a sister in the French service.'[12] Cadogan was by means of this pause able to scrutinise the complex defences, and others no doubt did the same. What they were able to glean and make beneficial use of so late in the day is far from clear, but their actions drew resentful comments from French officers nearby.[13] This fraternisation led to rumours that peace was at hand and that no battle would be fought. Cheering broke out in the lines from time to time, but it was just rumour, no more, and the resulting disappointment may have added to the bitterness with which the soldiers fought it out the following morning.

The Allied troops were roused from their bivouacs at 3.00 am to hear divine service. The kneeling soldiers sought their God before the regimental colours, piled on the drums. The plain and the woods round about were alive with the murmurings of many scores of thousands of men. By 7.15 am on 11 September 1709, all had eaten a hasty breakfast and gulped a tot of rum or genever gin (the French thought the attackers to be drunk), and were formed up and ready to attack.

Marlborough took a position with his staff just in rear of the British and Prussian infantry brigades under George Orkney, standing with a great battery of forty heavy guns (commanded by Colonel John Armstrong) opposite the French redans. Auvergne commanded the Allied cavalry here – German and Imperial squadrons, together with Lumley's British Horse and dragoons. In the deep woods on the right, Eugene had overall command of the German and Imperial troops who were to attack the Bois de Sars (rather confusingly, the Prince attacked on the right, although he was in command of the left Wing of the army). On the Allied left near the hamlet of Aulnois the Dutch infantry of the right Wing under the command of John Friso, the young Prince of Orange, was supported by Pallandt's Danes and a Scots-Dutch brigade under Colonel Gustavus Hamilton. Their particular task was to force the French line of defence in the Bois de Lanieres, and by threatening to turn the French right flank, firmly hold D'Artagnan's numerous infantry in place. In simple terms, Eugene would force the French left and Orange would fix their right. Marlborough would then decide the battle in the centre with his cavalry.

Shortly after 7.30 am Armstrong's great battery opposite the Gap of Aulnois opened fire with a terrific bombardment of both the French centre and a peculiar triangular shaped piece of wood facing outwards from the Bois de Sars towards the redans. The effect was immediate and devastating, with terrible damage caused to both the redans and the breastworks in the triangle. Casualties mounted rapidly amongst the defenders. Colonel De La Colonie, whose regiment was in reserve behind the Gardes Français in the redans, spoke eloquently of the terrible effect of the cannonade:

> Next morning [11 September] at break of day the battery of thirty [sic] cannon opened fire, and by its continuous volleys succeeded in breaching the entrenchments in the wood on our left, and the head of the enemy's infantry column made its appearance.

At this point a French battery came into play against the advancing troops. De La Colonie wrote:

> The fire of this battery was terrific, and hardly a shot missed its mark ... A gap was no sooner created than it was filled again, and they even continued their advance upon us without giving us any idea of the actual point determined on for their attack. At last, the column, leaving the great [Allied] battery on its left, changed its direction a quarter right and threw itself precipitately into the wood on our left, making an assault upon the portion which had been breached.[14]

The troops the Colonel was watching with such fascination were the British battalions of the Duke of Argyll's brigade (the Buff's, Webb's and Temple's Regiments), who formed the left hand echelon of Eugene's Wing going into the attack on the angle of the Bois de Sars.

Meanwhile, the grazing effect of the Allied cannon bombardment had serious consequences for the French cavalry on the plain behind their infantry defences. The 'overs' skimmed the parapets of the earthworks and ploughed through their ranks with ghastly results, cutting down men and horses. This early artillery success for Marlborough appears to have caught Villars unprepared. His gunners had no adequate reply, and the excellence of the Allied preparations in siting the batteries so well says a great deal for the efficient use to which the two-day delay was put by the Duke and his commanders.

While the cannonade thundered on, parties of Allied stormers –

grenadiers and pioneers with their hatchets and iron-tipped staves – crept forward under cover of the fire and a sheltering remnant of early morning mist. They began to hack and tear at the defences and obstacles to clear a path for their comrades gathering behind. An hour or so after the cannonade began, sometime before 9.00 am, the massed echelons of Eugene's German and Imperial infantry (under the command of Schulemburg and Count Lottum) moved forward through the outer thickets of the Bois de Sars, and the Allied attack began in earnest. The forty battalions under Schulemburg headed for the French breastworks on the forward edge of the north-easterly face of the Bois de Sars, while Lottum's twenty-two battalions advanced steadily to assault the eastern edge of the piece of woodland which jutted out towards the centre of the field. As they moved forward, the Allied soldiers could see hardly anything of their opponents, who crouched low in the shelter of their entrenchments. Lottum afterwards commented on the grandeur of the Allied advance but added that 'it seemed that they must make war on moles.'[15]

As the attackers entered the woods, clearly outlined against the bright morning light behind them, the French breastworks suddenly blazed with musketry. The fire was heavy, well directed and disciplined, and under its devastating lash the Allied infantry floundered through the first obstacle belt in the woods. This barrier had been imperfectly breached, despite the vigour and spirit with which the grenadiers and pioneers had plied their tools. There was a desperate and costly scramble through the entangle-ments as, regardless of the losses, the German and Imperial troops bravely struggled towards the forward line of breastworks. The battalions of the Régiment du Charost, on the French left, were overwhelmed and scattered, but the attackers lost all order in the smoke and noise, and could make no real progress in the face of the solid defence. Quickly losing their bearings, they milled around in confusion, and then streamed back out of the woods, looking for a place to re-form well away from the tormenting French fire.

The Allied losses in this sharp initial repulse were severe; the regimental commanders led by example, and many officers fell within the first few minutes of the attack. Mrs Christian Davies recalled that the attackers were also: '. . . exposed to the fire of their artillery, which swept down whole companies at a time.'[16] Some of Schulemburg's brigades soon had no surviving field officers on their feet, but Eugene, indomitable as ever, was close at hand, and was stung at so prompt a rebuff to his veteran troops. The soldiers were gathered back into their ranks and drawn up in fresh attacking formation for another attempt, while the artillery redoubled its fire and the French soldiers huddled low as their breast-works splintered and shivered in the storm of round-shot.

Eugene's troops gallantly went forward once again. Some soon got tangled in boggy ground in front of part of the breastworks, but they trampled over the tumbled bodies of their fallen comrades in order to get to grips with the French. The whole scene rapidly became chaotic; proper control of the advance was virtually impossible, with dense smoke hanging in the copses and the woods. Every tree seemed to conceal a sharpshooter, and the Allied officers fell with awful rapidity. Despite all this, the determination of the attackers gradually took effect, and the first line of breastworks were carried after a brutal and costly struggle, the soldiers desperately shooting and stabbing at each other across the barricades. The wounded were stamped on, bayoneted and plundered in the deadly frenzy of such a terrible struggle.

At the same time that the second attack went in on the Allied right, at about 10.00 am, Eugene urgently called on Marlborough for support. Orkney was immediately requested to detach a brigade of his British infantry from the position in the centre, and to move to their right, across the stretch of marshy ground, against the flank of the French defences in the triangle.[17] Here the Royal La Marine and La Sarre Régiments held firmly to their breastworks, but the French battery there had been quite overwhelmed by Armstrong's bombardment. Orkney responded promptly, and the 2nd English Foot Guards and the 1st Battalion of Orkney's own regiment were able to neatly turn the French first line, at about the same time that Lottum's attackers scrambled over the forward barricades nearby. The attackers were able to rush onwards towards the second line of French breastworks deeper in the wood, and they poured into these more thinly held defences, grappling with soldiers of the La Reine and Le Roi Régiments. Just then leading companies of the Béarn Régiment, drawn from the French centre, came hurrying through the trees to reinforce that very same position. Firing low through the smoke, the British and German troops drove them back into their third line entrenchments. To the right, Schulemburg's attack was now reinforced by the fresh brigade drawn from the force investing Mons, but the Allied progress was once again slow and ground was bitterly gained. The French and their allies contested every yard of the ground and the woods were carpeted with the dead and wounded, blue, grey, red and white uniforms lying thickly mingled together.

It seems rash for Marlborough to have lessened the infantry strength available to Orkney in the more open ground opposite the French centre. However, his intention plainly remained to exert maximum pressure upon the left Wing of the French army, and their grip on the woods was, perhaps, more resolute and stubborn than he expected. However, whatever freedom of action Villars enjoyed was being ruthlessly stripped away from him, and he was increasingly forced to commit what infantry battalions he had in hand to holding this threatened flank. The loss of two lines of defence was a shock for the Marshal and he grimly took rapid action to remedy the matter. First the three battalions of the Champagne Régiment, then the émigré Irish brigade, and lastly the four battalions of the Franco-Bavarian brigade under Colonel De La Colonie had to be sent from the French centre to the support of d'Albergotti's hard-pressed infantrymen in the woods on the left. De La Colonie wrote afterwards of his alarm at having to leave his position behind the redans almost defenceless, but he was promptly told to comply with the order or to hand over his brigade to an officer who would:

> When the first order was brought to the brigade-major, who reported it to me, I refused to obey it, and pointed out the absolute necessity that existed for our maintaining the position we were holding.[18]

Despite his protests, he had to move to the woods on the left, and by 11.00 am the centre of the French position was getting to be decidedly thin of infantry.

In this way, the Marquis de Chemerault, who commanded the left-most French redans gathered together twelve battalions, with the intention of delivering a sharp blow to Lottum's troops as they struggled to consolidate their grip on the triangle. With the added strength of the regiments drawn from the centre, Chemerault had the potential to split Eugene's attackers away from the rest of Marlborough's army; a sharp and well directed blow might do great damage. However, the Duke spotted the danger from his post near the great battery, and he brought Auvergne's leading squadrons of cavalry forward in reply, threatening to take the French troops in the flank as they advanced. Despite the difficult marshy ground they would have to cross, the Allied cavalry posed too much of a threat, and Chemerault had to let this fleetingly promising opportunity to strike at Lottum pass by. Instead the French infantry drew up close to the partially complete reserve line of breastworks near La Folie Farm.

Shortly after Eugene's troops began their attack on the Bois de Sars, away on the left of the Allied army the thirty Dutch battalions under the command of the Prince of Orange began their own attack, supported by the Danes and Scots. They surged forward past the Bois de Thiery towards the Bois de Lanieres, where the entrenched corps of French infantry under Boufflers and D'Artagnan awaited them. Orange's 25,000 troops were divided into five attacking columns. Two of these, comprising five Dutch, eight Swiss (in Dutch service) and Hamilton's two Scots battalions, under the immediate command of Baron Fagel, assaulted the Bois de Lanieres itself. The other three columns, with a total of seventeen Dutch battalions, moved resolutely across the gently sloping and more open ground towards the barricaded strongpoint of the Bleiron Farm. Near here lay the concealed French batteries.

At the outset Fagel's infantry attacked with such vigour that they were able to push the French Grenadiers back from their first line of entrenchments, forthrightly driving them deep into the woods at their back. The La Marck and Châteauneuf Régiments also withdrew, but they were not dismayed. Waiting there, in the copses to the rear, were three battalions of the Navarre Régiment, lean and ragged veterans of many battles, prudently placed in reserve by D'Artagnan. Quietly and quickly they rose from their shelter, and with a well controlled volley of musketry dashed forward in counter-attack. Fagel's disordered soldiers had to give way before the force of the French charge, and they fell back, surrendering the breastworks so preciously won only minutes before. De La Colonie, who at the time was still near the redans, saw all this and wrote:

> Our right withstood the enemy's attack with admirable firmness, disputing every foot of ground in the same manner as on our left. From the regiment of Navarre, which happened at that time to be composed of very short men, nearly in rags, who held our extreme right, and who behaved none the less marvellously well, to the regiment of Alsace, which extended thence to the centre held by the Gardes Francaise, everything went always in our favour.[19]

The Navarre Régiment may not have been smartly dressed, but evidently they were tough.

Meanwhile, on Fagel's right, the Dutch Blue Guards, so favoured and cherished by the late King William III, struggled forward into the teeth of a ferocious artillery onslaught from the concealed batteries near the Bleiron Farm. As the Dutch soldiers emerged from the dead ground of the approach, the patient and skilful French gunners under St Hilaire unleashed a storm of canister fire, and the attackers were tumbled down in their scores. Many of the Dutch battalions were caught in enfilade, with the guns firing down the length of their line, and great gaps were torn along the advancing ranks at each blast. Despite having the advantage of a rather more covered approach, the two attacking columns on the right of the Dutch Guards, under the immediate command of Generals Dohna and Spaar, fared no better against the battalions of the Alsace Régiment holding the Bleiron Farm itself. Although the Dutch soldiers resolutely pressed their assault onwards across the wreckage of their fallen comrades, they could not make an impression on the defence, and they too had to fall back to re-form.

With the Dutch retiring in considerable disarray, the immediate French counter-attack, by both the Navarre and Picardie Régiments, achieved some local success. Many Dutch officers had fallen and dangerous confusion loomed, so that Orange had to scramble his regiments back towards their cavalry supports. Prince Frederick of Hesse-Cassell was there, and he brought twenty cavalry squadrons walking slowly and impressively forward in an imposing mounted advance. The French had insufficient strength to press home their advantage without forming for a proper attack, so the elated soldiers returned to their breastworks and, checking flints and biting fresh cartridges, prepared to receive the next Dutch attack.

Sure enough, they came on again, encouraged by the Prince of Orange, who exposed himself without fear to the French fire. On the left, the Scottish soldiers of Hamilton's brigade (Tullibardine's and Hepburn's Regiments) had the benefit of the slightly better cover on the extreme flank, and they were able to fight their way forward from tree to tree to gain possession of part of the French position, boldly clearing the barricades with the bayonet. John Campbell, a Scottish soldier who fought at the breastworks that day, wrote that the men: '. . . skirmished pice by pice through the woods, exchanging shots with the enemy.'[20] This success was not substantial enough to withstand the inevitable and immediate counter-attack which came hurtling in – Hamilton's men were driven back by the German soldiers of the La Marck Régiment after desperate close-quarter fighting, in which Colonel Tullibardine, eldest son of the Duke of Atholl, was shot through the thigh. He refused to leave the field and, bleeding copiously from a terrible wound, led his Highland men into the attack on the woodline once more, where he was finally shot down. Colonel Hepburn was also killed in that attack, and the wrecked Scots battalions had not the strength to hold on to their dearly bought gains. They grimly fell back towards the shelter of Hesse-Cassell's massed squadrons, where they could rally with the Dutch.

On the right of the Dutch assault, General Pallandt with his seven Danish battalions took advantage of the cover of some scattered copses, and managed to storm the Bleiron Farm after a stiff and bloody fight. The gallant defenders of the Alsace Régiment were driven out at bayonet point. The French under Lieutenant-General Christian Birkenfeld were quick to respond to the dangerous loss of this strongpoint, and the May and Greder Suisse Régiments came charging forward in a fierce counter-attack. The volleys of the Danes staggered the attacking Swiss, but they resolutely formed again and renewed their assault. Pallandt had valuable support from the musketry of two Hanoverian battalions sent towards the Bleiron Farm by Jorgen Rantzau, whose brigade linked the Dutch corps with the centre of the Allied army. The Greder Suisse battalions promptly wheeled and lunged at them, and in the heavy fighting soon only three Hanoverian officers were left standing, and their troops fell back. Pallandt feared encirclement of his embattled Danes as the French counter-attack gained pace, but Rantzau felt he could do no more without specific permission from Marlborough to leave his allotted position in the centre. Urgent appeals from Deputy Goslinga failed to move the Hanoverian commander into committing his entire brigade, and the Danish soldiers had to withdraw and abandon their hard won position at the Bleiron Farm.[21]

To the left of the Danes, the second Dutch attack was mounted on a narrower front than previously, and was no more successful. The French gunners continued to extract an awful price from the Dutch as they came forward. Orange's staff officers were shot down around him, and he had at least two horses killed, but went forward on foot, encouraging and exhorting his men to fresh efforts in the hurricane of fire that faced them. The attacking soldiers showed the greatest determination and their assault was again and again pressed right through the abatti obstacles to the French breastworks. The left-most attacking column, comprising the 2nd and 3rd battalions of Dutch Guards, were particularly conspicuous for the bravery of their assault, but every soldier who laid hands on the barricades was shot down. At last the gallant soldiers could take no more, and they broke and poured back towards their starting point. Baron Fagel was amongst the dead, as were General Spaar and the valiant Swede Count Oxenstiern. Many Dutch battalions had no officers left in action, and a 130-strong company of Huguenot Cadets (all sons of noble émigré families) simply ceased to exist – only three of the young men survived the day unhurt. John Deane wrote afterwards in his journal of the slaughter: 'A great many other regiments on the Hollands sarviss being very much broak and shattered.'[22]

At this grim point, Boufflers might have taken advantage of the Dutch disarray, and by using superior numbers in this part of the field mounted a dangerous counter-attack to unhinge the left of the Allied army. That he did not do so indicates in particular his own formal training in the ways of war. He was not given to spontaneity and had no instructions for such an effort. It is also likely that the Marshal did not appreciate the local superiority he had, the reality of which (seen in hindsight) made a counter-attack an immensely attractive prospect. Subsequent criticism of Boufflers for not being more adventurous, particularly by French commentators, seems misplaced – the Marshal could not know what a numerical advantage he had.

Deputy Goslinga, who atoned for a lot of his past meddling nonsense by his gallant conduct this day, galloped over to Marlborough with a plea that the Dutch infantry be supported. Until now the Duke's attention had, of necessity, been entirely on the heavy fighting in the Bois de Sars. Now the attack on the left claimed his time. Calm as ever, he rode over to the scene of Dutch devastation, pausing briefly to instruct Rantzau to stand firm with his brigade and to anchor the Allied centre in front of the Bois de Thiery. He then spoke reassuringly to the distraught Prince of Orange, calming him, and commending the valour of his troops. At about 11.00 am, seeing that the indomitable Dutch soldiers were even then forming their ravaged ranks for another attack, Marlborough asked Orange to simply hold his ground and maintain a stout front to fix the French troops on this flank. The battle obviously had to be won on another part of the field. The young prince followed this instruction admirably, marshalling his brigades menacingly but just out of cannon shot, and making overt preparations for another attempt, when the chance should occur. [23]

All this time, in the Bois de Sars away on the Allied right, the infantry attacks ground forward at heavy cost and great pain. Musket butt, bayonet and sword were freely used, and the desperate and savage man-to-man fighting offered little opportunity for quarter to be shown by either side. Red John, 2nd Duke of Argyll, was once again in the thick of things with his brigade as it drove into the French flank in the Bois de Sars triangle. He was struck three times by spent musket balls, picking himself up after each blow. Hearing his soldiers mutter that he must be secretly wearing a breastplate under his clothes, Argyll furiously stripped off his laced coat and waistcoat so that all could see that he had no more protection than the common foot soldier. Sword in hand, and in his shirtsleeves and ruffled wrist bands, he then led his troops into the attack once again. Mrs Davies remembered:

> The Duke of Argyle went open-breasted amongst the men to encourage them to behave as became Englishmen; you see brothers, said he, I have no concealed armour, I am equally exposed with you.[24]

Soon afterwards Eugene was struck behind the ear by a musket ball, but he refused to have the wound dressed until the battle was won. He declared that if he survived the day it would be soon enough to have the wound attended to that evening, and if he did not survive it would not matter anyway.

During this part of the battle that redoubtable campaigner, Mrs Christian Davies, now serving as a sutleress in her husband's regiment, faithfully went forward into the roaring woods to take him a refreshing drink of beer. She complained afterwards that debris shot down from the trees caused her much discomfort. Her search was in vain and, failing to find him in the firing line, took to turning over dead bodies in her quest. She found her man, lying in a pile of the killed, in one of the copses in the wood:

> I entered the wood with small beer for my husband; though the shot and bark of trees fell thicker than my reader, if he has not seen action, can well imagine; not a few times pieces of the latter fell on my neck, and gave me no small uneasiness by getting down my stays. My dog howled in a pitiful manner, which surprised me as it was unusual. A man near me, who was easing nature, said 'Poor creature, he would

fain tell you that his master is dead.' I ran amongst the dead, and turned over near two hundred, amongst whom I found Brigadier Lalo, Sir Thomas Prendergast, and a great number more of my best friends, before I found my husband's body which a man was stripping. At my approach he went off, and left his booty.[25]

In the confused fighting, Donald McBane, a noted swordsman serving with Orkney's Regiment, carried his small son, who should have been left back in camp in the care of the wife of one of his comrades, in his knapsack. The boy was so quiet that McBane thought he had been killed by one of the musket balls that he felt pass through his clothing and accoutrements, but he found that the lad had only suffered a slight injury to his elbow. After seeing that the wound was dressed by the regimental surgeon, McBane returned the infant to his anxious foster mother at the end of the day.

At about 11.30 am, as the French were worn down, Eugene's infantry began to emerge from the far side of the Bois de Sars. Count August Wackerbarth, who commanded the leading German infantry, was wounded at this point, and had to be carried off the field. Still, the ousted French soldiers had to fall back into the more open country towards the La Folie Farm, where their partially complete final line of breastworks lay. At this critical point, when the tired attackers might have found it difficult to gather enough strength to break this further line, Withers arrived on the march from Tournai. His heavy column of infantry began to emerge across the open fields off to the far left of the French line, the menacing mass of newly arrived Allied infantry steadily taking shape as it came closer. As they advanced Withers deployed four infantry battalions towards the reverse edge of the woodline to cover his left, while the other fifteen battalions were boldly pushed towards the La Folie Farm, and the open flank of Villars' army.

Here was a masterstroke on the field of battle, as the French position was now completely turned; 10,000 fresh Allied soldiers were deploying for action in plain sight of the French commander, and a catastrophe threatened his army. The 'special effort' referred to by Eugene in his letter to the Emperor was now taking devastating effect. To add to Villars' problems, by about 12.00 noon, Schulemburg's artillerymen managed to drag a battery of seven 12-pounder guns through the woods, and they engaged the French infantry with round shot. The nearest cavalry squadrons were also fired on, causing them to retire farther towards the village of Malplaquet. Schulemburg wrote afterwards: 'I managed to bring up by a kind of miracle seven big guns which I had with me, by which I did not fail to do great harm to the lines of French cavalry.'[26] This particular feat of arms plainly indicates that the woods may not have been quite as tangled as is often supposed. The French defenders can be relied on to have cleared the underbrush to improve their fields of fire, and many of the trees were felled to make the breastworks and abattis. A more particular obstacle for the guns was probably the marshy ground underfoot.

The advance of Withers' corps was met with what strength Villars could hastily summon. He re-deployed those of Chemerault's infantry not in close contact and stripped still more battalions away from his already weakened centre with a ruthless disregard for the carefully constructed balance of his defensive arrangements. The Marshal had no choice but to form a fresh line 'refused' (or bent back) on his left flank. The troops scrambled into place just in time, and in heavy and merciless fighting, with charge and counter-charge coming fast upon each other, the French held back the advancing Allied infantry, around the La Folie Farm. Nearby, eight squadrons of French Carabiniers under the Chevalier de Rozel charged and routed a larger force of ten Hessian cavalry squadrons under Miklau. These had advanced faster than their infantry supports, and were caught as they attempted to deploy on the edge of the woods. Little quarter was shown to them, six of the Hessian squadrons being utterly broken and the troopers hacked down.

As Withers' infantry pressed forward the Royal Regiment of Ireland engaged their exiled Catholic countrymen in the French recruited Royale Régiment d'Irlandaise. The superior fire discipline of the British battalion decided the encounter and the émigré Irishmen were defeated and driven back. Captain Robert Parker (although not present with his regiment that day) heard many first-hand accounts of this action from his brother officers, and attributed much of the success, not just to superior fire discipline, but to the heavier musket ball in use in Marlborough's army.[27]

The robust reply to the threat against his left flank was a considerable tactical success for Villars, but the price his army paid was very heavy. Eugene's grimy infantry thronged the western edge of the Bois de Sars, rather disordered and weary, but still dangerous. They exchanged volleys with the French near La Folie Farm. At the same time, on the other flank, Boufflers' infantry, although magnificently successful in their stout entrenchments, were confronted still by Orange's corps (who, although terribly battered, showed signs of intending to attack again). Every battalion of infantry that Villars had was in the line and committed, yet the vital redans in the centre of his position were almost unoccupied.

Marlborough, who had returned from steadying the nerve of the Prince of Orange, now moved with Eugene to the forward edge of the Bois de Sars to view the French centre from a clearer angle. The forty or so French battalions, scraped together to bolster the left flank, could be plainly seen but they were not being deployed to fight for the redans. They were fully engaged in holding Withers off from La Folie Farm, or preparing for Villars' effort to retake the woods. The Duke then, rather pointedly, had his attention drawn by Schulemburg to the weakness of the French centre. It is not likely that he had failed to notice this for it was a major part of his plan, but he accepted Schulemburg's broad hint with patience, and ordered George Orkney's infantry forward. The hardest part of this advance was the boggy ground underfoot and Orkney wrote afterwards: 'It was about one o'clock that my thirteen battalions got to the entrenchments, which we got very easily.'[28]

Now, the French artillery commander, Armand de St Hilaire, hurried to Villars with the news that the very centre of the army was pierced. The nine redans in the open were, even as he spoke, falling into the hands of Orkney's British and Prussian infantry. Some of the guns had been dragged out and saved, but St Hilaire breathlessly explained that those left behind would be turned on the French cavalry before long. This was the risk that Villars had been forced to accept and now the true price was to be paid by his horsemen. Time might not be available for him to recover the balance of his army under the repeated blows of the Allied attack, but he dauntlessly began to draw together whatever battalions were to be had. A renewed effort was to be made to drive Eugene's infantry back out of the Bois de Sars, and to regain the initiative in that part of the field at the least.

While pondering all the grim possibilities, at about 1.30 pm, Villars' conspicuously mounted group of officers was swept by musketry from some Allied soldiers standing at the edge of the woods. Many in the French party were hit, and the Marshal was shot through the left knee. In agony, he was helped from his horse and carried to a chair brought out from a nearby cottage. Villars attempted to continue to direct his troops, but his distress was too great to allow him to do so. Fainting from loss of blood, the Marshal was carried from the field. Chemerault was killed in the same volley, and shortly afterwards Albergotti fell from his horse and fractured his leg, but whether this was an accident or caused by enemy fire is unclear. [29]

The paralysis in command that these sudden events inflicted on the control of the battle for the French left flank was stark. Word of the Marshal's fall ran through the ranks, and around the stricken group of senior officers the redoubtable defenders began to waver. Reportedly only the Irish regiments remained really firm. The Marquis de Puysegur (so perversely prominent at Oudenarde) hurried to the scene and he instantly recognised the gravity of the situation; unless a firm grip was taken there would be collapse on this flank. A stream of orders was issued, and within thirty minutes of Villars being wounded those of the French battalions around La Folie Farm that were still on their feet and fighting had fired their last shots and begun to withdraw from contact. They did so with a flourish and in good style, advancing boldly from their breastworks to loose off their volleys and then retire. The desired effect was achieved, for the Allied infantry momentarily drew back. Du Rozel's Carabiniers, flushed with their quick success over the Hessian cavalry, covered the withdrawal of the infantry here with efficient skill, and the disciplined ranks of the French troopers kept the Allied soldiers at bay, deterring any close pursuit. In any case, a properly co-ordinated harrying of the French battalions was probably not practical as Eugene's troops needed a breathing space. Puysegur managed something approaching a clean break on this flank – quite an achievement in the circumstances.

Meanwhile, an aide had been sent spurring away to the right Wing to find Marshal Boufflers, and summon him to take command of the army. Leaving D'Artagnan in command against any renewed Dutch assault, the elderly Marshal hurried to his new post in the centre of the field. As he did so he could see Orkney's infantry pouring through the gaps in the redans against virtually no opposition. The army Boufflers now commanded was in great peril – held tightly in place on the right and driven back on the left. Worse of all, the centre was pierced and what little artillery saved there was being hurried away by their crews running their pieces between the gaps in the cavalry massed on the Plain of Malplaquet. As predicted, those guns abandoned in the redans were at that very moment being turned upon their former owners by the British and German soldiers.

With his customary sound sense of timing, Marlborough had fixed the French army on both wings and forced his opponent to commit all his available infantry. He then attacked the most sensitive spot with troops carefully kept back for the purpose. All this he had done on other battlefields; it was his method. Orkney's battalions (two of them Prussian, and eleven British – the 2nd Foot Guards and a battalion of Orkney's Regiment having been detached earlier in the day to bolster the attack on the Bois de Sars triangle), were relatively few in numbers, but were quite strong enough to take and hold the redans.

The battalions of French and Swiss Guards, who were virtually all that remained to hold the French centre, now rather feebly took themselves off to avoid the dreadful cannonade directed against them. To add wings to their flight, some of the Guards made use of the untended horses of the Notat Dragoons who were just then moving forward to support them. The agitated and nervous attitude of these elite soldiers was widely commented on by observers at the time, and illustrates rather firmly the devastating effect of the prolonged Allied bombardment on this part of the French line. Had these Guards fought as well as they looked, the redans would have been held against Orkney's attack, and Colonel De La Colonie wrote scathingly of them: 'Some of our best dressed troops did not think it proper to hold this ground.'[30] The time was now approaching 2.00 pm.

The 176 squadrons of Allied cavalry, under the overall command of Auvergne, now began to pick their way across the marsh opposite the centre of the French line. The first line of Allied cavalry comprised Tilly's thirty Dutch squadrons; Lumley followed with the British Horse and dragoons, with von Bulow and the Prussian and Hanoverian cavalry in rear. The Imperial cavalry under the Duke of Württemberg and Count Vehlen formed the reserve. Simultaneously Hesse-Cassell advanced with his Dutch and Saxon cavalry of the right Wing, in support of a fresh effort by Orange's infantry. He took up a threatening position between the Bois de Thiery and the end of the redans. About 26,000 Allied horsemen were involved in this grand and intimidating advance.

Facing Auvergne on the Plain of Malplaquet were the 200 rather smaller French squadrons under the command of the Marquis de la Vallière (perhaps some 18,000 men strong). These troopers had suffered under the Allied bombardment all morning, and the drain on Villars' infantry resources as he fought to hold the Bois de Sars left them without adequate supports, as had occurred at Blenheim and Ramillies. This diminished their energy not one bit. As the kettle-drummers hammered their tattoo, the French horsemen came teeming forward, rank upon rank, charging towards the redans to ride down Tilly's squadrons before they could properly form on the open plain.

The Dutch troopers were caught at a disadvantage, for they were still engaged in drawing up into battle formation beyond the redans, and were not ready to receive the impetuous French charge. The two squadrons of Stair's Scots Dragoons were just behind them and they moved quickly forward in support, just in time to check the progress of the French squadrons. They broke the leading rank and threw them back, before recovering their own position in admirable order. In this way enough space was gained for Lumley and Tilly to bring their troopers fully into line before the action properly began. Jemmy Campbell, a squadron commander of the dragoons, was seen to distinguish himself in the hacking close-quarter contest that bought the necessary time for the Dutch. He decapitated an officer of the Gardes du Corps with a neat backhanded stroke of his sword, and was afterwards said by Orkney to have behaved in the action 'like an angell.'[31]

The cavalry battle rapidly sprawled out across the whole Plain of Malplaquet. There was little that was elegant about this bloody struggle, but the French fought with their usual bravery. As had become customary in Marlborough's army, the Allied troopers, when pressed or disordered, fell back on the nearby support of their infantry. The coolly delivered musketry volleys prevented the French subordinate commanders, the Comte de Beaveaude on the right and the Marquis de Montesson on the left, from pressing home whatever advantage they gained. All the same, it was a most determined and gallant effort by the French to tip the scales, and Marlborough wrote afterwards that although the Allied infantry had forced their way through the woods by one o'clock: 'Our horse then advanced into the plains, where the battle was resumed with great fury and lasted till three in the afternoon.'[32]

Orkney afterwards freely admitted that the repeated French onslaught was delivered with such dash that, had proper infantry support not been immediately at hand, the Allied squadrons must have given way. Still, this advantage was carefully delivered by Marlborough as a part of his overall plan, and his cavalry commanders put it to full use. There is no disgrace, and everything to be admired, in having superior tactical arrangements to your opponent. In this desperate battle, the Gardes du Corps under Montesson lost their celebrated banner, the Cornette Blanche, while the Chevalier de St George (Pretender to the English throne) was wounded by a sabre slash while fighting with the French cavalry. Six times de la Vallière's cavalry charged, and each time they were thrown back across the plain. Every time the Allied cavalry fell back to re-form, their batteries ravaged the French squadrons with unrelenting fury, roundshot and canister ripping their tired ranks. Moreover, as the afternoon wore on, Eugene was able to bring forward from the Allied right those Imperial squadrons of cavalry not so far engaged, and ten guns from Armstrong's great battery were dragged forward into the redans to add weight to the artillery onslaught on the French cavalry. Boufflers could see that the efforts of his gallant troopers were to no avail, while the Allied infantry, so disciplined and well handled, remained to support their own horsemen. At last the Marshal began to pull his battered squadrons back across the plain past the village of Malplaquet.

On the French right Wing, the solid infantry corps under D'Artagnan (soon to become the Marquis de Montesquiou) was slowly giving ground before the renewed advance of the Dutch infantry. D'Artagnan had three horses killed that day, and two musket balls struck his breastplate. Now Hesse-Cassell's cavalry were lapping around his left flank, threatening him with envelopment; before long the French infantry here might be pinned against the woods. At the Bleiron Farm, St Hilaire's smoke-grimed gunners, standing beside their pieces like blackened butchers, had exhausted their ammunition in the fierce artillery onslaught on the Dutch foot (a mere 400 rounds of ammunition remained in their caissons at the end of the day). It was time for the guns to go or be lost to the Allies. Accordingly, the orders were given and the withdrawal was well handled; the French artillery got away in the nick of time. In this skilful way, sixty-four guns were snatched away from the advancing Allies, and many of those that were abandoned had been disabled in the ferocity of the Allied bombardment. D'Artagnan's infantry covered the withdrawal of the guns towards Maubeuge and Bavai, while away on the left of the army, the infantry under de Goesbriand steadily fell back in good order towards Quiévrain. The French army had done all that its commanders demanded of it, now it really had to go.

As Boufflers drew his cavalry back, watched initially by only three fresh Danish squadrons, the Allied soldiers stood victorious on the bloody field of battle – victorious but exhausted. Marlborough's army could not follow the French with any vigour, for the effort and expense of the day had been too great. Withers' cavalry, although rather tired, were ordered to pursue, but Luxembourg's reserve corps of cavalry reappeared from its watch on the approaches to Maubeuge, and gave cover to the retreating French army. Withers closed with the French rearguard as it crossed the Hogneau Stream, but in a sharp little action fifteen French squadrons drove his leading troops back towards the Plain of Malplaquet.[33] At midnight, their task completed, Luxembourg withdrew his cavalry within the fortified lines of La Bassée.

That night a weary Duke of Marlborough added a paragraph to a letter he had begun to write to Sarah just before the battle began: 'I am so tired that I have but strength to tell you that we have had this day a very bloody battle, the first part of the day we beat their foot, and afterwards their horse.'[34] Meanwhile, Marshal Boufflers was at his field desk, writing to his King to explain the withdrawal of the French army, adding with sombre pride that rarely can misfortune have been attended by such glory.

Marlborough was rightly subdued after such a dreadful contest, for his troops had paid a mighty price for their victory. Over 20,000 Allied soldiers were casualties, amongst them many of the veterans who had shared the Duke's campaigns for long years. On the other side of the field Villars' gallant French army lost about 12,000 men, of whom only some 500 were unwounded prisoners. The Marshal afterwards claimed that his losses were much lighter, writing from his litter to Louis XIV that his army suffered only 6,000 casualties. This was preposterous and a poor compliment to his soldiers, implying that they could be driven from such a strongly entrenched position with merely trifling loss. In fact, on 20 September 1709 Boufflers wrote to Versailles that over 6,000 of their soldiers were still being tended for their wounds.[35] Naturally this figure takes no account of the dead left in the woods at Malplaquet, or those who had died of their wounds since the battle. As it was, the melancholy business of collecting and tending the wounded and burying the dead occupied many days. Marlborough sent William Cadogan to meet the Chevalier de Luxembourg at Bavai, and to arrange for parties of French to come forward and collect their own wounded.

A storm of indignation soon swept over Marlborough at the scale of the Allied losses, although the row was greatest in London where his political enemies were to be found, rather than in Holland whose troops had taken the hardest hammering. The Duke of Argyll, so valiant and fine in the reeking woods of the Bois de Sars, was soon swaggering about the coffee houses of London, swearing that the Queen had but to say the word and he would manhandle the Captain-General to the Tower, in front of his own troops, for his 'incompetence' at Malplaquet. The sickly old Queen was now estranged from the Duke and his fiery wife, but she did not approve such idle talk. Still, it was an unhappy episode.[36]

Meanwhile, the siege of Mons proceeded without serious interference from Villars and his battered army. The Duke of Berwick came forward to see what might be attempted in early October but drew off without forcing a battle. The Marquis de Grimaldi and his garrison of 4,500 men in Mons fought well, but the town was surrendered to Marlborough on 23 October 1709, once a breach in the defences was made. The expulsion of the French from the Spanish Netherlands was now practically complete, but there was no more time to campaign that autumn, and the Allied army went into winter quarters on 28 October.

In the short and bloody 1709 campaigning season, Marlborough had taken the fortresses of Tournai, St Ghislain and Mons, and the French field army had been mauled in the woods at Malplaquet. That was certainly something. At the cost of the lives of thousands of his cherished veteran soldiers, on 11 September the Duke drove his opponent back from an immensely strong entrenched position – a feat likened by George Orkney at the time to being equal to storming a fortress. This success was achieved with a distinct advantage in numbers, but not overwhelmingly so, and the tactical ability demonstrated by Marlborough and his generals under the most arduous circumstances was considerable. However, the damage to the Duke's standing, particularly in Britain where war-weariness was taking firm hold, was dangerous. Repeated references to a 'bloodbath' and to allegations of bungling on the field of battle, gave potent ammunition to Marlborough's enemies. This, when added to the very real cost in blood, was arguably too great a price to pay for the strategically limited success actually gained.

However, for years both Marlborough and Eugene sought to bring the French field army to decisive battle, and so often their opponents had eluded them. The challenging advance by Villars, plainly intended to disrupt the siege of the important fortress of Mons, seemed to offer the two commanders the chance they had sought for so long. To destroy Villars' army at this critical time would be a prize of immense value – potentially a war-winning stroke; one for which it was worth taking risks. These risks, for what they were, may have appeared to Marlborough to have been no greater than those faced on other critical occasions, as at Blenheim, and may have seemed far lower than those run to such good effect at Oudenarde the previous year. Whenever Marlborough fought the French he succeeded and, it could be calculated, the assault at Malplaquet should be no different. The delay in mounting the attack, firstly by having to bring up the artillery, then the uncertainty over the difficult ground, and lastly in waiting for Withers' corps to arrive, gave the French the chance to fortify beyond imagining the position they had taken up.

However, the Duke was confident of success, he had confidence in his generals and in his troops, and accordingly he was right to fight.

Marlborough may certainly be suspected of underestimating both the tenacity of the French soldiers and the strength of their entrenchments. However, his plan of attack was one that combined determination and imagination, mixing both brutal assault and subtle manoeuvre. His favoured technique was to exert maximum pressure and then strike where least expected – Withers' approach march against the French left flank at La Folie Farm is perhaps the most innovative example of this technique being put into practice. It is very likely, however, that the highly professional French commanders had studied his methods, and laid their own plans accordingly. The approach of the column from Tournai certainly was an unsettling shock for them, but they fought very well in other respects. The thought occurs that Marlborough, for once, underestimated his opponents' resourcefulness.

Perhaps also, the now mighty Allied army, over 110,000 men strong, was simply too large and unwieldy an instrument to be properly handled with the command and control techniques of the day. Even fine commanders such as Marlborough and Eugene could only spread their personal influence just so far, and much reliance had to be placed on lesser commanders who, of necessity, had command of large bodies of men. This army in 1709 was nearly twice the size of that at Blenheim or Ramillies. However, it is noticeable that subsequent operations with the Allied army, rapidly brought back to full strength after the battle, were carried out with skill and panache, so perhaps important lessons were learned at all levels.

The Dutch, who lost about 8,000 men killed and wounded in their ghastly assault on the French right Wing, were far less agitated at the cost of the battle than were the British. This indicates plainly that much of the criticism the Duke endured afterwards was motivated by political intrigue in London and professional spite amongst some of his British officers. Held in high esteem by the Dutch States-General, Marlborough retained their confidence, and they watched in forlorn dismay as his influence in London faded

Timing had been an important factor, and played a crucial role in the events surrounding the battle. Had Marlborough simply blocked Villars' approach to Mons on 8 September 1709, and tried to manoeuvre in order to fight the French in the open, well away from the constricting wooded belts where his greater numbers could really tell, it is likely that Villars would have slipped away. Had the Duke struck the French before his own arrangements were complete, when his guns were not up, and when Withers was still distant and unable to participate, his task would still have been enormous in having to force a passage between the woods. In either case he might then have faced accusations over delay on the one hand, and lack of preparation on the other. It seems entirely possible that his enemies in London would have placed a charge against the Duke of dereliction of duty, of failing to do his utmost in the face of the enemy.

The French tend to regard Malplaquet as a victory. This is quite understandable, but it is entirely wishful thinking. Marshal Villars and his army fought with magnificent tenacity, yet despite all their great efforts they had to quit their breastworks and leave the field by mid-afternoon – had they stayed they would have been destroyed. The Allied army stood tired but able and ready to offer battle that evening or the following day; the French did not, they hurried back to the protection of their defensive lines. Significantly, the prized fortress of Mons, for the security of which Villars fought the battle in the first place, was left to its fate. Yet the Marshal had plain instructions from Louis XIV that Mons was to be saved. These simple facts denote a defeat for the French, however honourable, not a victory. By so boldly offering battle at Malplaquet Villars openly attempted, and failed, to disrupt Marlborough's preparations for the siege. No French commander offering to fight a battle with the Duke on anything like level terms would go unchallenged; only in such a way could his true aim, the comprehensive defeat of the French field army and a valid peace, be accomplished. Given that the capture of Mons was a worthwhile aim for the Allies, the heavy cost to their army of fighting this grinding battle, deplorable though it undoubtedly was, could be justified.

Marlborough always had a care for his soldiers – not for nothing was he known in the army as 'Corporal John', the one who ensured they were fed and clothed and paid, the one who led them and gave them orders, the one who watched over them, by day on the hot and tiring march and by night in their sodden bivouacs. But Marlborough always recognised the importance of decisive battle above every other consideration, and there was an inevitable price to pay. Soldiers acknowledge this as a part of their lot in life, and the Duke's troops, although growing weary of war, kept their trust in his abilities and his care for them. Marlborough defeated Villars, both face to face on the dreadful battlefield of 11 September 1709 and always thereafter. The Marshal not once ever really challenged the Duke to battle outside defensive lines again. Only when Marlborough was at last dismissed by his ungrateful Queen did Villars dare to move out to attack the Allied army once more. This simple fact is more expressive than words.

The Malplaquet Battlefield Today

Lying squarely on the present-day border of France and Belgium, just to the south of the busy town of Mons, the Plain of Malplaquet has not been built over and spoiled. The fields, small farms and woods all around are largely untouched and it is not difficult to visualise the desperate fighting that took place there in the late summer of 1709. Unfortunately, it is no longer possible, as Winston Churchill could in the 1930s, to stroll about and find cannon-balls lying in the grass. However, the woods follow their ancient pattern, particularly in the north-western part of the battlefield, in the Bois de Sars, where Eugene's infantry fought with such tenacity, and Withers' column approached, unsuspected and unseen, to turn the left flank of the French army. The leafy woods are now silent.

In the centre of the battlefield, the main road southwards from Mons bisects the Plain of Malplaquet, and the customs-post is now vacant and unused. The French erected a monument in memory of the battle in 1909 (now rather dilapidated and in need of attention), and this stands at the roadside and provides a useful elevated spot from which to view the surrounding terrain. The fields are open (the plain is a watershed, with the land sloping gently away to both the north and south) and provided good going for the employment of cavalry. It was here that the tumultuous mounted battle was fought in the afternoon. The Bleiron Farm, near which the French sited the concealed battery which devastated the Dutch infantry, is visible a few hundred yards away, and the fold in the ground, running off to the north-east, along which those guns were sited to such good effect, can be clearly seen. On the Belgian side of the border the many small gulleys and streams Eugene mentioned in his letters are still evident, and indicate the broken and boggy nature of the ground which caused such difficulties for the Allies in preparing their attacks. Standing and looking towards France, the Plain of Malplaquet is in hidden ground, due to the terrain sloping away to the south from the watershed along the border. Armstrong's big guns, bombarding the French redans from this vicinity, would plainly tend to throw their projectiles over their target and into the dead ground beyond. This caused heavy losses to the patient French cavalry as the balls tore through their ranks throughout the long morning of the infantry battle.

Over on the right of the French position, the lane past the Bleiron Farm leads to the woods which mark the present extent of the Bois de Lanieres. The woods here are less dense than on the other side of the battlefield, and a little more imagination is required to see how the action developed. However, a good view is to be had to the north-east of the round copse which is the Bois de Thiery. There Rantzau stood with his Hanoverian brigade, anchoring the Dutch infantry to the British and Prussian troops in centre. Orange's troops surged past the wood in their doomed attacks on Boufflers' infantry position. The ground rises gently to the south and south-west, giving an additional physical advantage to the French defenders, both in their repulse of the Dutch, and in the surging counter-attacks that struck Orange's broken battalions as they fell back from their fruitless assaults.

NOTES

1. Letter from the Duke to Secretary of State Boyle, dated 13 September 1709, in Murray, G (ed.), *Letters and Dispatches of the Duke of Marlborough*, Vol IV, 1845, p. 597.
2. Louis XIV to Villars at the Council of State at Marly on 11 May 1709. See Sturgill, C, *Marshal Villars and the War of Spanish Succession*, 1965, p. 85.
3. Chandler, D, *Marlborough as Military Commander*, 1973, p. 251.
4. Churchill, W S, *Marlborough: His Life and Times*, Vol IV, 1947, p. 581.
5. Atkinson, C T (ed.), *Gleanings from the Cathcart Mss*, JSAHR, 1951, p. 98.
6. Coxe, W, *Memoirs of John, Duke of Marlborough*, Vol II, 1848, p. 434.
7. Corvisier A, *La Bataille de Malplaquet 1709*, 1997, p. 61.
8. Chandler, p. 254.
9. Churchill, pp. 595–6.
10. Chandler, p. 257.
11. De La Colonie, J (ed. W Horsley), *Chronicles of an Old Campaigner*, 1904, p. 337.
12. Letter from Matthew Bishop, in Hastings, M (ed.), *Oxford Book of Military Anecdotes*, 1985, p. 148.
13. Mrs Christian Davies reported that camp gossip had it that Marlborough himself went into the woods to converse with his nephew the Duke of Berwick, and that it was hoped he gave no secrets away. If that was so the gossip was very ill-informed, Berwick was nowhere near the battlefield. See Defoe, D (ed. J Fortescue), *Life and Adventures of Mrs Christian Davies*, 1929, p. 137.
14. De La Colonie, p. 338.
15. Coxe, p. 447.
16. Defoe, p. 129. The tactics for making such an assault were highly developed and well practised at this time; these veteran battalions were used to siege warfare when desperate attacks were very much the order of the day. The procedure adopted was to draw up the attacking battalions with the grenadiers forming the first rank. These men, and the pioneers (either attached from other units or drawn from volunteers within the battalions), would move forward and clear paths for the attacking troops, covered by fire from soldiers nominated by the commanding officer; once a way forward was clear the attacking wave of troops would be called on by their officers to give a cheer and to move into the assault. Groups of battalions, in ad hoc brigades, would usually carry out this procedure on a larger scale, with the grenadiers often grouped together for the task, as at the Schellenberg.
17. The British brigade detached to assist Lottum and Argyll in the attack on the Bois de Sars triangle consisted of the 2nd English Foot Guards and the 1st Royals (Royal Scots). Argyll's brigade was actually commanded in action that day by Colonel Richard Temple, although 'Red John' went in with the troops.
18. De La Colonie, p. 340.
19. Ibid.
20. Burn, W, *A Scots Fusilier and Dragoon under Marlborough*, 1936, JSAHR, p. 91.
21. Rantzau was quite right not to involve his whole Hanoverian brigade without orders. Orkney's infantry were already partially committed, rather unexpectedly, to the attack on the Bois de Sars triangle. With no strong reserves of infantry, Marlborough's centre was potentially vulnerable to any serious French counter-stroke. However inconvenient for the Dutch in their desperate attack, Rantzau's watch over the gap opposite the Bleiron Farm was crucial to the Duke. See Coxe, p. 452.
22. Chandler, D (ed.), *Journal of John Deane*, JSAHR, 1984, p. 94.

23. It is sometimes suggested that the Prince of Orange was only intended by Marlborough to make a dummy attack against the French right Wing, but that he lost his head in the heat of the battle and led his troops almost to destruction. See Edwards, H, *A Life of Marlborough*, 1926 p. 255, and *Gleanings from the Cathcart Mss*, p.100. That the Allied effort on the left was in far less strength than that on the right plainly indicates that the Duke's main effort lay with Eugene in the Bois de Sars, and comments that Withers was perhaps intended at first to pass behind the entire Allied army to join Orange in his attack are less than convincing. Too great a time and effort was entailed in such a move. Accordingly, the concentration of most effort on the right flank of the Allied attack is understandable and logical. However, pretended attacks were not at all in Marlborough's style – he preferred to mount maximum pressure on many points and then to take advantage of his opponents' unfolding lack of balance as command procedures were firstly put to the test, and then comprehensively overwhelmed. This was plainly seen with Orkney's infantry attack at Ramillies which fooled the French commander but was not, of itself, a dummy attack – had the chance offered, his local success would have been reinforced. At Malplaquet, while Orange was young and relatively inexperienced, he was certainly no fool and nor were the battle-hardened commanders around him. A comprehensive misunderstanding of the real role assigned to their attack is not credible. The Dutch losses, terrible though they were, say more for the highly proficient nature of the French dispositions, for the complexity of the defences and the vigour of the defenders, and of the admirable, if misplaced, perseverance of the attacking soldiers when faced with such extraordinary and insurmountable odds. See also Chandler p. 257; Bowen, H, *The Dutch at Malplaquet*, JSAHR, 1962; Trevelyan, G M, *The Peace and the Protestant Succession*, 1948, p. 25; and Coxe, p.451.

24. *Life and Adventures of Mrs Christian Davies*, p.138. Coxe believed that this incident actually occurred during the subsequent siege operations against Mons, but this is a misreading of the narrative. See *Memoirs of John, Duke of Marlborough*, p. 467 .

25. *Life and Adventures of Mrs Christian Davies*, p. 139.

26. Churchill, p. 614. This passage of the Allied guns through the woods indicates that the terrain was, in parts, nowhere near as tangled as is often thought. This makes perfect sense for the French soldiers would have cleared as much of a field of fire for themselves as they could, and many trees were felled to make up the abatti obstacles.

27. Chandler, D (ed.), *Captain Robert Parker and Comte de Mérode-Westerloo*, 1968, p. 89. Parker had been posted to Ireland, rather against his will, to teach the platoon firing method to the recruits there. He heard of the incident from his brother officers who fought at Malplaquet that day.

28. Churchill, p. 618.

29. Villars' knee never completely healed for the kneecap was shattered, and agonising attempts by the surgeons, while his aides held the Marshal flat to the table, failed to remove the ball. He eked out his tortured long life with the mangled joint held in an iron brace. Years later, Villars sadly commented, on hearing that his old friend James Fitzjames, the Duke of Berwick, had been neatly decapitated by a round-shot while on campaign: 'He always had luck that one.' See Petrie, C, *The Marshal, Duke of Berwick*, 1953, p. 334. The Irishman, Peter Drake, who fought with the French that day, said afterwards that Albergotti was actually shot through the body, causing him to fall from

his horse. See Burrell, S, *Amiable Renegade. The Memoirs of Captain Peter Drake 1671–1753*, 1960, p.165.

30. De La Colonie, p. 338. There was wide comment in France at the poor performance of these supposedly elite regiments. An anonymous French veteran wrote: 'We have lost the battle through the long-standing cowardice of the Régiment du Roi and the Gardes Français who were slack in the last battle.' (Author's own translation). See Corvisier, A, *Le Moral des Combattants*, 1977.

31. *Cathcart Mss, p.* 99. See also Churchill p. 625. Peter Drake left a vivid account of the bloody close-quarter mounted struggle around the redans. He used his carbine to blow off the head of a German trooper at close range, and received eleven musket ball strikes on his breastplate, and two more through the tails of his coats. In addition, he ended the day bearing five sabre slashes. See Burrell, pp.166–7.

32. *Letters and Dispatches of the Duke of Marlborough*, p. 505.

33. Marlborough's choice of Withers' corps to pursue the French, led by Danish squadrons of cavalry (apparently the only really fresh troops available) is interesting. It plainly indicates that, despite the bitter fighting around the La Folie Farm, this portion of the Allied army remained the most capable of acting as a striking force.

34. Churchill, p. 627.

35. Estimates of the casualties at Malplaquet vary widely, and there are almost as many available as there are authors on the subject. The Dutch reported that the total Allied loss, both killed and wounded, was 17,732. This is very precise indeed, but there is a list in the Public Record Office in Kew, Surrey, which gives Allied infantry casualties to be 18,353. If this is right, and again it is a very precise figure, then the total losses in Marlborough's army cannot be short of 20,000. The French, perhaps understandably, claimed that the true Allied figure was much higher, and Marlborough's enemies in London quickly picked up this theme. Regimental losses varied widely of course; the two battalions of the French Royal-Infantrie (who fought the Dutch from beside the concealed batteries at the edge of the Bois de Lanieres) suffered 450 killed and wounded – well over 50% of their bayonet strength; whereas the single battalion of the Royal Artillerie Régiment, who were nearby, lost only ninety-six men. See Corvisier pp. 120–4 for an interesting analysis of the differing reports on the scale of the casualties in both armies. M. Corvisier comes to the conclusion that the Allies lost 21,000 killed and wounded, while the French casualties amounted to 11,000. This seems about right, though may understate Villars' losses.

36. Memories are long, and during the 1715 Jacobite rising Argyll was removed from his post as Commander in Chief in Scotland by Marlborough, who had been reinstated as Captain-General by George I. The rather thin grounds for Argyll's removal were that he was not pursuing the rebels with sufficient vigour. Marlborough's close friend, William Cadogan, replaced Argyll and Joseph Sabine, an old comrade in arms from the Flanders campaign and veteran of the crossing of the Scheldt at Oudenarde, took over from Cadogan when he, in turn, went back to London.

CHAPTER XII

Like Hounds Upon a Hare
The Closing Campaigns and the
Fall of Marlborough

That we must part from such a man

The heavy cost to the Allies of the Battle of Malplaquet put fresh heart into the desperate French and, despite the loss of Mons in October 1709, their military efforts were invigorated. The armies of Louis XIV could look forward to the campaign in 1710 with new spirit.

There remained the slim prospect of a negotiated peace. Despite the heavily qualified success of his army in 1709, Louis XIV still earnestly wanted an end to the war. He continued to offer good terms, and even agreed to remove his troops from Spain, but he would not accept Clause 37. The Whig administration in London was failing but they and the Dutch, who were broken financially by the war, had not the ability to recognise the opportunity presented. The war had to go on. As the Whigs fell from favour in London, so gradually did Marlborough, but he put these troubles to one side and returned to the Low Countries in February 1710 to prepare for a new campaign.

That winter the Duke again pressed Queen Anne to appoint him Captain-General for Life. The old arguments were again presented – he felt this would secure him from political enemies and intrigue at home while he fought a war abroad; simultaneously such an appointment would boost his prestige in the capitals of Europe where any lessening of his authority (actual or perceived) would be damaging to the Allied cause. Marlborough's fine instincts did not often fail him, but this was one such occasion. He was thoroughly out of favour with the Queen, she had no hesitation in turning down his request, and the Duke was, once again, further weakened by the public knowledge that this was so. Meanwhile, Duchess Sarah, whose headstrong behaviour had done such harm, lost all her posts at Court, and the Duke, even when on his knees in front of Her Majesty, could not save her from dismissal.

Events in London were moving swiftly and Sidney Godolphin,

Marlborough's friend and ally, was dismissed as Lord Treasurer on 8 August 1710. The ungrateful Queen, who owed so much to this man's selfless skill, refused to grant Godolphin an audience to receive from his hands the wand of his office. Meanly, she sent him a message that he should just throw it away. Later that year, in October, the Whigs lost power to the Tories in the General Election and Robert Harley, the Earl of Oxford, at once brilliant and devious, came into office. Marlborough's power base at home was now entirely gone, and his offices within the army were steadily whittled away. Regimental colonelcies were granted without reference to him, contracts for the supply of the field army were arranged behind his back. Before long he was Captain-General no longer, and simply commanded the Allied army in the Low Countries. The year 1710 was generally unfortunate for the Allied cause. In Spain their forces were everywhere defeated and expelled, and those Spaniards who fought on the Allied side were abandoned. Meanwhile, along the Rhine the Allied armies were inactive and unenterprising, and operations in northern Italy stalled.

Towards the end of the year, the new Tory administration schemed in secret with the French to conclude a separate and advantageous peace. Much of this was known to Marlborough (although much more was hidden from him), but he could neither speak of it nor obstruct moves to abandon Britain's partners in the Grand Alliance. Throughout this increasingly unhappy time the Duke retained the affection and trust of his commanders and soldiers, but ready as they were to fight, they could not tempt Marshal Villars to risk an open battle. The French stuck to their defensive lines in Artois and Picardy, calculating quite correctly that time was on their side. Britain, whose war effort had been immense, was tired of the conflict, and looked for as good a peace as could be obtained.

In April 1711 the Emperor Joseph of Austria died and his brother, the Archduke Charles, who might once have been King of Spain in other circumstances, succeeded him. The uncertainty in the Empire removed Eugene and his army from Flanders, to kick their heels on the Rhine for much of that year's campaigning season. The French armies ranged against Marlborough, as a consequence, now outnumbered him, but the Duke schemed to surprise and take the great fortress of Bouchain. It seemed possible that this was just one prize of such worth that Villars might have no option but to stand and fight.

To attain this objective, Marlborough had to pierce the fortified Lines of Non Plus Ultra (reportedly a comment by Villars' tailor when asked to let out his breeches), which stretched from the Channel coast to the Sambre river. In a subtle and complex operation, the Duke fooled Villars into weakening his defences at the small village of Arleux not far from Cambrai. He then marched his army to threaten the Lines on the Plain of Lens in the shadow of Vimy Ridge. When Villars took the bait and shifted westwards, Marlborough suddenly counter-marched through the moonlit summer night back to Arleux to break the Lines and cross the Sensee river, with hardly the loss of a man. This formidable feat of marching covered forty miles in only eighteen hours. Although Villars galloped ahead with a party of French cavalry he could not prevent the Allied coup, and instead got involved in a wild mêlée with Marlborough's advanced guard, and lost his hat.

This delightful operation enabled Marlborough to draw his army into battle-array and defy Villars to accept battle outside Bouchain. The ground chosen was Bourlon Wood. As it was, Villars knew that he had been out-generalled, and meekly drew off to manoeuvre and try to hamper the siege of Bouchain which followed. The ambitious enterprise to take the town, in the face of a superior French army close by, was an epic operation and was Marlborough's last military triumph. Bouchain fell to the Allies on 12 September 1711. The Duke's requests for additional supplies to enable an advance further into France went unanswered, both in London and in Holland. But then, confidential negotiations for peace were under way, and there is a likely connection.[1]

Marlborough returned to London at the close of the 1711 campaigning season to face scheming, criticism, accusation and lies. On 31 December the Queen suddenly stripped him of all his offices; her letter of dismissal was flung into the fire by Marlborough in disgust, an unusually impetuous act for someone so self-controlled. Marching soldier Matthew Bishop, veteran of many of Marlborough's campaigns, wrote of the army's disgust and outrage at the news: 'That we must part from such a man whose fame has spread throughout the world.'[2] Accused of mal-administration in the handling of the large sums of money expended in financing his army's operations, the Duke feared a prosecution and felt obliged to live abroad. Late in 1712, after the death of his close friend, Godolphin, he sought sanctuary in Holland, and in Hanover with the Elector (who mistrusted him, but needed his aid to secure the throne of Great Britain on Anne's death). His great Quartermaster-General, William Cadogan, was amongst those who chose exile with him, refusing to return to England when the British troops were recalled from the war in 1712. In contrast to his treatment in England, the Duke and Duchess were received with honours and acclamation wherever they went on the continent.

James Butler, 2nd Duke of Ormonde, replaced Marlborough in command of the army in the Low Countries but he was a poor substitute, despite his well-meaning efforts and personal bravery. Ormonde had not the strength of character to resist the restraining orders that now arrived from London. These were imposed by the Tory Ministry, and required him not to employ British troops against the French, no matter what the threat might be. Infamously, Marshal Villars was made aware of these same orders. This crude deception was evident to the other Allied commanders and was a sad postscript to long years of campaign service together. At length, the red-coated soldiers were obliged to march off the field of war and leave their comrades in the lurch. They found all the towns of the Spanish Netherlands, except those few with British garrisons, closed against them, and were only allowed to find shelter in Dunkirk courtesy of King Louis XIV.

The German troops, so brave and steadfast in the British service, refused to leave their Dutch and Imperial allies. Despite mean threats by the British government that their arrears of pay would be withheld unless they marched off, they remained on campaign. Though they were, in a technical sense, mercenary troops, the Germans remained staunchly operational while the redcoats marched away with bitterness in their hearts.

Peace came to the weary nations with the Treaty of Utrecht of 11 April 1713, and the Peace of Rastadt of 7 March 1714 – better an imperfect peace than what was now a pointless war. King Philip (on whose behalf France had fought the war) remained on the throne in Madrid, but the power of France was immeasurably checked for a generation or more. Louis XIV was ailing and would soon die, to be succeeded by his great grandson (measles, and the peculiar medical techniques of the time, had ravaged the ranks of his children and grandchildren). By the two Treaties the Austrian Emperor Charles (who might have been King of Spain) got the Southern Netherlands, Sardinia and parts of northern Italy. Great Britain gained Gibraltar, Hudson Bay, Minorca and Newfoundland, with access granted to overseas trade at the expense of Holland. The Hanoverian succession to the British throne was also confirmed, more or less, by the foreign powers. The Dutch, although they regained many of their cherished Barrier Towns in 1715, were broken financially and exhausted by their efforts in war. They concluded their own peace with France and Spain, and then went into an irreversible decline as a world power. Over all this, the partition of the old Spanish Empire, one of the original aims of the Grand Alliance when forged by King William III and the Duke of Marlborough, was now achieved.

On the death of the bitter old Queen on 1 August 1714, Marlborough returned to London. He and his Duchess received a tumultuous welcome. The Duke was reinstated as Captain-General by George I, and regained his post as Master-General of the Ordnance and Colonel of the 1st Foot Guards. His relations with the new King were never particularly close, although they were civil enough. The post of Captain-General was now rather symbolic, and the Duke remained in London during the Jacobite Rising in 1715, but he safeguarded the army against needless peacetime cuts, and instigated useful army reforms. Amongst these was the creation of the Royal Regiment of Artillery in May 1716.

The Duke suffered a serious stroke, the first of several, on 28 May 1716, and this was possibly brought on by the death the previous month of his favourite daughter, Anne. Cadogan virtually took over as Captain-General (he did so officially in 1721). Increasingly Marlborough was obliged to give up his posts and duties, and he lived quietly in retirement with Sarah at the incomplete Blenheim Palace, at Marlborough House in London, and at Windsor Lodge. In increasingly fragile health, he last attended the House of Lords in November 1721. John Churchill, 1st Duke of Marlborough, died at Windsor Lodge early in the morning on 16 June 1722, attended by Duchess Sarah, who said prayers with him just before the end.

NOTES

1. Trevelyan, G M, *The Peace and the Protestant Succession*, 1948 p. 133.
2. Brereton, J, *History of the 4th/7th Dragoon Guards*, 1982, p. 79.

CHAPTER XIII
Time's Shadowy Fingers
Marlborough's Battles in Review

He was more than a match for all the generals of that nation[1]

The Duke of Marlborough never fought a major defensive battle. Whenever the opportunity came to engage the French field army, he attacked them without question or hesitation. He was impetuous and bold on these occasions, fearing that his opponents would slip away (as they sometimes managed to do). Still he was not rash, having a highly developed ability to calculate the odds rapidly and with judgement. This was in an age when generals were expected to operate at a more leisurely pace – sieges and marches were less expensive in money, lives and reputations, and were not so risky as accepting outright battle. The Duke therefore stands out as one of the very few army commanders of the time who would chance all on the basis of rapid and ruthless calculation. He shares this distinction with a handful of others – his great comrade Prince Eugene, the French commanders Marshal Villars and Marshal Berwick, and in the wider world Charles XII of Sweden. Marlborough had the ability to see, with shattering clarity, that only real battles would lead to real victories and an end to the war for Spain.

Of Marlborough's five big battles between 1704 and 1709 – Schellenberg, Blenheim, Ramillies, Oudenarde and Malplaquet, he enjoyed a numerical advantage in just three — Schellenberg, Ramillies and Malplaquet. In the other two, Blenheim and Oudenarde, he achieved a temporary local advantage by astute manoeuvering, and maintained that advantage long enough to unbalance and overwhelm his less adept opponents. The ability to do this is highly refined military skill, demonstrating an application and understanding of the very modern military concept of Find – Fix – Strike.[2]

The tactics that Marlborough employed were curiously similar on each occasion he fought a battle, once allowance is made for the differing force ratios, the varied topography and timescale. At each instance he rapidly summed up the situation by personal reconnaissance, completed his appreciation while moving his troops into place, and refined his plan. He then threw heavy infantry attacks onto his opponents to fix them in position. In this way he seized the initiative, and by maintaining the pace and tempo of the attacks, often at great cost (as with Eugene and Cutts at Blenheim), took care not to lose that advantage for long, if at all, as events unfolded. Once the enemy had responded to the growing crisis that the Duke's attacks brought on, and had committed the reserves that should have been kept back against a real emergency, Marlborough's own reserves were adroitly employed against the weakened sector. The collapse and flight of the enemy army followed. This overall technique may be seen in use in all the five big battles. Only at Oudenarde and Malplaquet did the final phase – collapse and flight – take less dramatic shape than previously; on the first occasion because the onset of night saved the French, and on the second the exhaustion of the Allied army permitted their opponents to get away in tolerable order.

The other significant difference at Malplaquet was that Marlborough, commanding a very large army with all the complications that were entailed, was impelled to wait while his artillery and his detachments (notably Withers) got to the scene. The Duke had to permit his foe ample time to prepare for what became a 'set-piece' battle, rather outside his usually preferred setting.

It is interesting that Marlborough achieved the most perfect tactical successes when he had everything under his own eye. Eugene faltered at Blenheim, although the task he was set with his small army was daunting, and no blame can be attached for the slowness of his progress. Overkirk's valiant Dutch cavalry were overthrown and chased back at Ramillies, until Marlborough hurried forward reinforcements from the right Wing. At Oudenarde, the critical spot was always the dangerously open left flank of the Allied battle-line as it hurriedly deployed along the Diepenbeek Stream. The Duke stationed himself there to oversee the fighting at that point. Eugene was permitted to command on the larger Allied right Wing, where the battle, although hectic, was not so critical for much of the afternoon.[3] This on-the-spot effect was not possible at Malplaquet – the sheer size of the Allied army, twice that at Ramillies, made such personal control impractical. Accordingly, the execution of Marlborough's perfectly valid plan was left to lesser commanders. These men were good soldiers, and their behaviour was valiant, but they did not, perhaps, have the Duke's touch. The conduct of the battle seems to have suffered accordingly – Marlborough was the missing ingredient.

The Schellenberg hill fight opened up the vast region of Bavaria to Marlborough's strategic offensive. This was the first such complete victory for an English commander in continental Europe for many years, and it caused a sensation. The Imperial Court in Vienna was amazed at the audacity and unexpectedness of the ruthless assault and pursuit. Marlborough was immediately marked as a serious commander, a man to be reckoned with. He was certainly criticised for the heavy losses his army incurred, and there was some feeling that D'Arco could have been edged out of position with careful manoeuvering. This is perhaps true, but it ignores the awful time imperative that the Duke was labouring under. Any delay meant that the Elector of Bavaria would join D'Arco with the likely result that a major set-piece battle, with hardly a prospect of success, would be required to force the crossing of the River Danube. In addition, it was now known that Tallard was on the march from the Rhine, and before very long the Elector would be powerfully reinforced. It was well worth Marlborough's while to push the pace and try and force a Bavarian submission before the new French army arrived.

A few weeks after the Schellenberg came the great victory over the combined Franco-Bavarian army at Blenheim on the banks of the Danube. This occasion marked an unheard of shift in military and political power and influence in Europe. The French army had a tradition of conquest and victory – it was the best in the field, its commanders were supreme, its soldiers were valiant. Now an English general, with a stolen army drawn from many nations, had leapt upon and utterly shattered a numerically stronger French force – had taken its commanders into his own coach, and seized dozens of guns and regimental colours, vast quantities of baggage and thousands of prisoners. The list of casualties testified to the bitterness of the fighting for both armies fought well; success was no foregone conclusion for Marlborough and he had anxious moments. Still, his mastery in planning and execution, allied to the devoted support of Eugene in tying down the more numerous armies of Marshal Marsin and the Elector, and the valour of his fighting soldiers, carried the day. The destruction of an entire French army was an unheard of thing, and men could not sleep in their excitement at the astounding news from the Danube valley. Marlborough was marked out as the greatest captain of his generation – England was made a world power that day. Blenheim was the wonder of the age.

Oudenarde ranks as a most unusual battle at any time. There were no pre-arranged dispositions, no tacit mutual agreement by opposing commanders to stand and fight a battle, no careful siting of batteries or drawing up in convenient and neat lines of the glittering array of fine armies to beat of drum and flourish on the trumpets. There was no review of the regiments by the army commanders, no speeches, no fine declarations. Instead there was the sheer sweating spontaneity of the approach marches and of the initial Allied attacks; the deft ad hoc grouping of the running battalions as they fed into the teeming battle, and the desperate selfless bravery of both French and Allied soldiers as they struggled face-to-face for mastery of the lanes and hedges beside the Scheldt river. These are all facets of a most unusual battle. It was impossible to fully control such an extraordinary event, but Marlborough had the skill to grip the tactical initiative with both hands. He marched his army close enough to strike, and then hurled his advanced guard under William Cadogan like a javelin into the flank of the temporarily indolent French army as it marched comfortably away. The Duke acted with utter confidence in his own abilities, and in the abilities of his officers and soldiers. His army responded in a magnificent way, and the crushing of the right Wing of Vendôme's army was utterly shattering to the morale of the French soldiers, no matter how bravely they had fought. No one could mistake the confident recklessness with which Marlborough's success was achieved. Had night not come, had Overkirk not been delayed, had the bridges over the Scheldt held, the war might have ended that evening. For ever after, the French walked in fear of Marlborough.

Malplaquet must always be regarded as a dark and controversial battle. The recently failed peace negotiations undoubtedly engendered a certain bitterness amongst the soldiers of both armies. Theirs were the lives which were the daily price paid for the lack of agreement in comfortable council chambers far away, and they felt it deeply. When planning his assault through the Bois de Sars, Marlborough was faced with difficult terrain and tedious problems in bringing up his heavy guns, and the delay this caused was used by the French to massively fortify their position. He was the commander, and it was ultimately his decision to wait – he bears the responsibility. When the Allied attack at last went in, appallingly heavy losses were endured before Villars' army was driven off the battlefield; and they managed to retire in good order, more or less. The accusations routinely directed at Marlborough by his enemies were now immensely strengthened by the slander of a bloodbath battle that day, charges of self-serving incompetence in the conduct of the campaign, and hints at corruption at the highest levels of the Allied army. However, the mark of whether a battle is a victory or not is hardly to be found in the scale of the losses. If these are proportionate to the resources available and to the advantage gained they may be acceptable, regrettable though they always must be. Soldiers who go to war may expect to be killed, it is a part of the deal – it is also a part of that same deal that their lives should not be wasted, and it is in this particular respect that questions arise regarding the delay in mounting the attack that mist-laden morning in September. Questions may also be asked concerning the effectiveness in the command and control of such large numbers of troops in the woods, and of the quality of some of the subordinate field commanders on the actual day. Perhaps it would have been better not to fight there, but hindsight is a valuable tool, enabling the observer to belittle the efforts of others.

Although chronologically it is in the wrong place, consideration of the Battle of Ramillies is left to the last. With the fight at the Schellenberg and the smaller engagement at Elixheim in 1705, this is the only victory where Marlborough commanded on his own, without the valuable assistance of Prince Eugene. It is accordingly of enormous importance to

Marlborough's reputation as a commander – despite the assertions of later commentators it shows that he did not depend on Eugene for victory, however closely they worked together on other battlefields.[4] At Ramillies that Sunday in May, Marlborough, not optimistic that Marshal Villeroi would risk a fight in open battle at all, suddenly came upon the French army when on the move. He had no hesitation in closing up to and grappling with his opponent. In the space of only four short hours, the Duke attacked Villeroi's fine and well supplied French army, which was deployed in a good defensive position and in virtually equal strength to his own. He splintered his opponent's force and drove it in utter rout for many miles. That night, as he lay down on the grass to sleep, Marlborough did not know where his army was, so headlong was the pursuit of his beaten foe. It was as if an unlatched door had swung open and his army had fallen through. Many French units did not stop running until they got to their own border, so great was the shock that had been endured. The splendid victory at Ramillies led Marlborough to conquer, in a matter of a few weeks, all of present-day Belgium. The history of Europe fundamentally changed that summer, and France's military effort in the war and for generations afterwards would not fully recover. In fact, a victory for the Grand Alliance lay on the table if someone had only had the presence of mind to pick it up. Well might one of Marlborough's marching captains write after the battle 'Give me grace, o lord, never to forget this great and glorious day'.[5]

NOTES

1. Chandler, D, *Marlborough as Military Commander*, 1973 p. 331.
2. Find: A commander will seek out his opponent and try to learn his intentions, while simultaneously concealing his own location and plans. At Blenheim, Marlborough and Eugene were well informed of the location of the Franco-Bavarian army, but their opponents were in ignorance of their movements.
   Fix: A commander will deny an opponent freedom of action, by obliging the enemy commander to conform to his own actions. At Ramillies Marlborough achieved this by rapidly closing up to the French army, while a plan of attack was still being formed in his mind.
   Strike: Once a commander has taken the initiative, set his opponent up and unbalanced his arrangements, he will strike with all of his available force to secure victory. At Oudenarde Marlborough seized the initiative with his march to the Scheldt, and then, as his troops arrived, struck again and again at the numerically superior, but confused, French army.
3. After the Marquis de Biron was released from Allied captivity, he remarked to St Simon that, on the day of battle at Oudenarde: 'Prince Eugene took command wherever he went by courtesy of Marlborough, who preserved the entire authority.' See Churchill, W S, *Marlborough: His Life and Times*, 1947, Vol III, p. 386.
4. See Henderson, N, *Prince Eugen of Savoy*, 1964 and McKay, D, *Prince Eugene of Savoy*, 1977 for interesting comments on this topic.
5. Trevelyan, G M, *Ramillies and the Union with Scotland*, 1948, p.117.

CHAPTER XIV
The Sound of a Distant Drum
Marlborough's Army

The Generals began their contest every year in Spring.[1]

The Duke of Marlborough, as Captain-General of Queen Anne's Land Forces, and de facto Commander of the forces of the States-General of Holland, had field command of a huge confederate army.[2] The largest national contingents came from Britain and Holland, but considerable numbers of Allied troops served under the Duke, and these came from the Protestant states of Germany – Hesse-Cassell, Prussia, Hanover, Saxony, the Palatinate and others. Denmark and the Protestant cantons of Switzerland also provided fine troops. In addition, the Duke often had command over Imperial troops from Austria and Germany (usually under the immediate command of Prince Eugene or the Margrave of Baden). This rich mixture of military talents and capabilities often retained their national characteristics in uniform and chains of command – it was not unknown for the commander of a national contingent to have to refer to his prince before responding to Marlborough's orders on campaign. The example of the Danish cavalry hurrying to join the Allied army at Ramillies, in defiance of their orders, is an interesting case of local initiative being used to excellent advantage.

Military tactics and techniques were changing fast in western Europe at this time. The pike had all but disappeared, and cumbersome matchlock muskets had given way to the more effective flintlocks with socket bayonets. Firing by whole ranks, which was normal practice with matchlocks, was both inefficient and difficult to control (particularly as soldiers have a tendency to fire high), and the effectiveness of musketry when firing by ranks was shockingly feeble at even the modest usual range of about sixty paces. This outdated practice was steadily being replaced by the innovation of firing by groups of platoons. This method enabled commanders to maintain an almost continuous rolling and well directed fire upon the enemy, who would have no rest from the tormenting musketry directed at them. This was a Swedish innovation originally, taken up by the Dutch, and was highly favoured by

Marlborough who spoke of introducing the 'Dutch system' of platoon firing into his regiment as early as 1689.

Although an improvement on firing by ranks, this new method would have been difficult enough to control. The general roughness of ground, obscuring smoke and deafening noise of battle, and the excitement of the soldiers wishing to hit their opponents hard before they tried the same thing, would all hamper efforts by officers and sergeants to maintain control. A certain raggedness in musketry firing must have been inevitable after the first few volleys.

The French, contrary to general belief, were not far behind Allied practice, and platoon firing was unofficially used by their commanders from 1705 onwards, being adopted generally in 1708. In addition, during a firefight, the Allied troops seemed to have an in-built advantage, in that their musket ball was slightly heavier than that of the French opponents. This ball would fly straighter and farther, and would hit with more effect at the other end; Robert Parker comments on this phenomenon in his account of his regiment's fight in the woods at Malplaquet. Hand grenades were not much used outside entrenchments, but grenadier companies were generally regarded as elite troops, bigger and stronger and, theoretically at least, braver than others. They were often employed in the first wave of an assault, the long-handled hatchets which many still carried having a useful role in clearing obstacles.

There were no fully designated light troops, and light companies were not introduced into infantry battalions until later in the 18th century. However, it is apparent that troops were extensively used in a 'light' role – patrolling, scouting, raiding and skirmishing during Marlborough's campaigns. The use of sharpshooters was not unknown. The general idea that the armies in Marlborough's day always operated in uniformly rigid lines is plainly mistaken. Such a method of movement would not work, other than in full scale battle when the complexities of controlling huge numbers of infantry soldiers over a limited period required such a technique (and would continue to do so for another 150 years). In other phases of battle things were more fluid – Tom Kitcher remembered British skirmishers clearing the French out of the copses on the approach to the Petite Gheete Stream at Ramillies. De La Colonie wrote of the deadly night patrols creeping through the dark woods before the Battle of Malplaquet and the Scots regiments skirmished forward 'pice by pice' in that attack.

A British infantry battalion would have about 900 men at full strength (usually thirteen companies of sixty men apiece, plus officers), while French battalions were rather smaller, with about 700 men on the rolls. On campaign, casualties, absence and sickness would reduce these numbers significantly. British regiments tended to have just one battalion, the common tactical unit, but other armies had multi-battalion regiments (sometimes, misleadingly, referred to as brigades the next larger tactical formation). The Gardes Français had six battalions in 1704. It was common practice on both sides that a regiment would be 'owned' by a senior officer, and would carry his, or in the case of royalty (e.g. Queen's Regiment of Horse) her name. These appointments could change frequently, and keeping track of which regiment was engaged where and when, and what it was actually called with differing titles being used year on year, can be tricky. These senior officers would rarely serve with the regiment, having other command or staff duties.

Artillery in the early 18th century was fairly heavy and immobile, and once placed on the battlefield would usually stay there throughout the day. The weight of the gun carriages at this time was a distinct handicap in moving the guns. In addition the gunner tactics of the day could be likened to a battering ram, intended to blast holes in the rigidly drawn up lines of opposing infantry. Lighter guns, 'battalion' pieces such as those which accompanied Cadogan on his march from Lessines to Oudenarde, were fairly mobile and, attached two per battalion, could be deployed in flexible fashion. Their calibre, 2 pounder or so, meant that they were only effective at close range when the gunners themselves would be liable to be shot down by the opposing infantry. The bigger guns, up to 32 pounder on the battlefield, were laboriously dragged into position by ox-teams, and the crews fought their pieces from that spot. Mobility was not improved by the civilian teamsters, usually on short-term contracts, who were used to get the guns dragged from place to place. The esprit de corps of such men is unlikely to have been high. However, on occasions, such as at Blenheim when Blood got his guns across the Nebel Stream, or at Malplaquet when Lottum's batteries were manhandled through the woods, an enterprising commander would move his batteries as tactically necessary.

Round-shot was used at medium and long range (out to about 4,000 yards, visibility permitting), while at closer range, and particularly against massed troops, canister-shot (rather charmingly called partridge-shot), consisting of cans of musket balls which sprayed from the cannon mouth shotgun-like, were cruelly effective. Grape-shot, a naval weapon utilising clusters of larger 'grape' sized balls, was not usually used on land, although its use is often referred to. Case-shot, or explosive shell, tended to be unreliable because of faulty fuses, but was widely used by high angle howitzers and mortars. Horse artillery was an arm that was yet to be developed.

Cavalry remained the battle-winning arm of war, by virtue of mobility and shock action. The infantry did not have the tactical ability, in most cases, to stand against properly deployed cavalry.[3] Still horsemen were expensive to equip, train and maintain. Here also tactics and techniques were changing as armour was fast disappearing, although breastplates were still used, and were reintroduced for the British cavalry in 1708. A

British cavalry regiment comprised six troops (usually grouped into two squadrons). Each troop fielded sixty-two men. This gave a full regimental strength, counting twenty-four officers, of 396 all ranks, but this number would rarely be achieved on campaign. The use of firearms from horseback was rapidly diminishing, as the feebleness of pistols and carbines compared with the stark effectiveness of charging home with the sabre was recognised; the overthrow of the French cavalry at Blenheim owed much to the loss of impact of their halting to fire off carbines at the Allies, and thereby losing impetus in their advance. Nonetheless, the notion of charging home does not imply a full blooded gallop, as this would tire the horses and lead to confusion, stalemate or disaster. A more modest canter or trot forward was the norm, and this enabled commanders to control their troops to greater effect. Steadily the pace was increased until the moment of impact when the faster moving, and better closed up, formation would usually succeed. Shock action was sought, with the resulting collapse of morale and flight of the beaten opponent. A great deal of energetic sword-swinging could produce few injuries, but an enemy in full flight without hope of recovery meant victory.

Dragoons, originally mounted infantry armed with musket and bayonet, were increasingly used as cavalry, and before long the distinction between true cavalry 'Horse' and dragoons would disappear. 'When on horseback they are to fight as the Horse do.'[4] Status and rates of pay for dragoons would not match those of cavalrymen for some time yet. Light cavalry was used in increasing numbers, but the role which they would come to fill, that of scouting and screening, fell mostly to the dragoons at the time of Marlborough's campaigns. Foraging was an everyday pursuit, and raiding, while not yet a major function for cavalry in western Europe, fell to the dragoons to perform by virtue of their mobility (hence the derogative expression 'goon').

There was no British corps of engineers as such at this time, but engineer officers (who held rank in other combat arms at the same time as their technical appointments) had a valuable role in enabling an army on the march to have mobility, by laying bridges and clearing obstacles. In defence the preparation of entrenchments, obstacles and barriers was their responsibility, and allotted squads of soldiers and conscripted peasants would labour at these tasks. The pontoon bridge trains (often referred to as 'tin-boats'), were particularly valuable, and could be laid at great speed, as was demonstrated by Cadogan's engineers at Oudenarde.

The supply and maintenance of armies is an enormous enterprise, and is an activity often overlooked. It appears to be a drab and mundane activity, and is superficially rather less exciting than the cut and thrust of the fighting troops on the battlefield. A great deal of this was in the hands of civilian contractors, but Marlborough gave it his constant close attention. Without adequate supply soldiers cannot fight, and he was aware how vital was the routine business of feeding, clothing, housing and paying an army.

The care of the sick and the wounded tended to be quite rudimentary; soldiering was always a tough trade. Regiments had surgeons and surgeons' mates, and Marlborough had the 'widows' of the army deputed to act as nurses after major battles. From 1705 onwards a Commissioner for Sick and Wounded was an established post at Marlborough's headquarters. Still these arrangements could be overwhelmed. Donald McBane lay wounded on the turf outside Blindheim village for hours after the battle passed on, and was stripped by marauders and tormented by raging thirst before he was found by friends. The woods at Malplaquet were thick with the wounded for a week after the battle. Arrangements had to be made with the French to tend and remove their own wounded and to alleviate the burden for the Allies. Such problems persist after battles to the present day, in varying forms.

Marlborough's organisational abilities, his careful eye for detail, and his concern for the troops and capacity for hard work, all stood his army in good stead on campaign. Still, however good the administration might be, things inevitably go wrong. Mrs Christian Davies remembered an occasion when 'The Corporal having received the company's money, instead of paying it them, lost it at play, and then desperately shot himself through the head.'[5]

The command and control of an army, whether in peace or at war, is a vast and complex undertaking. The movement of troops, the routes to be taken, the timetable to be adopted, the order of march, the shelter for the night and the stockpiles of food, ammunition and forage, all have to be prearranged. This must be a part of a coherent plan which, in time, will bring the army close to an active and dangerous enemy in pitched battle. These are just a few of the dozens of tasks to be undertaken every day, day after day, by the commander of an army, and for which there is a body of staff officers to assist. Marlborough had an enormous capacity for hard work, and a considerable ability to absorb minute details. He discharged his duties with a very small staff. In action, the Duke kept everything under his own eye, and occasionally this put him greatly in harm's way, as at Ramillies when he was ridden down by the French cavalry. His aides, intelligent young officers, scoured the battlefield taking his commands and bringing him information, while the running footmen, flexible, discreet and enterprising, gave him a keen insight into the unfolding drama of the fatal contest.

Discipline in armies at this time could be harsh, although only Swedish, Russian, Austrian and Turkish armies actually had regimental executioners. Dragoon John Yeoman was made to run the gauntlet through his comrades twice for insulting the regimental quartermaster while on the march to the Danube. The severest penalties for desertion and mutiny and other major crimes were freely in use, although an intriguing latitude was sometimes allowed soldiers – as with those who had become captive in Spain yet returned to serve in the Allied army after the Battle of Oudenarde. The Irishman Peter Drake, slipping easily from one army to another, seems to have led a charmed life. It appears that the harshest penalties were applied to make an example from time to time, as with Marlborough's periodic orders that looters would meet the noose if apprehended.

Soldiers are a lively lot, and they sometimes take their revenge. An officer in Howe's Regiment, who treated his men badly, promised them that he would mend his ways if they behaved well at the Battle of Blenheim. As the French in Blindheim Village capitulated, he turned to his soldiers, doffed his hat to them and called for a cheer. 'Gentlemen,' he cried 'the day is ours.' At that moment a shot rang out through the twilight and the officer fell mortally wounded. The fatal musket ball did not seem to come from the French.[6]

Marlborough had a secret service – not just the scouting and intelligence gathering activities of an active army, or the deserters, talkative prisoners of war, informers and turncoats to be found in any prolonged military campaign. The Duke had a highly placed and remarkably prolific informer at the French Court itself, who kept the Duke posted regarding the goings on at Versailles. The correspondence sent was enormous, over 800 communications being received by Marlborough between 1708 and 1710 alone, and the information imparted was of enormous value. Who that informer was is not known.

NOTES

1. Boulenger, J, *Essay on Warfare*, quoted in Martin, C, *Louis XIV*, 1975, p.37.
2. Marlborough held no formal appointment in command of Dutch troops. The arrangement was that he had the field command of the Anglo-Dutch army when it campaigned together. Queen Anne's army consisted of the English, Scots and Irish Establishments each with their own budgets. For simplicity I have largely referred to the Queen's troops in this individual way up to the Union of England and Scotland in 1707, and as British troops thereafter. Although they had no separate army establishment, many Welshmen also fought under Marlborough.
3. The feebleness of infantry against well handled cavalry is demonstrated by the scattering of Rowe's otherwise fine regiment by the Gens d'Armes outside Blindheim Village. In the same vein Boufflers felt unable to advance against the temporarily broken Dutch infantry at Malplaquet when he was confronted by the proximity of Hesse-Cassell's massed cavalry. See Chandler, D, *The Art of Warfare in the Age of Marlborough*, 1974, p. 124.
4. Brereton, J, *History of the 4th/7th Dragoon Guards*, 1982, p. 53.
5. Defoe, D (ed. J Fortescue), *Life and Adventures of Mrs Christian Davies*, 1929, p. 106.
6. Hastings, M (ed.), *Oxford Book of Military Anecdotes*, 1985, p. 147.

Marlborough's British Regiments

The British regiments in Marlborough's service during the War of the Spanish Succession (with 1881 and 1914 titles in brackets) were as shown. Unless otherwise noted, they fought in all the Duke's campaigns in Germany and the Low Countries:

<u>Cavalry and Dragoons</u>

Queen's Regiment of Horse/Lumley's Horse (King's Dragoon Guards)
Wood's Horse (3rd Dragoon Guards)
Cadogan's Horse (5th Dragoon Guards)
Wyndham's/Palmes' Horse (6th Dragoon Guards)
Schomberg's Horse (7th Dragoon Guards)
Raby's (Royal) Dragoons (1st, Royal Dragoons) 1702–3
Hay's/Stair's Royal Scots Dragoons/Grey Dragoons (Royal Scots Greys)
Ross's Royal Dragoons of Ireland (5th Royal Irish Lancers)
Kerr's Dragoons/Queen's Own Regiment of Dragoons (7th Hussars) 1711 onwards

<u>Foot Guards</u>

1st English Foot Guards (Grenadier Guards)*
2nd English Foot Guards (Coldstream Guards)* 1708 onwards

* These two regiments were often brigaded together for security duties at army headquarters

<u>Infantry</u>

Royal Regiment/Orkney's (1st/Royal Scots)
Churchill's/Argyll's/the Buffs (3rd/Queen's Own Royal West Kent Regiment)

Webb's/Queen Dowager's (8th/King's Regiment)
Steuart's (9th/Royal Norfolk Regiment) 1702–3
North & Grey's (10th/Lincolnshire Regiment)
Stanhope's/Hill's (11th/Devonshire Regiment) 1702
Livesay's (12th/Suffolk Regiment) 1708
Barrymore's (Pearce's Dragoons/13th/Somerset Light Infantry) 1702
Howe's/Somerset's (15th/East Yorkshire Regiment)
Derby's/Godfrey's (16th/Bedfordshire & Hertfordshire Regiment)
Bridge's/Blood's (17th/Leicestershire Regiment) 1701–2
Royal Irish/Hamilton's/Ingoldsby's (18th/Royal Irish Regiment)
Erle's (19th/Green Howards) 1710–12
Rowe's/Mordaunt's/De Lalo's/Scots Fuziliers (21st/Royal Scots
    Fusiliers)
Ingoldsby's/Sabine's (23rd/Royal Welch Fusiliers)
Seymour's/Marlborough's/Tatton's/Primrose's (24th/South Wales
    Borderers)
Cameronians/Ferguson's/Borthwick's/Stair's/Preston's
    (26th/Cameronians)
De Lalo's/Mordaunt's/Windsor's (28th/Gloucestershire Regiment)
    1704–6
Farrington's (29th/Worcestershire Regiment) 1704–6 and 1708
Huntingdon's/Leigh's (33rd/Duke of Wellington's Regiment) 1702–3
Lucas's/Hamilton's (34th/Border Regiment) 1708 onwards
Meredith's/Windress's (37th/Hampshire Regiment)

The following were 'hostilities only' regiments, for they all disbanded at
the onset of peace. Those raised by 1704 were not present at the Danube
campaign, being engaged on garrison duties in the Low Countries.

Stringer's/Argyll's/Orrery's/Sibourg's
Temple's/Newton's
Evans'
Macartney's/Sutton's 1704 onwards (except 1707–Spain)
Prendergast's/Macartney's 1708 onwards
Wynne's 1708 onwards
Townshend's/Honeywood's 1708 onwards
Johnson's 1708
Moore's 1708
Dormer's 1707–9
Creighton's 1708.

APPENDIX II
Who was Who on Marlborough's Battlefields

Albergotti. Francois-Zenoble-Philippe, Comte de (1654–1717). Lieutenant-General. Italian officer in French service. Commanded left Wing at Malplaquet.

Anhalt-Dessau. Leopold, Prince of (1676–1747). Prussian officer. Commanded Eugene's infantry at Blenheim and German Infantry at Oudenarde, Malplaquet. 'The Old Dessauer' of Frederick the Great's campaigns.

Anjou. Philippe, Duc de (1683–1746). Grandson of King Louis XIV. Became King Philip V, King of Spain in 1700.

Argyll. John Campbell, 2nd Duke of (1678–1743). Known as 'Red John'. Fought with Marlborough at Ramillies, Oudenarde and Malplaquet. A political rival of the Duke, he was influential in the negotiations that led to the Union of England and Scotland.

Armstrong. John, Major-General (1674–1742). Chief of Engineers in Marlborough's army (1704). Surveyor-General of the Ordnance 1723.

Auvergne. François Egon De La Tour, Lieutenant-General of Cavalry in the Dutch service at Malplaquet.

Baden. Louis-Guillaume, Margrave of (1655–1707). Commanded the Imperial troops at the Schellenberg. Died from long-lasting effects, possibly gangrene, of a wound to the foot received there.

Berwick. James Fitzjames, Duke of (1670–1734). Marshal of France. Natural son of James II (when Duke of York) and Arabella Churchill, Marlborough's older sister.

Biron. Charles Armand de Goutant, Marquis de (1663–1736). Commanded French flank guard at Oudenarde where he tried without success to drive in Cadogan's bridgehead, and was taken prisoner.

Blood. Holcroft, Brigadier-General (1668–1707). Commanded Marlborough's artillery at Schellenberg and Blenheim. His father attempted to steal the Crown Jewels from the Tower of London.

Boufflers. Louis-François, Chevalier, Marquis and Duc de (1644–1711). Marshal of France. Veteran French commander. Out-manoeuvred by Marlborough in 1702 and 1703. Defended Lille in 1708, and took command of French army at Malplaquet when Villars was wounded.

Burgundy. Louis, Duc de Bourgogne (1682–1712). Grandson of Louis XIV. Nominal French commander at Oudenarde, then Dauphin of France. Died of measles.

Cadogan. William, Lieutenant-General (1665–1726). Marlborough's Irish Quartermaster-General and Chief of Staff. Commanded Allied advanced guard at Oudenarde. Became Major-General of the Ordnance on Marlborough's death.

Churchill. Charles (1656–1714). Younger brother of Marlborough. General of Infantry. Fought at the Schellenberg, Blenheim and Ramillies.

Clerambault. Philippe de Pallnau, Marquis de (died 1704). Lieutenant-General. French commander in Blindheim village. Reportedly drowned in River Danube.

Cutts. John, Baron (1661–1707). General of Infantry, commanded British infantry at Blenheim. Nicknamed 'the Salamander' for his liking of being in the hottest fire. Died in Ireland, in comparative poverty.

D'Arco. Comte. Piedmontese officer in Bavarian service. Commander of the Franco-Bavarian corps against Marlborough at the Schellenberg, and of the Bavarian infantry at Blenheim.

D'Artagnan. Pierre Comte, Marquis d'Montesquiou (1709). Marshal of France. Commanded French right Wing at Malplaquet.

Davies. Mrs Christian, also known as Mother Ross (died 1739). Enlisted in the Irish army in 1683, as Christopher Walsh. Fought at Schellenberg (wounded) and Blenheim, and was wounded again at Ramillies. Served as sutleress for rest of Marlborough's campaigns. Subsequently became a pensioner at the Royal Military Hospital in Chelsea. Author of lively reminiscences of her campaigns.

De La Colonie. Jean, Colonel. French officer in Bavarian service. Served at Schellenberg, Ramillies, Oudenarde and Malplaquet. Author of informative memoirs.

Dopff, Daniel Wolf, Baron (1665–1718). Dutch cavalry commander and Quartermaster-General.

Eugene. Prince François-Eugene of Savoy (1663–1736). Imperial Commander and President of Imperial War Council. Great friend and colleague of Marlborough. Refused a commission by King Louis XIV in the French army, he fought for Austria instead. Blenheim, Oudenarde and Malplaquet. Victor of Battle of Turin 1706.

Goor. Johan Wigand van (1647–1704). Dutch engineer officer, General of Infantry. Killed leading the initial Allied assault at the Schellenberg hill 1704.

Goslinga. Sicco van (1644–1731). Frisian Field Deputy. Brave but meddling, an arch critic of Marlborough.

Grimaldi. Honore, Marquis de (1675–1712). Lieutenant-General. Commander of French left Wing cavalry at Oudenarde. Fought at Malplaquet.

Hay. Lord John. Colonel of Dragoons. Fought at Schellenberg, Blenheim and Ramillies. Died of fever at siege of Menin 1706.

Hompesch. Graf Reynard Vincent van (1660–1733). Dutch Lieutenant-General. Defeated at Höchstädt battle in 1703. Served with Allied cavalry in all Marlborough's major battles.

La Motte. Louis-Jacques de Fosse, Comte de. French Major-General. Commanded Greder Suisse Regiments at Ramillies, and the flying column sent by Vendôme to seize Bruges before Oudenarde, July 1708.

Lottum. Philip Karl, Count (1650–1719). Prussian General. Commanded Prussian and Hanoverian infantry at Oudenarde, and the German and British infantry of the Allied left Wing at Malplaquet. Became Field Marshal 1713, and commander of the Prussian army.

Lumley. Henry (1660–1722). Major-General (1696), General (1711). British cavalry commander, present at all Marlborough's major battles.

Luxembourg. Christian-Louis de Montmorency Chevalier and Duc de (1675–1746). Lieutenant-General. Commanded French reserve cavalry at Malplaquet. Marshal of France (1734).

Marsin. Ferdinand, Comte de (1656–1706). Marshal of France. Commanded French left Wing at Blenheim. Killed at Battle of Turin in 1706, soon after receiving a premonition of his own death.

Mérode-Westerloo. Eugene-Jean-Philippe, Comte de (1674–1732). Walloon officer in French service until 1706, and then served with the Allies after Ramillies. Author of highly entertaining and informative memoirs.

Mordaunt. John, Viscount and Brigadier-General (1706). Son of Charles, Earl of Peterborough, the Allied commander in Spain. Mordaunt commanded the forlorn hope at Schellenberg, and lost an arm at Blenheim.

Nangis. Louis-Armand de Brichanteau, Marquis de (1682–1742). Marshal of France. Saved cavalry of French left Wing after Oudenarde.

Natzmer. Dubislaw (1654–1739). Prussian Major-General, cavalry commander defeated at Höchstädt (1703). Fought at Blenheim (captured), Oudenarde and Malplaquet.

Orange. John Friso, Prince of Orange and Nassau-Dientz (died 1711). Dutch infantry commander at Malplaquet. Drowned in River Rhine estuary.

Orkney. Lord George Hamilton, Earl of (1666–1737). General of Infantry, Governor of Virginia 1715, Field Marshal 1736. Fought at the Schellenberg, Blenheim, Ramillies and Malplaquet. Commanded the force covering Brussels during Oudenarde campaign.

Overkirk. Hendrick Van Nassau, Count (1640–1708). Dutch Veld-Marshal, close colleague of Marlborough. Ramillies and Oudenarde. Died of strain during siege of Lille.

Oxenstiern. Count (died 1709). Swedish officer in Dutch service. Fought at Oudenarde, killed at Malplaquet.

Palmes. Frances, Lieutenant General (1650 – 1719). British cavalry brigade commander who routed French Gens d'Armes at Blenheim.

Puysegur. Jacques François de Chastenay, Marquis de (1655–1743). Lieutenant-General, Marshal of France. Oudenarde and Malplaquet. Influential military author.

Rantzau. Jorgen (1652–1733). Major-General. A Holsteiner, he was the Hanoverian Cavalry Commander at Oudenarde, and commanded an infantry brigade at Malplaquet.

Sabine. Joseph (1662–1739). Major-General. Fought at Schellenberg, Blenheim and Ramillies. Commanded brigade at Cadogan's crossing of River Scheldt, Oudenarde. Succeeded Cadogan as Commander in Chief in Scotland in 1715.

St Hilaire. Armand de Marmes de (born 1651). Commanded French artillery at Blenheim, Oudenarde and Malplaquet. Skilled exponent of aggressive artillery tactics.

Schulemburg. Matthias-Johan, Count (1661–1743) Hanoverian Lieutenant-General, commanding Saxon troops in Allied service. Commanded infantry attack on right flank at Malplaquet. Defended Corfu against Turks in 1711, and settled there.

Tallard. Camille d'Houtun, Comte and Duc de (1652–1728). Marshal of France. French commander of right Wing at Blenheim. Held prisoner for eight years in Nottingham Castle.

Tilly. Claude-Frederick de Tserclaes Comte de (died 1723). Lieutenant-General, commander of Dutch cavalry at Oudenarde and Malplaquet

Vendôme. Louis-Joseph, Duc de (1654–1712). Marshal of France. Commanded French army at Oudenarde. Grandson of King Henry IV of France.

Villars. Claude Louis Hector, Duc de (1653–1734). Marshal of France. Commanded French army at Malplaquet. Marshal-General (1733).

Villeroi. François de Neufville, Duc de (1644–1730). Marshal of France. Commanded the French army at Ramillies.

Von Zurlauben. Beat-Jacques de la Tour-Chatillon, Comte de (died 1704). Swiss Lieutenant-General. Commander of French first line cavalry of the right Wing at Blenheim, killed in action that day.

Withers. Henry (died 1729). Lieutenant-General. British infantry commander. Schellenberg, Blenheim, Ramillies, Oudenarde. Commanded the turning movement at Malplaquet.

Wittelsbach. Maximilian Emmanuel, Elector of Bavaria (1679–1736). Governor-General of Spanish Netherlands. Defeated at Blenheim and Ramillies. Restored to his estates by the Treaty of Rastadt in 1714.

Württemberg. Prince Karl Alexander, Duke (1661–1741). Commander of Danish cavalry at Ramillies, Oudenarde and Malplaquet.

BIBLIOGRAPHY

(*JSAHR – Journal of the Society of Army Historical Research, London*)

Addison, J, *The Campaign* (poem), London, 1704.

Alison, A, *The Military Life of John, Duke of Marlborough*, London, 1848.

Ashley, M, *Marlborough*, London, 1939.

Atkinson, C T, *Marlborough and the Rise of the British Army*, London, 1921.

——, *History of the Royal Hampshire Regiment*, Glasgow, 1950.

——, *Marlborough's Sieges*, JSAHR, 1933.

——, *Marlborough and the Dutch Deputies*, JSAHR, 1935.

——, *Marlborough's Order of Battle*, JSAHR, 1936.

——, *A Royal Dragoon in the Spanish Succession War*, JSAHR, 1938.

——, (ed.), *Gleanings from the Cathcart Mss*, JSAHR, 1951.

——, *Queen Anne's Army*, JSAHR, 1958.

——, *Ramillies Battlefield*, JSAHR, 1960.

Barnett, C, *Marlborough*, London, 1974.

Barthorp, M, *Marlborough's Army 1702–1711*, London, 1980.

Belfield, E, *Oudenarde 1708*, London, 1972.

Belloc, H, *The Tactics and Strategy of the Great Duke of Marlborough*, London, 1933.

Bowen, H, *The Dutch at Malplaquet*, JSAHR, 1962.

Brereton, J, *History of the 4th/7th Dragoon Guards*, Catterick, 1982.

Burn, W, *A Scots Fusilier and Dragoon under Marlborough*, JSAHR, 1936.

Burns, A, *The Malplaquet Battlefield*, Royal Artillery Journal, Woolwich, 1933.

Burrell, S (ed.), *Amiable Renegade. The Memoirs of Captain Peter Drake 1671–1753*, London, 1960.

Burton, I, *The Captain-General*, London, 1968.

Carleton, G, *Military Memoirs*, London, 1728 and (ed.) 1929.

Carman, W, *The Siege of Lille 1708*, JSAHR, 1940.

Chandler, D, *The Art of Warfare in the Age of Marlborough*, London, 1974.

——, (ed.), *Journal of John Deane*, JSAHR, 1984.

——, *Marlborough as Military Commander*, London, 1973.

——, (ed.), *Captain Robert Parker and Comte de Mérode-Westerloo*, London, 1968.

——, (ed.), *Oxford History of the British Army*, Oxford, 1994.

Churchill, W S, *Marlborough: His Life and Times*, London, 1947.

Corvisier, A, *La Bataille de Malplaquet 1709*, Paris, 1997.

Le Moral des Combattants, Paris, Revue Historiques des armées, 1977.

Cowles, V, *The Great Marlborough and His Duchess*, London, 1983.

Coxe, W, *Memoirs of John, Duke of Marlborough*, London, 1848.

Cronin, V, *Louis XIV*, London, 1964.

Dalton, C, *English Army Commission Lists & Registers 1661–1714*, London, 1898–1904.

Defoe, D (ed. J Fortescue), *Life and Adventures of Mrs Christian Davies*, London, 1929.

De La Colonie, J (ed. W Horsley), *Chronicles of an Old Campaigner*, London, 1904.

Dickinson, H, *Bolingbroke*, London, 1979.

Dickson, P, *Red John of the Battles*, London, 1973.

Edwards, H, *A Life of Marlborough*, London, 1926.

English Historical Review, *Letters of the First Earl Orkney*, April 1904.

Fortescue, J, *History of the British Army*, Vol I, London, 1889.

——, *Marlborough*, London, 1932.

Frances, D, *The First Peninsular War*, London, 1974.

Green, D, *Blenheim*, London, 1974.

——, *Queen Anne*, London, 1970.

——, *Sarah, Duchess of Marlborough*, London, 1967.

Hamilton, F, *History of the Grenadier Guards*, London, 1877.

Hastings, M (ed.), *Oxford Book of Military Anecdotes*, Oxford, 1985.

Haswell, J, *James II*, London, 1972.

Henderson, N, *Prince Eugen of Savoy*, London, 1964.

Hopkinson, M, *Anne of England*, London, 1934.

Johnston, S (ed.), *Letters of Samuel Noyes*, JSAHR, 1959.

Jones, J, *Marlborough*, London, 1993.

Kearsey, A, *Marlborough's Campaigns 1702–1709*, Aldershot, 1911.

Lang, G, *Private papers on the order of battle at the Schellenberg*. Seen by the author January 2000.

Lediard, T, *Life of John, Duke of Marlborough*, London, 1736.

Lee, A, *History of the Tenth Foot*, London, 1910.

Leslie, N, *Succession of Colonels of the British Army*, JSAHR, 1959.

Liddell Hart Centre, King's College London, *Papers of Major Peter Verney*.

MacFarlane, C, *Life of Marlborough*, London, 1854.

Martin, C, *Louis XIV*, London, 1975.

Maycock, F, *An Outline of Marlborough's Campaigns*, London, 1913.

McBane, D, *The Expert Swordsman's Companion*, Edinburgh, 1728.

McKay, D, *Prince Eugene of Savoy*, London, 1977.

Miller, H, *Colonel Parke of Virginia*, Chapel Hill, 1989.

Mitford, N, *The Sun King*, London, 1966.

Murray, G (ed.), *Letters and Dispatches of the Duke of Marlborough*, London, 1845.

Norton, L, *First Lady of Versailles*, London, 1978.

———, (ed.), *St Simon at Versailles*, London, 1958.

Nosworthy, B, *The Anatomy of Victory*, New York, 1992.

Petrie, C, *The Marshal, Duke of Berwick*, London, 1953.

Phelan, I, *Marlborough as Logistician*, JSAHR, 1989.

Rogers, H, *The British Army of the 18th Century*, London, 1977.

Rowse, A, *The Early Churchills*, London, 1956.

Sautai, M, *La Bataille de Malplaquet*, Paris, 1910.

Scouller, R, *The Armies of Queen Anne*, Oxford, 1966.

Snyder H, *The Duke of Marlborough's Requests for Captain-Generalcy for Life*, JSAHR, 1967.

Southey, R, *The Battle of Blenheim* (poem), London, 1794.

Stadtarchiv Donauwörth Papers, *Die Schlacht am Schellenberg 1704*.

———, *Die Schlachten auf dem Schellenberg und bei Höchstädt/Blindheim 1704*.

Sturgill, C, *Marshall Villars and the War of Spanish Succession*, Kentucky, 1965.

Taylor, F, *The Wars of Marlborough 1702–9*, Oxford, 1921.

Thompson, G, *The First Churchill*, London, 1979.

Tipping, C, *The Story of the Royal Welch Fusiliers*, London, 1915.

Trevelyan, G M, *England under the Stuarts*, London, 1938.

———, *England in the Reign of Queen Anne*, 1948 (three vols): *Blenheim*

———, *Ramillies and the Union with Scotland*

———, *The Peace and the Protestant Succession*.

Van der Zee, H and B, *William and Mary*, London, 1973.

Verney, P, *The Battle of Blenheim*, London, 1976.

Wace, A, *The Marlborough Tapestries at Blenheim Palace*, 1968.

Weaver, L, *The Story of the Royal Scots*, London, 1915.

Wilcox, W, *Historical Records of the 5th Lancers*, London, 1908.

Williams, N, *Redcoats and Courtesans*, London, 1994.

Wolseley, G, *The Life of Marlborough*, London, 1894.

Wykes, A, *The Royal Hampshire Regiment*, London, 1968.

Young, P, *The British Army 1642–1970*, London, 1967.

INDEX

Abercromby, James, 78
Act of Union, 127
Albemarle, see Keppel
Albergotti, Marquis di, confronts
  Marlborough at Goycke, 134;
  176, 178, 182, 189,
Anhalt-Dessau, Leopold, Prince
  of, leads assault on Bavarian
  great battery, 66–8, 73
Anjou, Philip, Duke of (King
  Philip V of Spain) 9, 10, 164
Anne Stuart, Princess and Queen
  of England, 7, 8, 12, 20, 22, 44;
  learns of Blenheim victory, 79,
  88, 119, 129, 156, 159, 201; death,
  204
Antwerp, 15, 122, 131, 160
Argyll, John Campbell, 2nd Duke
  of, 108, 111, 116; Oudenarde,
  143, 145–8; Malplaquet, 186, 193
Arleux (see Lines of Non Plus
  Ultra)
Armstrong, Colonel John, 178, 181
Athlone (see Ginkel), 13, 15
Aulnois (Malplaquet) Gap, 171–2,
  176
Auvergne, Lieutenant-General,
  171–2, 178, 182, 190
Averock, Brigadier-General, 71

Baden, Louis-Guillaume,
  Margrave, 20, 23, 25–7, 30, 32,
  35–44, 50; on devastation of
Bavaria, 50; besieges Ingolstadt,
  53; wounded foot, 54; 58, 82,
  88–9, 95, 128
Barrier Treaty and Towns, 12, 128,
  168
Bavaria, Elector of (see
  Wittelsbach)
Bavarian infantry, 30–4, 37–41, 43,
  51; stout defence of Lutzingen,
  66–7, 73, discipline at Elixheim,
  91
Bedmar, Isidore, Marquis de,
  19–20, 22
Belville, Colonel, 75, 77–8
Berensdorf, Count, 37, 41, 70–1
Berg village, 35–7, 39
Berwick, James Fitzjames, Duke
  of, 19, 128–9, 135–6, 156–8, 163,
  167; methods, 207
Biron, Marquis de, 141–2
Bishop, Corporal Matthew, 178
Blackadder, Major John, 90
Black Forest, 16, 25, 49, 51
Blenheim, battle of, 49–82; losses
  in equipment, 80; scale of
  victory, 81; 208
Blenheim Bounty, 88
Blenheim Dispatch, 79
Bleiron Farm, 174, 176, 182–5,
  192
Blindheim village, Cutts' attack,
  64–6; packed with infantry, 65;
  French capitulation, 77–8

Blood, Colonel Holcroft, 37, 62, 71, 73, 215

Bois de Lanieres, 172, 176, 182,

Bois de Sars (triangle), 170, 180, 185, 187, 190, 193

Bois de Thiery, 172, 185,

Borthwick, Colonel, 111; killed, 116

Boser Couter hill, Overkirk's turning movement at Oudenarde, 149–52

Bothmar, Count Johan von, 134

Bouchain, 203

Boufflers, Louis-François, Duc de, 13–15, 19, 163; joins Villars at Malplaquet, 176, 185, 188; takes command of the army, 190, 193; writes to Louis XIV, 193

Boussu Gap, 171

Bringfield (Bingfield), Lieutenant-Colonel James, 111

British infantry, assault on Ramillies ridge, 107–8, 112–13, 116

Brouwaan Château, 148, 150

Bruges, 122; loss to French, 133–4, 158; recapture by Allies, 163

Brussels, submission to Marlborough, 120; 132, 137, 156, 160, 163

Burgundy (Bourgogne), Louis, Duke of, on campaign with Vendôme, 131; Oudenarde campaign, 131–60.

Butler (see Ormonde)

Cadogan, William, 1st Earl, 32, 63, 98, 102, 112–13; at Oudenarde 136–47, 151, 153, 178, 193

Calcinato, 95, 115, 122

Camaret Bay letter, 6–7

Campbell, Major James, 112; conduct at Malplaquet, 191

Campbell, John (see Argyll)

Campbell, Captain John, describes skirmishing at Maplaquet, 184

Caraman, Pierre-Paul, Comte de, 91–2, 98, 122

Cathcart, Captain Charles, 136, 144

Chamillart, Michel de, 96; 119–20

Chanclos, Brigadier-General, reinforces Oudenarde, 134, 155

Charles II, King of England, 1–4

Charles (Carlos) II, King of Spain, 9

Charles, Archduke of Austria, King Charles III Spain and Charles VI of Austria, 9, 118, 127, 133, 164; becomes Emperor, 202

Chemerault, Marquis de, 133, 182, 188–9

Chevalier de St George (the Old Pretender), 12, 148, 192

Churchill, Lieutenant-General Charles, 54, 62, 70, 75, 77, 102

Churchill, Admiral George, 129

Churchill, John (see Marlborough)

Clause 37, 165

Clerambault, Philippe, Marquis de, 65, 69, 73

Cutts, Major-General John, Baron 64–6; forces French to reinforce Blindheim, 66; 77–8

D'Alègre, Yves, Marquis, 91, 98

Danish cavalry, 49; join Marlborough at Ramillies, 97, 102; at Malplaquet, 193

D'Arco, Count, 30–44, 59, 67

D'Artagnan, Pierre, Comte (Montesquiou), 176, 179, 182, 190, 192

Davies, Mrs Christian, 36, 50, 62, 80, 117, 152, 164; at Malplaquet, 180; searches for husband, 186; 217

Deane, Private John, 144, 151, 155

De Blainville, Jules-Armand, Marquis, 70–1
De Blanzac, Marquis, 78
De Frequelière, Marquis, skilled handling of French artillery, 59
De Guiche, Major-General, 108, 113, 174
De La Colonie, Jean, 32, 37–8, 40–4, 51, 76, 105–7, 109–10, 178–9, 182–3, 190, 214
De La Vallière, Marquis, 72, 192
Dender river, marching campaign to secure, 134–7
De Rozel, Chevalier, 188, 190
Deserters, 32–3, 217
Devastation of Bavaria, 50–1
Dillingen, 30, 42–3, 54
Donauwörth, 29–44, 53
Dopff, Daniel, Baron, 98, 172
Drake, Captain Peter, 115, 218
DuBordet, Colonel, 35–6, 40–2
Dutch Field Deputies, 15–17, 19, 88
Dutch Guards 103–5, 107, 114; devastated by French artillery, 182–5
Dutch States-General 8, 12–13, 19, 92, 127, 131, 195
Dyle river, 95–6, 101, 117–18, 120

Elixheim (see Lines of Brabant)
Eugene, Prince of Savoy, 24–7, 30, 51; shadows Tallard through Black Forest, 52; combines with Marlborough, 54; Blenheim campaign, 56–82; Italian campaign, 93, 127–8; March from Moselle valley, 132; joins Marlborough for Oudenarde campaign, 135, 137, 149; refuses to support invasion of France, 160; wounded at Lille, 163; Malplaquet campaign, 167–96, letter to Emperor before battle,

173; methods similar to Marlborough's, 207

Fagel, Baron 182–3,
Fascines, 35, 37–8, 64, 107, 143
Ferguson, Brigadier-General James, 36, 41, 58, 64
Feversham, Louis Duras, Earl 4–5
Field Symbols, 41, 116
Franquenay, 104, 109
French dragoons, foiled counter-attack at Schellenberg, 40; defence of Blindheim, 59, 64; routed at Taviers, 105–7
French infantry, destroyed on Plain of Höchstädt, 75, capitulate in Blindheim, 77–9, sturdy defence of Ramillies and Offuz, 111–12, bravery at Oudenarde, 148
French Maison de Roi cavalry, 65, 101, 106, 110, 115, 151–2, 176
Fugger, Count, reluctantly assists Dutch attack, 70–1

George, Elector of Hanover (George I), 131
George, Electoral Prince of Hanover (George II), at Oudenarde, 143
Gheet Stream, 96, 98, 100, 102, 107–8, 214
Ghent, 120; loss to French, 133–4, 145, 156–8; recapture, 163–4
Ghent–Bruges canal, 158
Gibraltar, 164
Ginkel, Godart van, Earl of Athlone, 13,
Glanders (German sickness), 52
Godolphin, Sidney, Earl, 4, 96, 201
Goor, General Johan van, 22, 24, 37, 39, 43, 87
Goslinga, Sicco van, 98, 118, 140, 168, 185

Grand Alliance, 8, 12, 19, 20, 87, 128–9, 164–5
Grand Dauphin (see Louis)
Great Frost, 163–4
Grimaldi, Honore, Marquis de, defence of Mons, 194
Groenewald, defence of, 145–6
Guiscard, General, 103, 105, 110, 113

Haine river 168, 170
Hamilton, Brigadier-General Gustavus, 178, 184
Hanoverian cavalry, charge down Swiss infantry at Oudenarde, 143
Hare, Rev Francis, 39, 63, 67, 76
Harley, Robert (see Oxford)
Hesse-Cassell, Prince Frederick of, 168, 183–4, 191–2
Höchstädt, battle at, 16, 54, 56; 61, 75, 128
Holstein-Beck, Prince of, 70
Hompesch, Lieutenant-General Graf Reynard, van, 35, 44, 71, 77
Horn, Count, 35–6, 40
Hulsen, Brigadier-General, 58, 70–1, 77
Humières, Marquis de, 74
Huyshe, 140, 144, 153

Imperial Grenadiers, turn Bavarian flank at Schellenberg, 40–1
Ingolstadt, 53, 82
Irish regiments (in French service), 70, 108, 188

James II, Duke of York, King of England, 1–5, 6, 7
Joseph I, Archduke and Emperor of Austria, 89, 93, 202

Keppel, Arnold von Joost, Earl

Albemarle 7, 136
Kitcher, Private Thomas, 107–8, 113, 117, 214

La Folie Farm, 188–9, 195
La Motte, Louis-Jacques, Comte de, 133
Leopold, Austrian Emperor, 15, 20, 25; death, 89
Lessines, 137, 145
Liège, 14, 89
Ligonier, Major John, 89
Lille, 135, 160, 163
Lines of Brabant, 90, 98, 102, 160
Lines of La Bassée, 167, 193
Lines of Non Plus Ultra, 202–3
Lines of Stollhofen. 30, 51, 128
Lottum, Count Philip, 148–9, 157–8, 180, 182
Louis XIV, King of France, 2, 3; the Spanish Succession, 9–13; 16, 20; advice to Marshals, 23, 25; 29, 103, 145; on Swiss regiments, 52; 58, receives news of Blenheim defeat, 81; urges Marshals to give battle, 96; 118, 119; raises new regiments, 121; understanding towards failed generals, 121; 128; sends Burgundy to campaign with Vendôme, 131; 133; waits for news from Oudenarde, 156; recognises need for peace, 164; rejects Clause 37, 165; urges Villars to save Mons, 168, 196
Louis, Dauphin of France, 10, 165
Louvain, 96, 120
Lumley, Major-General Henry, 35, 58, 103, 108, 149, 151, 155, 191
Lutzingen, 59, 66–8, 70, 81
Luxembourg, Christian-Louis, Chevalier de, 171; detached to cover Mauberge, 172–3; 193

Lys river, 157, 159, 167

Maastricht, 2, 22, 96, 158
McBane, Private Donald, carries son into attack at Malplaquet, 187
Maffei, Alessandro, Count, 40, 115–16
Malplaquet, battle at, 167–96; state of the ground, 173; casualty numbers, 193; qualified victory 194–6; 208
Marlborough, John Churchill, 1st Duke of, early life and education, 1–2; service at Court, 1–2; active service abroad, at sea, and with French army 1–3; marriage to Sarah Jennings, 3; Sedgemoor campaign, 4; deserts James II, 5; campaign in Ireland, 6; dismissal, 6; Camaret Bay letter, 6; reinstatement, 7; negotiations with Dutch, 8; appointed England's Captain-General, 12; 1702–3: becomes Duke, 14; campaign in Low Countries, 14–16; threatens retirement, 16; 1704: 19; plans the march to Danube valley, 20; preparations for the march, 21–2, 24; tactics on the march, 24–6; 30; at Schellenberg fight, 29–44; partnership with Eugene, 25; on devastation of Bavaria, 51; Blenheim campaign, 56–82; triumphal return to London, 88; 1705: passage of the Lines of Brabant, and success victory at Elixheim, 90–1; 1706: Ramillies campaign, 95–122, ridden down by French cavalry,111; conquest of Spanish Netherlands, 120–2; 1707: offer of Governor-Generalcy of Spanish

Netherlands, 127–8; fruitless campaign against Vendôme, 129; 1708: ill-health 136; Oudenarde campaign,131–60; fails to gain Eugene's support for invasion of France, 160; capture of Lille; 1709: requests for Captain-Generalcy for Life, 164, 201; dismay at failed peace negotiations, 165; army in readiness, 166; Capture of Tournai and St Ghislain; Malplaquet campaign 167–96; accepts need for delay in attack, 172–3; keeps Withers' corps in reserve, 173; 1711: Lines of Non Plus Ultra 202–3; capture of Bouchain, 203; 1712–13: loss of offices and dismissal by Queen Anne, 202–3; exile, 203; return and reinstatement, 204; 1714–22: ill-health, semi-retirement and death, 204–5; tactical methods, 207–11; modern concept of operations, 207; partnership with Eugene, 210–11; confederate nature of army, 213; command and control, 217; secret service, 218
Marlborough, Sarah, Duchess of, 6, 22, 50, 119, 129; quarrels with Queen Anne, 159–60, 164, 193; dismissed, 201; with Duke at his death, 205
Marsin, Ferdinand, Comte de, 20, 25–6; at Blenheim, 57–82, defence of Oberglau, 70–1; retreat to the Rhine 89; 95, reinforces Villeroi, 95–6, 209
Matignon, Charles, Comte de, 142, 153
Medical services, 43, 217
Mehaigne river, 96, 105

Menin, 133, 135, 138
Mérode-Westerloo, Eugene,
    Comte de, 59, 61–2, 72–5, 79, 133
Mindleheim Principality, 88
Minorca, 164
Mons, 122, 132, 157, 168, 170, 181,
    194, 201
Montesquiou (see D'Artagnan)
Mordaunt, Brigadier-General
    John, 35, 38, 46
Moselle, 16, 19, 22–2, 88–90, 131,
    135–6
Murray, Major-General, Swiss
    brigade shelters Marlborough at
    Ramillies, 111

Namur, 15, 90, 96, 118
Nangis, Marquis de, salvages
    French cavalry after Oudenarde,
    154
Natzmer, Major-General
    Dubislaw, 58, 140, 150–1
Nebel Stream, obstacle to
    Marlborough's assault, 60–1
Non Plus Ultra (see Lines of)
No Peace Without Spain, 165
Nordlingen, 30, 43, 63
Norken Stream, 138, 144, 148, 152
Noyes, Rev Samuel, 38

Oberglau, 59, 64, 69–70
O'Brien, Charles, Viscount Clare
    116
Offuz, 100, 102, 112, 114, 116
Orange, John Friso, Prince of, at
    Malplaquet, 178, 182–4, 185–6,
    188
Orkney, George Hamilton, 1st Earl
    of, 75, 77, 90, 102, 107–8, 112,
    117, 122, 141, 178, 181; pierces
    French centre at Malplaquet,
    189–90, 191–2, 194
Ormonde, James Butler, 2nd Duke
    of, 203

Ostend, 15, 122
Ottomonde, 105, 114
Oudenarde, 120; reinforced by
    Marlborough, 134; 135; battle at,
    140–60; spontaneous nature,
    159; 208
Overkirk, Veld-Marshal, Hendrick
    van, Count, 15, 23; at Lines of
    Brabant 89–92; at Ramillies, 98,
    109, 113–14; 136; Oudenarde
    campaign, 149–50, 152; death
    during siege of Lille, 163
Oxenstiern, Lieutenant-General,
    Count, 151–3; killed at
    Malplaquet, 185
Oxford, Robert Harley, Earl of,
    201

Pallandt, Major-General Johan,
    Baron, 168, 178, 184
Palmes, Lieutenant-General
    Francis, 69
Parke, Colonel Daniel, 79–80
Parker, Captain Robert, 24, 114,
    129, 188, 214
Partition Treaty (see also Ryswick)
    9
Peer, 14
Pfeiffer, Major-General, 141
Platoon firing (see Tactics)
Plattenberg, Brigadier-General,
    138, 141, 143
Pontoon bridges, 63, 141, 144
Pope, Lieutenant Richard,
    comments on Schellenberg
    losses, 44
Prussian infantry, storm
    Lutzingen, 66–7, 73
Puysegur, Marquis de, at
    Oudenarde, 142, 148, 150, 153;
    withdraws left Wing at
    Maplaquet, 189–90

Quiévrain, 170, 192

Ramillies, battle at, 100–22, 127;
stunning effect on campaign,
208, 210

Rantzau, Major-General Jorgen
von, at Oudenarde: 141, 143;
charge along the Ghent road,
144; 146, 151; holds Allied centre
at Malplaquet, 184–5

Rastadt, Peace of, 204

Rowe, Brigadier-General
Archibald, 57, 64

Royegem, 148, 153

Ryswick, Treaty of, 9

Sabine, Major-General Joseph, 138,
141, 143

Scarpe river, 167

Schaerken, 143, 145, 151

Scheldt river, 120, 137; crossings at
Oudenarde battle, 131–60; 167

Schellenberg, battle at, 29–45,
49–50; Eugene fortifies hill, 54,
visit by French officers, 128; 208

Schulemburg, Matthais-Johan,
Count, 102, 180–1, 187–8

Schwenningen, passage of defile,
57–8, 64

Scots-Dutch brigade, 108, 111, 116,
141

Sedgemoor, Marlborough at
battle, 4

Silly, Marquis de, probes Allied
advance prior to Blenheim, 57

Slangenberg, General, 15, 92

Spaar

Spanish Netherlands, 10, 15, 19,
20, 90, 117–18, 120–1, 127, 155,
194

Stair, John Dalrymple, 2nd Earl of,
116, 144, 156

St Ghislain, 168, 170, 172–3, 177,
194

St Hilaire, Armand, Marquis de,
189

St Simon, Louis de Rouvroi, Duc
de, comments on new
regiments, 121

Swiss Troops, in French service,
52; routed at Ramillies, 104–6;
141, 184

Sybourg, Colonel Charles, 69

Tactics, Cavalry, 65, 69, 72–3, 104,
109, 115, 191, 215–6; dragoons,
216: Infantry, 47, 64, 104, 146,
180, 213–14; light troops, 214:
Artillery, 36, 47, 49, 59, 62, 179,
187, 215; Engineers, 63, 141, 144,
168, 216

Tallard, Comte de, in London, 12;
19–20, 23, 25, 36, 45, 49–51;
combines with Marsin and
Elector, 56; conduct at Blenheim
57–82, battle tactics, 61, taken
prisoner; return to Versailles,
81

Tapfheim, 56

Taviers, 90, 100, 103, 106, 109, 114

Tilly, Claude, Comte de, 150, 152,
191

Toulon, 128

Tournai, 135, 167–8, 170, 187, 194

Turenne, Vicomte de, 3

Turin, 129

Unterglau village set on fire by
Tallard, 59

Utrecht, Treaty of, 204

Vendôme, Louis-Joseph, Duc de,
95, 129; Oudenarde campaign,
131–60; incredulity at Allied
approach, 142; impetuous
advance, 145–6, insults
Burgundy, 154; untruthful battle
report, 156; 165, 167, 210

Vienna, 16–17, 20, 24, 43, 51

Villars, Claude-Louis-Hector, Duc

de, 2, 16, 89, 95, 128; takes command of French army in Flanders, 165; Malplaquet campaign, 167–96, 210; manoeuvres behind woodland belt, 172–3, defensive tactics, 176–7; wounded, 189; wariness of Marlborough, 196; 202, 203; methods, 207

Villeroi, François de Neufville, Duc de, 15, 23, 25, 89–90; Ramillies campaign 95–122, options available, 101; reasons for defeat given, 121; return to Versailles; 211

Visoule Stream, French and Swiss routed, 106

Von Zurlauben, Beat-Jacques, Comte de, 62, 68–9, mortally wounded, 72

Walcourt 6

Walloon Troops in defence of Offuz, 107; defections after Ramillies 118; in Mons, 168

Week, Major-General, 150

Welheim Farm, artillery emplacements, 66, 70

Wertmüller, Colonel, 103–7, 109, 113

Widows of the Army, 217

William III (William of Orange), King of England, Stadtholder of Holland 4, 5

Wilkes, Major-General, 57, 69

Withers, Lieutenant-General Henry, 35–6; flank march at Malplaquet, 170, 172, 177, 187–8, 193, 195

Wittelsbach, Maximilian Emmanuel, Elector of Bavaria, 12, 15, 19–20, 23–4, 26, 29–30, 49–52; at Blenheim 57–82, loss of all estates, 81; campaigns in Low Countries, 89, 97; at Ramillies, 101, 114–15, 117; 209

Wörnitz river, 32–3, 35–6

Wratislaw, Johann Wenzel, Count, 20

Württemberg, Karl-Alexander, Duke of, 66, 68, 97; joins Allied army at Ramillies, 102, 109, 113–15

Yssche river, 92